MIGRANT MODERNISM

MIGRANT MODERNISM

Postwar London and the West Indian Novel

J. Dillon Brown

Distributed in Canada by
SCHOLARLY BOOK SERVICES, INC.
289 Bridgeland Ave, Unit 105
Toronto ON M6A 1Z6
www.sbookscan.com
orders@sbookscan.com or call 1-800-847-9736

University of Virginia Press
Charlottesville and London

University of Virginia Press
© 2013 by the Rector and Visitors of the University of Virginia
All rights reserved
Printed in the United States of America on acid-free paper

First published 2013
9 8 7 6 5 4 3 2 1

Library of Congress Cataloging-in-Publication Data
Brown, J. Dillon, 1971–
    Migrant modernism : postwar London and the West Indian novel / J. Dillon Brown.
        p.   cm.
    Includes bibliographical references and index.
    ISBN 978-0-8139-3393-1 (cloth : acid-free paper)—ISBN 978-0-8139-3394-8
(pbk. : acid-free paper)—ISBN 978-0-8139-3395-5 (e-book)
    1. West Indian fiction (English)—History and criticism. 2. Caribbean fiction—
History and criticism. 3. Postcolonialism in literature. 4. Modernism (Literature)—
England—London. 5. London (England)—In literature. I. Title.
    PR9214.B76 2013
    813.009'9729—dc23

                                                                    2012035610

Dedicated to the memory of Rick Brown (1945–2009)

Every text is an act of will to some extent, but what has not been very much studied is the degree to which texts are made permissible.

—Edward Said, *The World, the Text and the Critic*

Contents

Acknowledgments

This project has an embarrassingly long lineage, hearkening back to two classes, one taught by John Bishop and the other by VèVè Clark, coinciding one fortuitous, long-ago semester. Some years later, Joseph Clarke rekindled my interest in Caribbean literature, for which I am grateful. My primary debt of gratitude is to Jim English, whose patience, insight, wisdom, and humor have been instrumental at every stage. Memorably for me, the contours of the project took shape only after Jim crisply summarized, in one sentence, what I had spent the previous half hour desperately trying to articulate. The depth and incisiveness of his intellect have proven similarly important to my thinking ever since, if primarily as aspirations. The unbounded generosity and erudition of Jean-Michel Rabaté and the perceptive, considerate criticism of Ania Loomba likewise deserve more thanks than can adequately be expressed here.

Initial research for this project was enabled by a grant from the J. William Fulbright Association. Brooklyn College's Leonard & Clare Tow Faculty Travel Fellowship, the Brooklyn College New Faculty Fund, a PSC-CUNY Grant, and a British Studies Fellowship from the Harry S. Ransom Center have also provided generous and much appreciated support for research specific to this project.

Colleagues in the English Department at Brooklyn College—especially James Davis, Joseph Entin, Claire Joubert, Nicola Masciondaro, Geoff Minter, Martha Nadell, Roni Natov, Ellen Tremper, and Joy Wang—provided a rich and welcoming environment in which to do intellectual work. My current colleagues at Washington University in St. Louis have likewise been a blessing, and indeed my friendships with so many make it impracticable to acknowledge them all individually here. Those who have provided commentary and guidance specifically on this project include Daniel Grausam, Marina MacKay, William Maxwell, William McKelvy, and Vincent Sherry. Both institutions also provided important research time and have my sincere thanks for that.

Further afield, my time in Barbados was enriched by the kindness of the literature faculty at the University of the West Indies, Cave Hill, especially Jane Bryce, Ian Craig, Mark McWatt, and Evelyn O'Callaghan. Philip Nanton, though he absconded to Grenada for the year, also deserves mention. At the University of the West Indies, Mona, I would like to thank Michael Bucknor, Victor Chang, and, especially, Nadi Edwards and Schontal Moore for their unaccountable hospitality and intellectual camaraderie. Bill Schwarz and Rebecca Walkowitz were initial, helpful supporters of my work on this project, and I would also like to thank Peter Kalliney for providing early feedback to which I may still not have fully done justice. Matthew Hart has graciously suffered through much of this project's long genesis, offering intellectual inspiration or the distractions of drink, as necessary. I am also deeply grateful to Cathie Brettschneider at the University of Virginia Press for her support of this project and to the anonymous readers of the initial manuscript, whose insights have helped to make this book a vastly better one than it would otherwise have been.

Two parts of chapter 3 have previously been published. "Exile and Cunning: The Tactical Difficulties of George Lamming" was originally published in *Contemporary Literature* 47.4 (Winter 2006) and is held in copyright by the Board of Regents of the University of Wisconsin System. It is reproduced, in revised form, courtesy of the University of Wisconsin Press. "Changing the Subject: The Aesthetics and Politics of Reading in the Novels of George Lamming" was originally published in *The Locations of George Lamming*, edited by Bill Schwarz and published by Macmillan Caribbean in 2007. It is reproduced, in revised form, courtesy of the publisher. I am thankful for these permissions to reprint.

Finally, I would like to acknowledge my family. My parents have, to my amazement, never ceased offering love and support. My brother and his family have always been welcoming and encouraging, despite the arcane nature of my chosen pursuits. Rosenfelds near and far have likewise been patiently supportive of my work. Most important to me, indeed the grounding source of value for anything I do, are Jessica Rosenfeld and Samantha Rosalind Brown—sine qua non.

Introduction

At first glance, the central contention of this book might seem uncomplicated: that the Windrush novelists, West Indians living and publishing in London after World War II, emerged into prominence via an overt affiliation with literary modernism.[1] Indeed, as this book hopes to show in the pages that follow, when these influential Anglophone Caribbean novels are read within the historical and geographical context of their production, their affiliation with modernism becomes not simply evident but indispensable to an understanding of their complex literary-political aims. However straightforward it appears, though, such an assertion quickly becomes entangled in a constellation of literary-critical discourses—modernist, postcolonial, Caribbean—that have divergent, often antagonistic conceptions of both the nature and the function of their respective critical protocols, as well as the literature to which these protocols are applied. Part of the aim of this book, therefore, beyond merely illustrating how these foundational (and clearly anticolonial) West Indian novels developed through a relation to British modernism, is to model a critical framework that recognizes the mutually reinforcing interconnection between these apparently discrete literary (and literary-critical) phenomena. In excavating the convergences between West Indian novels and their modernist predecessors, that is, I hope to illustrate how the prominent postwar emergence of Anglophone Caribbean literature is best understood as a process unfolding—alongside and in contention with the legacies of modernism—within a transnational literary space.[2]

Of course, to lay claim to the term *modernism* is, from the outset, to invite disagreement from one's scholarly peers. Modernism, as Astradur Eysteinsson has observed, is a "highly troublesome signifier" (*Concept of Modernism,* 6), troublesome not least because of the chaotic variety of aesthetic movements, styles, and philosophies that have operated under its mantle. A further, equally vexing difficulty is involved in assigning either a period of time or a geographical area to which its production can usefully, let alone authoritatively, be limited. The title of Peter Nicholls's 1995 study—*Modernisms: A Literary Guide*—suggests with eloquent concision the irreducible multiplicity one must confront in navigating the tangled terrain of what we call modernist literature. In his preface, Nicholls positions the book against what he identifies as a prevailing critical tendency to reduce the complexities of modernism to caricature, to "a sort of monolithic ideological formation" (vii) used largely as a foil for postmodernism. Nicholls's self-consciously internecine critical foray, then, highlights a third factor complicating any effort at definitively characterizing literary modernism—the markedly variable history of the meanings that critics themselves have attached to this aesthetic phenomenon. As Eysteinsson has also emphasized, the critical concept of modernism has altered continually over time, taking on different values and characteristics as different comparative and historical frames are employed in its analysis.[3]

For this book, an illuminating index of modernism's taxonomical shiftiness can be descried in the space between two similarly titled critical attempts to evaluate literary modernism—Harry Levin's 1960 *Massachusetts Review* article, "What Was Modernism?," and Maurice Beebe's 1974 introduction to a special issue of the *Journal of Modern Literature,* "What Modernism Was." Beebe's piece begins with explicit reference to the "provocative essay by Harry Levin" (1065), but as his titular modification suggests, Beebe is much more certain of his answers. His article defines modernism in precisely the way that Nicholls subsequently reproves: as a one-dimensional backdrop against which postmodernism can be seen, much to the latter's advantage. Beebe characterizes modernism as "detached and aloof" (1076), dismissing it as an arid, solipsistic, form-obsessed practice and opposing it to a valorized "Post-Modernist literature which will reflect a more democratic and popular view of literature" (1078). Such views, especially given the time period in which they are advanced, are hardly surprising. Of more interest here is the fact that Beebe's article engages so minimally with its alluded-to predecessor. Beyond its initial acknowledgment that the question posed by Levin's title is worth asking, Beebe's article never refers back to its critical namesake, and indeed, the modernism that Levin actually describes in his article is radically different from that which Beebe sees a short fourteen years later.

In his use of the past-tense "was," Levin certainly signals his sense that modernism has been superseded, but unlike Beebe's, his attitude to this decline is one of wistful regret. For Levin, the imminent demise of experimental modernism, which he calls "one of the most remarkable constellations of genius in the history of the West" (620), is an occasion for mourning rather than celebration, and he notes with palpable disapproval that in 1960, the novel "seems to be regressing toward the plane of documentary realism, where at best it may be indistinguishable from reportage or good journalism" (625). In answering the question posed by the title of his article, Levin advances a case for modernism as a revolutionary phase of intellectually stimulating literature, which, in his view, serves as an ethical bulwark against the thoughtless acceptance of the status quo and the too-easy embrace of contemporary notions of technological and commercial progress. In stark contrast to Beebe's view of modernism as politically and ethically unavailing, Levin's article concludes in affirmation, proposing that modernist authors "have created a conscience for a scientific age" (630). In the midst of his resigned acceptance of the inevitable ebb and flow of cultural movements, Levin assertively holds up modernism as a socially involved, morally inclined cultural practice characterized by a stance of principled intellectual resistance.

While Levin speaks, interestingly, as an American commentator on British culture, his views find confirmation in contemporaneous British assessments of modernism.[4] Stephen Spender's 1963 monograph, *The Struggle of the Modern,* provides an important example. Spender, whose career as a writer and commentator serves as a crucial bridge between the prewar and postwar literary culture of Britain, offers a view of modernism—or what he calls "the modern"—strikingly coincident with Levin's. Spender names an essentially identical canon of modern authors—James Joyce, D. H. Lawrence, T. S. Eliot, Virginia Woolf (75)—and, like Levin, credits them with an adamant rejection of regnant social values and assumptions.[5] The modern(ist) writer is opposed in Spender's schema to the "contemporary" writer, who, even though strongly critical of society, "fundamentally . . . accepts the forces and values of today" and even embraces "the same weapons of power, ideology and utilitarian philosophy" employed by the dominant class (77). Spender betrays suspicion of such intellectual submissiveness, and though he attempts a scrupulous even-handedness in discussing his categories of the modern and the contemporary, it is clear that his sympathies lie primarily with the former. Like Levin, Spender affirmatively describes the moderns' resistance to the instrumental- izing forces of the present day, observing that "to the modern, it seems that a world of unprecedented phenomena has today cut us off from the life of the past," while making sure to distinguish this disposition from the merely re- actionary (78). In the closing pages of the book, Spender presents an elegiac assessment of modernism, one in which the echoes of Levin are unmistakable: "The significance of the modern movement looked back at from today is not just that it produced some masterpieces, nor that it extended the boundar- ies of idioms, techniques, and forms, but that in certain works a fragmented civilization was redeemed within the envisioned memory of the greatness of its past. To achieve these poignant states of remembering great unifying beliefs and art while confronting chaos and destruction, safe positions of sheltered certainty were avoided, whether they were based on the kind of reasoning which goes with belief in progress and technology, or on religious dogmas" (265). The rousing tones employed by Spender in this summation rhetorically underscore the grandeur, in both purpose and achievement, he attributes to the now eclipsed modernist project. For influential critics in the early 1960s, then, modernism could still be summoned (if largely in retrospection) as a su- perlative instantiation of the redemptive energies of social, political, and aes- thetic opposition—a sense of modernism far removed from what Beebe's later article imagines.

It is, in part, modernism's semantic inconstancy in the critical arena to which the book's title, *Migrant Modernism,* gestures. For in the literary milieu on which this book focuses—1950s London—modernism was even less con- solidated than critics such as Levin or Spender, let alone Beebe, can assume. Indeed, the decade beginning in 1950 takes shape as a period of deep literary and cultural crisis in Britain, with debates about modernism very much at the fore. Articles in both academic and popular journals discussing the status and function of the postwar British novel struggle even to name what has come to be called modernism—with labels including "self-conscious literature," "su- preme fiction," "experimental fiction," "non-conformism," and "mandarin- ism"—let alone its definitive value or place in the cultural field.[6] The title's second connotation arises from the particular group of writers the book ex- amines—George Lamming, Roger Mais, Edgar Mittelholzer, V. S Naipaul, and Samuel Selvon—novelists from the English-speaking Caribbean, newly arrived to Britain and responsible for a remarkable literary efflorescence in these postwar years, one that has generally been considered the founding moment of the Anglophone Caribbean literary tradition. Although their singular importance as founders has recently come under productive critical scrutiny,[7] the sheer number of novels published by West Indian writers in the United Kingdom in the postwar years (over seventy between 1950 and 1962 by Kenneth Ramchand's count), as well as the awards and critical attention accorded the Windrush writers (including Guggenheim Fellowships and the W. Somerset Maugham Award), suggest a phenomenon whose importance to the establishment of Anglophone Caribbean literary culture in the twentieth century would be difficult to deny.[8] With regard to these writers, the title references the book's central claim: that the novels of these migrant authors evolved out of an affiliation that both embraced and productively altered the oppositionality of modernist practice registered by Levin and Spender. Taken as a whole, then, *Migrant Modernism* signifies two intersecting contentions with regard to modernism. The first is that modernism's self-reflexive, counterdiscursive impulses migrated into the very foundations of Anglophone Caribbean fiction. The second is that these migrant Windrush writers constitute an important, alternative strain of modernist practice, different from and far less pessimistic than the inward-turning late modernism posited by critics such as Tyrus Miller and Jed Esty.[9]

In articulating this alternative strain, I have taken encouragement from Laura Doyle and Laura Winkiel's *Geomodernisms: Race, Modernism, Modernity*, which suggests the need for "configuring more global and longer histories for modernism than is typical" (14). Explicitly positioning itself against more traditional understandings of modernism as a solely European practice limited to the early twentieth century, Doyle and Winkiel's volume emphasizes the diverse ways in which non-Western writers have deployed and engaged with modernism. The expansive impulse of their book resonates with a disciplinary formation in modernist scholarship that has come to be identified as the new modernist studies. Tentatively codified by Douglas Mao and Rebecca L. Walkowitz in 2008, this critical tendency is characterized by a willingness to broaden understandings of modernist practice well outside the categories of time, space, and medium within which it has conventionally been studied. With reference especially to the first two of these three classificatory boundaries, Mao and Walkowitz delineate an indisputable "transnational turn" in modernist criticism that ventures beyond the familiar European internationalism of prewar modernism, into what has normally been considered the province of (postwar) postcolonial literature.[10]

Customarily, of course, this province has not been particularly welcoming to such critical incursions: as Patrick Williams has argued, postcolonial literary critics originally defined their field by a "reaccentuation" ("'Simultaneous uncontemporaneities,'" 13) of modernism as an antithetical discourse, and as Simon Gikandi has observed, "for almost fifty years, postcolonial critics and scholars have treated modernism with suspicion" ("Preface," 421). Certainly, as postcolonial literary studies emerged as a theoretically consolidated discipline, its contours were often established via an oppositional contrast with modernism. For example, Stephen Slemon, in a special issue of *ARIEL* devoted to a discussion of the postcolonial-postmodern divide, describes these avenues of inquiry as "the two critical discourses which today constitute themselves specifically in opposition" to modernism ("Modernism's Last Post," 4).[11] This opposition, for Slemon, is natural for postcolonial criticism, since he understands modernism to be an artistic practice founded on "the wholesale appropriation and refiguration of non-Western artistic and cultural practices" ("Modernism's Last Post," 3). A founding theoretical text of postcolonial studies, *The Empire Writes Back,* sets up a similar contrast, asserting that "the self-critical and anarchic models of twentieth-century culture which modernism ushered in can be seen to depend on the existence of a postcolonial Other which provides its condition of formation" (Ashcroft, Griffiths, and Tiffin, *Empire Writes Back,* 158).[12] In establishing the boundaries of the discipline, then, there was an early tendency, as Charles Pollard sees it, to rely rather easily on an assumption that "modernism is to postmodernism as colonialism is to postcolonialism" (*New World Modernisms,* 9).[13] Williams proffers a convincing historical explanation for this drive for differentiation, surmising that "one of the reasons for post-colonial animosity towards modernism is no doubt the fact that post-colonial critics encounter modernism as already *in situ,* an institutionalised, would-be hegemonic, seemingly reactionary presence, and one which even in its self-reflexive moments appears obsessively concerned with the condition of the West" ("'Simultaneous uncontemporaneities,'" 18). Following the historicizing logic of Williams's assessment, I examine the historical particularity of the postwar London literary scene. In doing so, I hope to illustrate that for these early West Indian authors, modernism was not, as postcolonial criticism sometimes assumes, merely an alien literary force to be rejected, but a potentially liberatory aesthetic with strategically useful cultural connotations.

In this way, this book finds common cause with the increasing number of postcolonial literary critics willing to acknowledge the affinities between post-colonial and modernist literature. Gikandi, not least, provocatively asserts that it is mainly "in the language and structure of modernism that a postcolonial experience came to be articulated and imagined in literary form" ("Preface," 420). In her synoptic account of the field, *Colonial and Postcolonial Literature,* Elleke Boehmer has similarly suggested the need for scholars to "recognize that aspects of colonized and colonial expatriate reality were distinctively, per-haps in some cases even definitively modernist" (119), while Jahan Ramazani's *A Transnational Poetics* starts from a view that the "disciplinary boundaries between postcolonial and modernist studies have tended to veil the overlap, circulation, and friction between postcolonialism and modernism" (xii).[14] The language Ramazani employs to describe these aesthetic and critical junc-tures is worth noting. In studiously avoiding the language of unproblematic assimilation, it evokes instead an apposite sense of differential connection and contention as the features characterizing the relation between the postcolonial and the modernist. It bears emphasizing here, in agreement with Ramazani, that to interrelate elements is not to make them identical: the flattening out of all differences between the postcolonial and the modernist would threaten to duplicate a long history of the reinscription of nonmetropolitan resources into a metropolitan frame for the benefit of the latter's self-understanding. When making such connections, it is imperative always to keep in mind the vast im-balances of power that structure the cultural field.

It is, in fact, via the theoretical concept of a cultural field—influentially established by Pierre Bourdieu—that I seek to articulate the emergence of the Anglophone Caribbean novel with British modernism. For Bourdieu, *field* is a term used to describe the complicated social matrix within which particular-ized forms of human activity occur. The cultural field is thus meant to indicate the array of institutional structures through which culture, in a given social grouping, comes into being, including "not only the direct producers of the work in its materiality (artist, writer, etc.) but also the producers of the mean-ing and value of the work—critics, publishers, gallery directors and the whole set of agents whose combined efforts produce consumers capable of knowing and recognizing the work of art as such" (*Field of Cultural Production,* 37).[15] In this way, Bourdieu seeks to find a balance between the view of art as mere superstructure directly determined by the interests of the economically and politically dominant and the view of art as an absolutely free space of aesthetic creativity: artists, that is, cannot be seen to create in a sociocultural vacuum, but neither can they be seen *simply* to reflect their sociocultural environment. In Bourdieu's thinking the cultural field is an unstable, fluid structure that simultaneously defines and is defined by the contrasting positions taken up within it by individual actors at a particular moment in time. At stake always, in the positions within any given cultural field, is legitimacy—what "counts" in terms of style, content, genre, or political disposition. Specifically distinguished from a vague "spirit of the times" or a rigidly determinative structure, the cultural field takes the form of a "space of possibles, a system of different position-takings" (*Rules of Art,* 200), through which the regnant definition of cultural legitimacy is constantly defined, contested, and overhauled.

In terms of the specifically literary field, Bourdieu observes that the object of struggle "is the monopoly of literary legitimacy, that is, among other things, the monopoly of the power to say with authority who is authorized to call himself writer (etc.) or even to say who is a writer and who has the authority to say who is a writer" (*Rules of Art,* 224), a discursive power struggle with obvious pertinence to thinking about the arduous emergence of postcolonial Anglophone literatures. Bourdieu, of course, employs France for his illustration of the literary field, such that it becomes useful as well briefly to consider Pascale Casanova's *The World Republic of Letters,* which expands Bourdieu's concepts beyond French national borders to encompass what Casanova defines as "world literary space" (82). Although Casanova's larger account of this space is somewhat weakened by its reliance on a schematic teleology (at times strongly resembling a diffusionist discourse of development), it is insightful in establishing that the structuring hierarchies Bourdieu finds in the French literary field should be seen to operate on an international scale.[16] Significantly, Casanova's analytic system entails a global purview, suggesting that "the link between literary form and political history requires that texts be considered in relation to the national and international literary space that mediates political, ideological, national, and literary stakes" (322). As important, for the purposes of this book, both Bourdieu and Casanova argue that merely *engaging* in the struggle for literary stakes is not only an acknowledgment of the basic validity of the field but a necessary aspect of its constitution. As Bourdieu observes, "the generative, unifying principle of this 'system' is the struggle, with all the contradictions it engenders (so that participation in the struggle—which may be indicated objectively by, for example, the attacks that are suffered—can be used as the criterion establishing that a work belongs to the field of position-takings and its author to the field of positions)" (*Field of Cultural Production,* 34). Similarly, Casanova asserts that "no literary project, not even the most formalistic, can be explained in a monadic fashion: every project must be put in relation to the totality of rival projects within the same literary space" (320). Looked at this way, even postcolonial texts engaged in the most vehement disavowals of metropolitan mores nevertheless come into view as position-taking participants in a larger literary field, unified with their apparent antagonists by virtue of sharing the same disputed cultural terrain.[17]

Accordingly, this book highlights the contested literary field—centered in London, but by definition transnational—out of which postwar West Indian novels emerged. Focusing on the Windrush novelists who first established a publishing foothold there, the book maintains that these pioneering figures, far from writing in splendid, anticolonial isolation, were necessarily enmeshed in the local politics of British literary production. The nature of these local politics is established via examination of contemporaneous reviews of the relevant novels in the British literary press. Although for Bourdieu the institutional mechanisms of a field extend much deeper than such largely ephemeral texts—into longer-term stakes of publishing, prestige, and ultimately canonization in the academy—both the reviewers and reviews are nevertheless crucial, initial gatekeepers to legitimation in the literary world. More important for the case being made here, they offer the most reliably documented source for how the literary field was immediately *experienced* by Windrush writers: the reviews explicitly reveal how influential figures in the British literary establishment understood and assessed early West Indian literature. While the writers discussed here surely kept a close eye on how they were received at home in the Caribbean, their letters, manuscripts, and published writing all indicate they also (by necessity, given the prerogatives for continuing to be a published author) kept well apprised of their British reception.[18] Thus, employing a basic framework suggested by Bourdieu and Casanova, I hope to show how these writers were obliged to negotiate an ostensibly colonial publishing structure in order to tender their own anticolonial message—in a form recognizable within that very structure. Within this context, an elective affinity with modernist practice was a crucial strategic position, lending the Windrush writers literary legitimacy without compromising their oppositional political aims.

It is by now not entirely unusual to associate Anglophone Caribbean literature and modernism, even though, in parallel with postcolonial criticism as a whole, criticism devoted to Caribbean literature has not always been comfortable with this association. Gikandi's *Writing in Limbo: Modernism and Caribbean Literature,* the first book-length treatment of Caribbean literature's modernist investments, for instance, is expressly motivated by a desire to counteract the "strong critical resistance to modernism . . . in the study of Caribbean literature" (252).[19] However, as Gikandi's book decisively illustrates, "Caribbean writers cannot adopt the history and culture of European modernism, especially as defined by the colonizing structures, but neither can they escape from it" (3). Following Gikandi, several more recent monographs have explicitly attempted to make connections between modernist and Anglophone Caribbean literature: Pollard's *New World Modernisms: T. S. Eliot, Derek Walcott, and Kamau Brathwaite* and Mary Lou Emery's *Modernism, the Visual, and Caribbean Literature.*[20] Pollard's book convincingly traces the Eliotic influences underpinning the work of Brathwaite and Walcott. Directly countering claims of Caribbean literature's antipathy to modernism, Pollard argues that the English-speaking Caribbean's two most heralded poets "seem less anxious to sweep away the burden of modernism and more anxious to exploit its resources for new purposes" (19). Focusing on the politics of visual representation, Emery's book likewise asserts the possibilities Caribbean writers have located in modernist practice, arguing that it has enabled them "to offer trans-figurative countervisions" (19) to a colonial system intent on fixing Caribbean subjects in an objectifying gaze.[21] At a fundamental level, these books by Emery, Gikandi, and Pollard all register the crucial recombinatory possibilities offered to Caribbean literature by modernist aesthetics, what J. Michael Dash has described as modernism's fluid "cross-cultural ideal that privileges neither ossified sovereignty nor the uniformity of universalizing sameness" (*Other America,* 163).[22] What they do not register very strongly, however, is a sense of the particular historical context in which these possibilities could seem so attractive to the Windrush generation.

Peter Kalliney's consideration of the BBC radio program *Caribbean Voices,* in contrast, puts a great deal of emphasis on the immediate cultural currents influencing West Indian literary production in London.[23] Examining the role the program played in facilitating the publishing and critical successes of Windrush writing, Kalliney demonstrates how alignment with the BBC "allowed black colonial writers (in very limited, particular circumstances) to interact with, even join, London's cultural establishment" ("Metropolitan Modernism," 94). Although building on Kalliney's convincing description of the mutually beneficial institutional alliances that formed between Windrush writers and well-positioned champions of prewar modernism, I argue that the period's politics of form go well beyond the almost accidental confluence of aesthetic agendas Kalliney suggests. Indeed, although the forces structuring the British literary field clearly helped pave the way for postwar West Indian writers' modernist stylings, the counterconventional impulse of modernist form also lent itself to the kind of anticolonial critique-from-within engaged in by Windrush novels. If Vincent Sherry is correct in identifying early Anglo-European modernism's primary significance as the "reenacting of the end of Old World values, attitudes, and practices" occasioned by World War I (*Great War*, 322), an analogous suspicion of rational (imperial) discourse might be descried in the formal techniques characteristic of the Caribbean authors examined here. The pages that follow will suggest that at this crucial postwar moment of both literary and political change, West Indian novelists not only embraced the contemporary cultural legibility and prestige of modernist writing but also found something particularly resonant in its mobile forms of self-aware critique.[24]

This book thus undertakes a thickly descriptive account of how literary modernism was deployed by the earliest and most influential of the Windrush novelists at a particular place and time—London, in the years immediately following World War II. The first chapter details the cultural backdrop against which the rest of the book's readings can be understood, delineating the governing taste of *Caribbean Voices* under the editorship of Henry Swanzy in conjunction with an examination of Kingsley Amis as the dominant British voice of the era's significant (if sometimes exaggerated) reaction against modernism. This initial chapter establishes the complicated cultural currents of the period, within which, for a young, nonwhite author from the colonial provinces, an affiliation with modernism could provide some distinct institutional advantages while also conveying an equally distinct literary-political message.[25] The following chapters examine the output of the first four Windrush writers to publish novels in Britain—Mittelholzer, Selvon, Lamming, and Mais, respectively—focusing on their diverse engagements with modernist aesthetic forms and the cultural valence attached to them by British literary reviewers.[26]

It is important to observe here that all of the authors treated in this book are men. Belinda Edmondson has made the case that the early nationalist authors from the Anglophone Caribbean articulated their claims in terms that were overwhelmingly masculine.[27] It is hard to argue otherwise: although a good deal of work has been done to excavate the unsung role of women in European modernism, a parallel project would not be as practicable in the case of Windrush-era novels. For a variety of reasons, including simply the demographic fact of primarily male participation in the initial stages of postwar migration, discouragingly few West Indian women published novels at this time (though many did publish short stories and poems in *Caribbean Voices* and in the region's little magazines).[28] Those who did—namely Phyllis Shand Allfrey, Lucille Iremonger, and Ada Quayle—were associated with the white planter class or the colonial administration. As such, they faced quite different challenges in the cultural sphere—they were not at the time grouped with the major Windrush figures, nor do their political prerogatives fit easily into dominant postcolonial narratives.[29] Critics such as Alison Donnell, Evelyn O'Callaghan, and Leah Rosenberg have all made strong cases for the important function of women's writing before the Windrush era, but this influential postwar generation of novelists is unmistakably comprised of Caribbean men.[30]

Notwithstanding their gender uniformity, the individual writers treated in the following chapters deploy modernism in quite different ways, to quite different ends. Mittelholzer, for example, embraces formal experimentation in a conscious embodiment of T. S. Eliot's ideas of tradition, suggesting that a new, West Indian literary aesthetic could be recognized as distinctive only through mindful reference to the British tradition from which it wished to separate. Lamming, on the other hand, uses his pugnaciously difficult style as an assertive strategy to signal an unexoticized, intellectually valid West Indian difference while simultaneously highlighting the possibility, however arduous, of intercommunal understanding. Selvon, far different in personal and political temperament, employs modernist forms as an argument for the recognition of a rooted cosmopolitanism, signaling the universal without wholly subsuming the local in the former's abstracting force. Finally, Mais's experimentation enacts a self-reflexive meditation on the political efficacy of language and literature, providing a Caribbean echo of modernism's bedeviled attempts to harness the consciousness-changing potential of aesthetic production. The book's coda reflects on the early critical and editorial work of Naipaul, showing how his rising prominence in the decade was instrumental in steering British-based Anglophone Caribbean literature away from its modernist roots, into a more placidly British style. It also briefly considers the fragmented legacy of

the Caribbean Artists Movement, in terms of its split into culturally nationalist Black British and Caribbean forms, suggesting that this split has led to
the most prominent inheritors of the Caribbean modernist tradition, Kamau
Brathwaite and Wilson Harris, being perceived in radically different critical
frames that serve to obscure the significance of their predecessors' modernist
entanglements.

The book's final aim is in some sense an archaeological one: to excavate
the influences and practices instrumental in these early postcolonial novels'
emergence, demonstrating that the contemporary West Indian canon in fact
established itself via a strategic engagement with modernist forms. Against
an origin narrative of West Indian literature (like that of most postcolonial
literatures) that is normally conceived through a frame that directs attention
to the formation of an autonomous, autochthonous national-literary tradition, I propose an account that recognizes the densely transnational forces
through which these Windrush novels took form.[31] In my critical emphasis
on London—the inaugural site of this generation's startlingly prolific and influential literary production—I aim to question the strict territorialization of
both Anglo-modernist and Caribbean literature, highlighting the (still) hierarchical literary space they indubitably share. In doing so, I hope to point not
only to the consciously crafted modernist affiliations of these migrant West
Indian writers but also to the ways in which they can be seen to have shifted
traditional understandings of modernism. The later stages of modernism influentially characterized by critics such as Miller and Esty involve an anxious
turning in toward the condition of England and its native inhabitants. While
demonstrably imbricated in the cultural trends of the British majority, the migrant modernism analyzed here displays a much more buoyantly optimistic
oppositionality characteristic of an earlier prewar modernism, a disposition
that might be seen to manifest itself in multiple forms and locations outside of
Europe over the course of the century.[32] The fact that such an overtly anticolonial project found expression through a willingly intertextual dialogue with
forms readily identified as metropolitan should not be seen as politically dis-
honorable or somehow off-putting. Instead, I suggest, these pioneering Windrush novels stand as an important example of how a non-European literature
shrewdly entered (and thus in some ways altered) the well-fortified realm of
high literature, taking modernist techniques of critique and developing them
in a more politically and racially expansive—or, put another way, postcolonial—direction.

1   At the Scene of the Time
Postwar London

> But the Movement is interesting. It is interesting, like other movements,
> not only in itself, but because of the light which it throws upon the
> work of writers who are outside of it, perhaps opposed to it.
>
> —J. D. Scott, "In the Movement"

Early in his 1960 volume of essays, *The Pleasures of Exile*, George Lamming
fixes his sharply analytical eye on "an English critic, Mr. Kingsley Amis, discussing West Indian novelists in the *Spectator*" (28). The discussion in question, Amis's 1958 "Fresh Winds from the West," treats eight recently released
books by Caribbean authors and stands as a testament to the high visibility
of Windrush writing on the British cultural scene at the time. However, Lamming is not particularly pleased by the type of attention represented by Amis's
article, which he dismisses as ill considered and virtually bereft of literary
discernment. Lamming's irritation attaches most strongly to his impression
that Amis, despite occupying a high cultural position as novelist, critic, and
university teacher, displays the "type of mind [that] cannot register the West
Indian writer as a subject for intelligent and thoughtful consideration" (29).
Aggrieved at this lack of intellectual seriousness, Lamming proceeds to dissect
Amis's critical assumptions, revealing a great deal about the obstacles facing
West Indian authors in Britain in the process. For example, Lamming rebukes
Amis's comfortable conceptions of Englishness and its inherent superiority,
describing how Amis accepts "the privilege so natural and so free of being the
child and product and voice of a colonising civilisation" (30). Amis's lack of
political engagement and maturity is bitingly condemned, characterized as an
ethos of "shouting, in mockery, the adolescent privileges that are the theme
of any Mr. Don't-really-care-a-damn-except-to-be-as-decent-as-possible" (30).
Lamming also hints at the tacit racism of such a view, imagining that a black
writer expressing the pallid decency Amis advocates might be "regarded as a

simple, articulate boy," based on the British assumption of colonialism "as a development and later as an improvement on slavery" (30). The lengthy example from Amis's article with which Lamming begins his caustic assessment suggests one final point of disagreement—one regarding literary form. The passage included by Lamming is the article's opening paragraph, an extended diatribe on literary experiment, a stylistic practice Amis dismisses as risibly fraudulent and misguided. Although Lamming does not explicitly address this aspect of Amis's article, the very style of *The Pleasures of Exile* (not to mention the four novels Lamming had published by this time) stands in a relation of silent but poignant dissent from Amis's dismissal of the usefulness of experimental prose. Lamming's implicit disagreement points to an important dynamic in postwar literary London, in which younger writers were rebelling against the techniques of prewar modernists such as Woolf and Joyce (both derisively referred to in the passage of Amis's Lamming provides). Lamming's brief excursus on Amis in *The Pleasures of Exile* in fact encapsulates some of the most crucial issues confronting Windrush writers in Britain, issues revolving around social privilege, politics, race, and—refracted through all of these—literary form. Although Lamming, even here, generally disavows any meaningful interest in Amis, or indeed any other English critics, his very inclusion of Amis in the text suggests the role the British cultural field had in helping shape West Indian literary production in the postwar years.[1]

As Kenneth Ramchand observes in his seminal study *The West Indian Novel and Its Background,* during these formative postwar years London "is indisputably the West Indian literary capital" (63), and certainly, following Ramchand, the awkward irony of such an important generation of anticolonial writers working in the metropolitan heart of empire has frequently been noted. However, beyond simple acknowledgment, critics have focused relatively little attention on the ramifications arising from the fact that this pioneering generation of West Indian authors lived and published almost exclusively in London. Most critical accounts that do focus on Windrush writing in London, such as John Clement Ball's *Imagining London: Postcolonial Fiction and the Transnational Metropolis* or John McLeod's *Postcolonial London: Rewriting the Metropolis,* concentrate their discussion on how this influx of migrant writers affected British literature and culture. They do not extensively consider the ways London, in turn, worked to mold these writers' literary output.[2] And while a good deal of attention has rightly been put on the BBC's *Caribbean Voices* by insightful commentators like Laurence Breiner and Glyne Griffith, their accounts tend to emphasize the separate, Caribbean-oriented community in the heart of empire that the show's production worked to form rather than examining interactions between Windrush writers and the surrounding British literary culture.

More recently, critics such as Peter Kalliney and Gail Low have focused scholarly attention on the important ways in which the demands and politics of publishing affected West Indian writing in the metropolitan setting of London.[3] Focusing on the Windrush writers' alignments within the British literary system, Kalliney and Low both insist on viewing that system as a malleable, if unavoidably constitutive, feature of West Indian literary production, rather than merely a sinister or oppressive force. This emphasis is fruitful: it acknowledges that the institutional and geographical placement of the Windrush generation has more than a passing thematic or historical significance to an understanding of their work and hence the emergence of postwar Anglophone Caribbean literature itself. Taken in this context, these novelists can be seen working toward the goals of cultural and political autonomy in the Caribbean—as they surely were—but doing so within the formidable constraints imposed by the London literary landscape. As this chapter hopes to show, this landscape is one that became increasingly influenced by the prerogatives of a group of writers originally referred to as the Movement.[4] Composed of English writers such as Amis, Donald Davie, Phillip Larkin, and John Wain, the Movement had cultural convictions—proudly philistine, aggressively nationalist, and anxiously concerned with the changing dynamics of class (not race) within Great Britain proper—that were largely antithetical to the concerns of the Windrush writers. If, as this chapter's epigraph suggests, the Movement can be of interest "not only in itself, but because of the light which it throws upon the work of writers who are outside of it, perhaps opposed to it" (J. D. Scott, "In the Movement," 400), considerable light can be thrown upon the Windrush writers active in London simultaneous with the rise of the Movement. Indeed, a close examination of the combative field of postwar literary London suggests that these pioneering West Indian writers overtly occupied positions both outside and in opposition to the Movement.[5] An analytic emphasis on London—undoubtedly the center from which postwar West Indian writing emanated—thus brings the transnational sophistication of the Windrush writers' achievements more properly into view, showing how, even in its most overtly nationalist stage, Anglophone Caribbean literature was inescapably imbricated (but not imprisoned) in metropolitan circuits of exchange and reception.

It should be emphasized here that Windrush literary production cannot be reduced solely to a reflexive response to the London literary world's governing tastes. Certainly, in Bourdieu's terms, the field is not an inert, impersonal force, but a flexible social space continually constituted via an accumulation of individual actions. These actions, of course, are themselves structurally informed by the all but imperceptible dispositions individuals bring to bear on their choices, a concept for which Bourdieu employs the term *habitus.*[6] In abstract terms, the mutually constitutive interactions between field and habitus—delicately balanced between determinant structure and individual choice—are the process whereby social life unfolds in Bourdieu's system of thought. In more particular terms, this necessitates an acknowledgment that Windrush writers did not come to London as blank screens upon which the modes and mores of the metropole were straightforwardly projected. Certainly, there already existed a legacy of modernist literary practice from the region, embodied in the work of authors such as Alejo Carpentier, Aimé Césaire, Claude McKay, Jean Rhys, and Eric Walrond. Although the Windrush writers manifest little if any overt knowledge of such a cultural inheritance, its very existence suggests that what Dash describes as "the spirit of intellectual dissidence, imaginative restlessness, and dialectical struggle" (*Other America,* 15) characteristic of the region's modernism emanates from a far-reaching array of influences in both spatial and temporal registers. A multitude of thinkers—including Sidney Mintz, Tzvetan Todorov, and most importantly C. L. R. James—have considered the Caribbean itself to be the inaugural ground of what we think of today as modernity, such that the region can be conceived as a space in which the social forces of alienation, disjuncture, rootlessness, and denaturalization often thought to catalyze modernist aesthetics are present long before the formation of European modernism.[7] Along these lines, David Scott's description of (C. L. R. James's depiction of) Toussaint l'Oeverture as a tragic figure of modernity might double as a relatively fitting description of a (male) modernist writer: "inescapably modern as he is obliged by the modern conditions of his life to be, he must seek his freedom in the very technologies, conceptual languages, and institutional formations in which modernity's rationality has sought his enslavement" (*Conscripts of Modernity,* 168). In some ways, then, as critics such as Dash, Gikandi, and Scott suggest, the critical self-reflexivity characteristic of modernist aesthetics resonates with long-established strategies of Caribbean self-expression and survival.[8]

At a more individual level, it is clear that Lamming, Mais, Mittelholzer, and Selvon had already established (in various ways, to differing degrees) a self-aware, antibourgeois, oppositional disposition characteristic of their modernist predecessors while living in the Caribbean. Lamming, for example, seems to have developed his proclivity for literary iconoclasm well before he arrived in London in 1950. As he has remarked in interviews, his reading tastes were formed in his teacher Frank Collymore's private library, largely in reaction to the school curriculum, which Lamming describes as "Jane Austen, some Shakespeare, Wells's novel *Kipps,* and so on . . . whatever the Cambridge Syndicate demanded" (interview, by Munro and Sander, 6).[9] In opposition to this curriculum, one of the most important discoveries Lamming made at this age, in his account, was of Joseph Conrad, whose writing he consistently names as an influence, one that inculcated "a reinforcement of that relation to the word, the word as instrument of exploration," rather than a merely transparent vehicle of already created thought ("George Lamming Talks," 11).[10] Lamming's early letters to Collymore from Trinidad likewise suggest a keen interest in literary revolt, mentioning his close study of earlier models of rebellion such as T. S. Eliot and William Wordsworth, while drawing comparisons between them and the expressly experimental aims of himself and his peers. In another letter, he invokes the term *enfantes terribles* to describe his generation of West Indian authors, specifically identifying them as conscious inheritors of a tradition of modernist insurrection.[11]

Alison Donnell's *Twentieth-Century Caribbean Literature* demonstrates the similarly domestic development of Mais's rebellious literary sensibility, via his critical contention with a locally influential Jamaican poet, J. E. C. McFarlane. For Donnell, Mais's disagreement with McFarlane prompts him into the "recasting of a culturally relevant modernist manifesto" (43) for his own aims. Citing passages from a 1940 article Mais wrote in *Public Opinion,* "Where the Roots Lie," Donnell observes Mais "echoing the fierce guidelines of Ezra Pound in 'A Few Don'ts by an Imagiste'" (48). In this literary call to arms, Mais, like Lamming, is interested in repudiating complacent understandings of "the school syllabus," identifying heretical energies in the English literary canon itself: "If only you would wake up for long enough to give the matter some thought you would realise that these men in their day were the last syllable in modernity! Chaucer broke new ground and a lot of traditions, so did Milton, so did Shakespeare" (quoted in Donnell, *Twentieth-Century Caribbean Literature*, 48). Early examples of aesthetic philosophizing from Selvon, such as his 1947 *Evening News* (Trinidad) column, "Michael Wentworth Contends," or Mittelholzer's recollections in *A Swarthy Boy*—which closes with the pugnacious artistic credo of his youth, "Victory or death!" (151)—also underscore that the Windrush writers' aesthetic nonconformism was inaugurated in the Caribbean, well before they arrived in London.[12]

Nevertheless, in the examples above, the fact that both Lamming and Mais figure their acts of literary insurgence *through* reference to British forebears introduces an important, if familiar, complication to the perceived autochthony of these writers' aesthetics. As the shared allusions to the educational system also underscore, the Caribbean space in which the Windrush generation became literate, let alone literary, was thoroughly permeated by a British-derived view of cultural value.[13] The habitus these writers brought with them to London, then, appears as a complicated mixture of reverence for the literary tradition of England and animosity (enhanced by the racism encountered on arrival) toward the imperial attitudes such a tradition continued to underwrite. The affective ambivalence of the Windrush writers' position is captured in Lamming's formulation of "the dubious refuge of a metropolitan culture" to which his generation migrated (*Pleasures of Exile*, 22) and later by a pessimistic description of the limited choice he and his peers faced between the "eternal dispossession" of exile in London and "the ignorant sneer of a Victorian colonial outpost" back home (47).[14] As Lamming famously observed in this same essay, the West Indian writer (at least during the postwar era he was describing) "writes always for the foreign reader" (43). To take this claim merely at face value would be a mistake—Lamming clearly envisions the eventual emergence of a home audience as both possible and desirable. To write it off entirely, on the other hand, would be to ignore Lamming's point about how powerfully geopolitical and economic forces structured the ways in which West Indian culture could at that time be produced. The concentration on London in the pages that follow, then, is not meant to suggest that the Caribbean is unimportant to these writers, whether as an originating source or as an ultimate horizon of value. It is, however, an acknowledgment that the underlying structural features of the British literary field cannot be lightly dismissed. Indeed, it is only through a negotiation of this field that the Windrush writers were able to establish the basis of what we now think of as Anglophone Caribbean literature, a fact emblematic not of cultural subjugation or defeat, but rather of the complex, mutually constitutive nature of the relation between British and West Indian, in the cultural (not to mention the economic and political) sphere.[15]

Caribbean Voices in the Belly of the Beast

The arrival of the SS *Empire Windrush*—a decommissioned troop transport ship officially carrying 492 Caribbean passengers—at Tilbury docks on 22 June 1948 has become an iconic moment in British history, symbolizing the inauguration of large-scale migration from the territories of the British Empire that led inexorably to Britain's contemporary self-presentation as a multicultural polity.[16] Although the Caribbean was not the only region to experience considerable emigration to the "mother country" during this time, its migrants (estimated at around 250,000 in total) attracted a great deal of the attention accorded this population of newcomers to England in the postwar period, and the "Jamaicans," as they were often erroneously generalized, tended to dominate the media portrayals of England's changing demographics.[17] The United Kingdom to which Windrush migrants arrived, however, was most certainly not the proud, invincible nation that had traditionally been promulgated abroad for the edification of Britain's colonial subjects. Ravaged by the war, and deeply in debt to both its colonial holdings and the United States, Britain was uncomfortably coming to terms with the emerging Cold War powers' eclipse of its previously unrivaled international influence in matters economic and political. As the British historian John Montgomery somberly observed in 1965, the nation's share of worldwide trade by 1955 had been more than halved to 15 percent since 1899, and there seemed little hope of stemming the decline. Such economic vulnerability manifested itself throughout the 1950s by recurrent hard currency crises that threatened the nation's solvency and undermined national confidence. Norman Mackenzie, writing in 1959, captures his generation's sense of beleaguered bewilderment that Britain's world position was far different from its accustomed dominance: "Two world wars, punctuated by a great depression, have made it impossible for the British to compete on equal terms with America or Russia, or even to hold what they have" (*Conviction*, 12). Long accustomed to a leading role on the international stage, the United Kingdom after World War II was in a palpably precarious position, rapidly losing influence around the world while finding itself without the financial or military resources to preserve even a semblance of its old preeminence.[18]

Internal to the country, circumstances were likewise uncertain and unstable in the postwar years. Wartime rationing continued well into the 1950s for several basic commodities, and the destructive effects of the Blitz on the nation's housing stock remained visible and acute. Moreover, between the years 1945 and 1951, Clement Attlee's Labour government was engaged in its historic attempt to break down the traditional barriers of British class privilege by instituting a host of innovative social and economic programs, including the creation of the National Health System; the vast expansion of access to a university education through scholarships and the establishment of new "redbrick" universities; and the nationalization of many key industries such as transport, utilities, coal, communications, and banking. Although the ultimate effects of this attempt at dislodging the entrenchment of upper-class hegemony should not be overestimated, concrete social and economic effects were certainly felt, and the subsequent uncertainty resulting from a partial unmooring of status markers was more or less inevitable.[19] As Malcolm Bradbury asserts, "in the aftermath of war Britain went through a deep and fundamental revolution, a shift of social power" (*Modern British Novel*, 269).

This potent combination of external and internal destabilization, it is generally agreed, led to a social world that was unsettled, uncertain, and shot through with a shifting mass of competing cultural, political, and economic agendas that left the British populace struggling to reconsolidate a viable image of national identity. Historian David Childs describes the mood of the country upon Winston Churchill's return as prime minister in 1951 as markedly unstable, noting that "in this changing world Britain experienced difficulty in finding its place, clarifying its position and renewing its identity" (*Britain since 1945*, 55). Swinging from the social-reform-minded age of austerity immediately after the war to the age of consumer affluence that Tory prime minister Harold Macmillan confidently proclaimed by the end of the 1950s, British life in the early postwar years appears as unusually unpredictable and unsettling, experienced at the time as "a diffuse social unease, as an unnaturally accelerated pace of social change, as an unhingeing of stable patterns, moral points of reference" (Hall et al., *Policing the Crisis*, 321). Domestic turmoil, coupled with insecurity on the international stage, is commonly presumed to have inspired the somewhat anxious call for national recovery characteristic of much political, social, and cultural discussion in the 1950s, an urgency only further exacerbated by a widespread fear of cultural invasion by American mass culture—especially rock-n-roll and jazz—aroused by the expanding economic and political power of Britain's Cold War partner. Gikandi has observed, moreover, how the arrival of immigrants from the former colonies intensified the perceived crisis of postwar Englishness. In his account, the new immigrants become "a real presence and cultural threat to the pastoral image of England as an island" while the decline of empire "nullifies the value previously invested in colonial subjects and spaces" (*Maps of Englishness,* 70). While the newly arrived Windrush writers would be actively concerned with the continuing ramifications of Britain's imperial role, Britain's own uneasy public discourse would increasingly concentrate on more insular, domestic matters.

This anxious, inward turn registered discernibly in the cultural trends of the era as well. As Arthur Marwick suggests, "it could reasonably be said that in the forties and early fifties British political and social thought was inward-looking, concentrating, for instance, on the Welfare State, on the British vision of the brave new world. . . . The novels of the time, too, have a national, even parochial, quality" (*British Society since 1945,* 76). Similarly, Marina MacKay and Lyndsey Stonebridge's introduction to *British Fiction after Modernism* describes the collective mood of British writing in terms of a growing insularity, observing that "as their island shrank, mid-century writers became more domestic and domesticated" (1). John Rosselli's plaintive 1958 observation in the *London Magazine* about the generation's limited literary purview captures a common critique of the day: "now our novelists seem almost extravagant in their refusal to push anywhere far from bed and board and the Sunday paper" ("Mood of the Month," 39). Robert Hewison has noted that one of the key themes of postwar cultural politics in Britain was "the promotion of a conservative image of English identity" (*Culture and Consensus,* 45), an uneasy shoring up of national character captured most revealingly in the wholehearted glee with which the entire nation celebrated the 1953 coronation of Queen Elizabeth II as cultural commentators proclaimed the inauguration of a "new Elizabethan age." In a 1960 article, Rayner Heppenstall aptly captures the conservative elements animating the revitalized national feeling, noting "the recrudescence here in the past ten years of an Englishry based on bowler hats and moustaches, churchgoing and dressing for theatres, the re-investment with glamour of Eton . . . [and] the reconstitution of a royalist mystique which had been long forgotten" ("Divided We Stand," 45). From the opposite end of the political spectrum, figures like Richard Hoggart were attempting to formulate a definition of Britishness via the assertion of a vibrant, vernacular (and uniquely British) working-class culture.[20] Across a broad range of motivations and political alignments, then, the postwar cultural field in Britain finds unity in its collective restiveness about the viability of Britain's national identity.[21]

In the literary arena, the era's cultural-national disputes were most frequently framed as a confrontation between modernism and realism. The modernist experimentation dominant before the war still attracted powerful cultural adherents, but its influence was clearly on the wane. In self-conscious contrast to the far-reaching ambitions of their modernist predecessors, the decade's proponents of realism consistently portrayed their aesthetic stance to be in keeping with the more modest, inward instincts of the postwar nation, signaling their alignment "with 'good old English tradition' (empiricism, common sense, social comedy along the lines of Fielding and Dickens)" (Gasiorek, *Post-war British Fiction,* 4). Although this struggle for cultural supremacy never reached any permanently decisive conclusion, the decade's neorealist antagonism to modernism ultimately came to predominate the postwar literary discussion in Britain: the broad tenor of the era's literary opinion conveyed in the title of Rubin Rabinovitz's 1967 study, *The Reaction against Experiment in the English Novel, 1950–1960,* matches most critical accounts and, more important, represents the common perception of the period's literary currents held by writers and commentators at that time.[22] Hewison describes the period being subject to a "general call to order, for a return to tradition away from modernism, that had gone out on all fronts in the early 1950's" (*In Anger,* 122), while D. J. Taylor assertively identifies the main current of the decade's novels as antiexperimental: "almost without exception their tone is anti-modernist, self-consciously opposed to the 'serious' fiction of the pre-war era, its characters and the attitudes they espoused" (*After the War,* 71).[23] Although this critical insistence on the antimodernism of the period can be overdone, it seems fair to say that influential critic and prolific novelist Angus Wilson was correct in declaiming in 1954 that "external observation, social setting, character set firmly in narrative and scene have once again returned" ("Arnold Bennett's Novels," 60) to literary fashionableness.[24] Indeed, by 1958, Francis Wyndham could unequivocally describe the dominant tendency of the decade's literature as "frankly anti-*avant-garde,* with its self-conscious Philistinism, its emphasis on picaresque narrative, slapstick humour and journalistic prose, it is a *reduc-*

tio almost *ad absurdum* of the reaction against Bloomsbury" ("New West Indian Writers," 188).[25] Thus, the literary scene in which the Windrush authors found themselves after World War II was characterized by an overt "principle of reaction against modernism in the emerging dominant style" (Head, *Cambridge Introduction*, 224), a style that was polemically associated with a return to older, more traditional English values.

If not in the ascendant, however, modernism still permeated the literary scene in important ways. Bradbury, for example, asserts that "though Modernism had begun to disappear . . . it had also never been more influential" (*Modern British Novel*, 273).[26] The process of consecrating modernism in the academy was becoming increasingly evident, and in the contemporary publishing sphere the discussion was by no means one-sided: a variety of critics (mostly associated with prewar literature) defended the tradition of Joyce, Kafka, Proust, and Woolf. Harry Ritchie, particularly, in his account of the period, takes note of the literary "Mandarins," well-placed critics and writers such as Cyril Connolly, John Lehmann, Stephen Spender, and Phillip Toynbee who had established their careers before the war, held prominent and influential positions as tastemakers in the world of letters in the postwar years, and maintained allegiance to the highbrow aesthetic principles of prewar modernism.[27] Lehmann, the editor of *London Magazine*, assembled a book of essays in 1956, *The Craft of Letters in England*, which was generally sympathetic to the idea of experiment and a more intellectually inclined type of fiction.[28] Toynbee contributed an article to this volume directly addressing the controversy, in which he criticizes the prevalent notion that "the better young novelists in England are at least agreed that the day of the experimental novel is over" ("Experiment and the Future," 69). Toynbee's article argues against "those critics who insist that the only good style is a plain style," maintaining that "to be plain in the manner of our modern plainness is simply to be hackneyed and inexpressive" (72). Similarly, in a 1957 article in *Twentieth Century*, L. D. Lerner takes up a defense of "self-reflective" writing, pleading that "we should not merely deplore this as modern oversophistication" ("Literature as the Subject," 555).

To depict a view of the decade as characterized by a monolithic rejection of modernist tenets, then, would be to overstate the case. A more accurate lens would register the fact that at midcentury "modernism lingered in the literary imagination" in more complex ways than simply as an anachronistic, discredited, and exhausted foreign nuisance (MacKay and Stonebridge, introduction,

2). John Wain gives a sense of this lingering presence in a 1956 *London Magazine* piece, using an extended cricket metaphor to describe the influential shadow cast by modernist writers: "a writer setting up business in the 1950's is like a batsman going out to the wicket as fifth or sixth man, to follow a succession of giants who have all made centuries" ("Writer's Prospect—IV," 60). Nevertheless, as even Bradbury observes, in the 1950s, realism was the regnant mode: "It was a decade of realism, when the post-war world and the post-war generation saw itself newly depicted in fresh fiction. It was a time of return to the 'liberal' novel, the novel of character and personality, and a time of the reconstruction of the tradition, when writers of an earlier period of realism, the Victorian and Edwardian ages, were recuperated and made visible" (*Modern British Novel,* 358). While still part of the postwar cultural scene, supporters of modernism were surely embattled, fending off aggressive charges of superannuation by critics like J. D. Scott, who in noting the emergence of the Movement in 1954 asserted that anyone still invested in prewar modernist culture belonged to a passing age. For him the sentiment of the times was readily observable: "it's goodbye to the Little Magazines and 'experimental writing'" ("In the Movement," 400).

It was this cacophonous and contentious cultural scene that Windrush writers entered upon arrival in Britain. Importantly, however, their initial relation to this scene was largely mediated in advance through Henry Swanzy, editor and producer of the BBC Overseas Service literary magazine radio program *Caribbean Voices.*[29] There can be little doubt that *Caribbean Voices* played a formative role in the postwar publishing of Caribbean literature: nearly every major Caribbean literary figure of the 1950s and 1960s (and beyond) can be found on a list of contributors to the program, including Michael Anthony, L. E. (Kamau) Brathwaite, Wilson Harris, Lamming, Mais, Mittelholzer, Naipaul, Andrew Salkey, Selvon, and Derek Walcott. Low, in an article on the publishing practices relating to 1950s West Indian writing, forcefully advocates the importance of the show, asserting that "the contribution of the BBC *Caribbean Voices* programmes in helping to establish the circle of Caribbean writers in the fifties cannot be overestimated" ("Publishing Commonwealth," 80–81). The program provided a pan-Caribbean literary forum for the discussion and reception of Caribbean literature and served as an incubator for aspiring writers by providing encouragement, regional exposure, contacts with London publishers and agents, and even financial support (both for reading on the program and for submitting pieces that were accepted). Lamming relates in

The Pleasures of Exile a commonly held view of Swanzy: "no comprehensive account of writing in the British Caribbean during the last decade could be written without considering his whole achievement and his role in the emergence of the West Indian novel" (67). Significantly, Swanzy himself had sympathies with the aims of prewar culture, and *Caribbean Voices*, under Swanzy's influence, advocated a literary philosophy that encouraged precisely the type of self-aware experimentation and critical engagement associated with modernist literary practice.

While a great portion of the material that was initially presented on *Caribbean Voices* was not remotely experimental—indeed, much of the earliest work is ineptly derivative in the worst sense—items appearing as early as 1949 were displaying tendencies matching those then understood as experimental, including a stream-of-consciousness story called "Taxi Mister" by Daniel Samaro Joseph and poems by Lamming such as "Birth" and "Prelude," which display surrealist strains and were described on the program as "impressionistic" and "not easy" to understand (*CV*, 9 Jan. 1949).[30] The next year, Roy Fuller, a regular critic on the show, though lambasting the Dantesque pretensions of Walcott's verse in general, nevertheless praises the poet for engaging in a literary practice of "healthy experimentation" (*CV*, 28 May 1950), and in June, Swanzy dedicated the entire month to programs of experimental writing, in which Lamming, Mittelholzer, and Selvon are significantly represented.[31] Mittelholzer regularly contributed pieces that had a varying and notable range of narrative techniques and points of view, such as his "Amiable Mr. Britten," an overtly self-reflexive short story about the writing process and authorship that employs stream-of-consciousness narration; pointed deviations from proper grammar; and a long series of fragmented, impressionistic prose phrases (*CV*, 5 Feb. 1950). In reviewing an issue of *BIM* for the program, Mittelholzer editorially advances the cause of literary experiment by singling out Selvon's story "My Girl and the City" as his best work yet and praising it for its experimentation (*CV*, 6 Oct. 1957). Indeed, under Swanzy's tutelage, *Caribbean Voices* encouraged and presented experimental works as crucial to the process of realizing any kind of authentic Caribbean literary identity.[32]

The prevalent notion of experimentation as vital and healthy for Caribbean literature was undoubtedly connected at one level with the uncertain status of a Caribbean literary tradition. Swanzy in particular saw *Caribbean Voices* as an important conduit for building such a tradition by providing a forum for on-air publication as well as professional critique and discussion. Addressing

West Indian poets early in his editorial tenure, Swanzy explains, "this need to discover tradition is the trouble of all pioneers: you don't always realise it, but you are making your own tradition, and later poets will benefit by reference to you" (*CV*, 27 July 1947). Indeed, Swanzy saw his role in the program (often tinged with a sense of liberal guilt) as one of facilitating the creation of West Indian literature, noting after one of his first on-air six-month summaries of the program that increasing the discussion, quality, and quantity of Caribbean writing was crucial in determining "whether a Caribbean literature develops or not" (*CV*, 11 Jan. 1948). *Caribbean Voices* certainly provided one of the most important forums for airing the widespread regional discussion of what could be considered a properly Caribbean tradition, and Swanzy's open encouragement of experimentation was at one level a frank acknowledgment that Caribbean literature was still in its incubation period. More important for the discussion to follow, Swanzy's open-ended and searching approach to literary creation aligned itself much more readily with the internationalist tendencies of modernist experimentation than the largely unquestioned English jingoism so characteristic of the Movement's return to realism.[33]

More pragmatically, the Windrush writers, upon arriving in Britain, found allies among Ritchie's literary "Mandarins," who maintained a receding but still viable institutional power in the publishing world at the time. As Kalliney observes, this older generation of literati seemed to welcome the Windrush writers as vital new standard bearers of the highbrow modernist aesthetic of the prewar years. Given the anxieties concerning British culture, the newly arrived authors from the Caribbean "helped London's extant modernists preserve the continuity of high culture in a city at a moment of widespread pessimism" ("Metropolitan Modernism," 91).[34] Swanzy's contacts in the publishing world were instrumental in the initial publications of most, if not all, of the early Windrush novelists, so this alignment of tastes seems more than simply fortuitous. If the Windrush writers are indeed the progenitors of a new West Indian literary aesthetic, this aesthetic emerged out of an intimate, if agonistic, relationship to wider tendencies in postwar British literature.

The Importance of Not Being Amis

While literary experimentation was welcomed by London's "Mandarins" and on *Caribbean Voices*, modernism's attractions for the Windrush generation also seem to lie just as importantly in its still-resonant cultural valences.

These valences, not coincidentally, were loudly rejected by Movement writers over the course of the 1950s. The most audible and influential of the Movement writers was none other than Amis, who seems to have had an outsized role in characterizing the views of the decade's new generation of British writers. Bradbury asserts that "Amis himself was central" to the new sensibility of the 1950s and that his "impact on the 1950s came to rival that of Waugh on the 1920s" ("No, Not Bloomsbury," 65, 63), while D. J. Taylor observes that "no discussion of the post-war novel can journey very far without acknowledging Amis's enormous importance" (*After the War*, xxv). Ritchie, too, remarks that Amis stands out in the decade as "a continuously influential presence," making it "difficult to overestimate the importance of Amis's literary career in the fifties" (*Success Stories*, 64). Amis, as has been well documented, carried no torch for his modernist predecessors; in the words of Bernard Bergonzi, "Amis has shown himself to be assertively anti-modern, anti-experimental, anti-cosmopolitan, to at least the same degree as [C. P.] Snow or William Cooper" (*Situation of the Novel*, 162).[35] As Bergonzi suggests here, Amis and his Movement peers expressed an (often exaggerated) abhorrence for the foreign and the fancy, which they largely associated with modernism. For Windrush writers, in contrast, modernism's perceived cosmopolitanism—a blend of internationalism and associations of cultural sophistication—is a much more amenable outlook: Amis's aesthetic insistence on plain old English culture did not align easily with their prerogatives.

Amis's first novel, *Lucky Jim*—published in 1954 and perhaps the emblematic novel of the decade—displays a marked scorn for high culture and any pretensions to intellectualism or aesthetic sophistication, directly associating it with the irremediably foreign. For example, the professor L. S. Caton, who becomes something of a running joke in Amis's next few novels, is made an object of derisive fun for editing "a new historical review with an international bias, or something" (14), implying with the careless afterthought the unimportant dreariness of Caton's pretentious endeavor. A similar opinion emerges in the novel's portrayal of Professor Welch's children, Bernard, a loud, self-ordained artist partial to berets, and his younger brother, whom the narrator dismissively describes as the "effeminate writing Michel" (250).[36] Amis emphasizes the pretentiousness of their French names—contrasting them with the real, earnest, masculine, and lively hero Jim Dixon—and associates their artistic inclinations with empty, posturing conceit. Endorsed by the novel, the gruff Dixon dismisses any artist figure as someone who manifests a "desire to range himself with children, neurotics, and invalids" (141) and thinks that anybody claiming any type of aesthetic exceptionalism "could be readily gratified with a tattoo of kicks on the bottom" (141). While it is true that *Lucky Jim* takes aim not at artists and writers in general (it is a novel itself, after all) but at the pretentiousness often associated with such people, Amis makes abundantly clear that people whose cultural tastes extend too extravagantly beyond his own protagonist's appreciation for, in the estimation of one of Amis's contemporaries, "beer, England, and common sense" (Raven, "Kingsley Amis Story") are to be deplored and shunned.[37]

Amis's 1958 novel, *I Like It Here,* can be taken as a further, resonant example of this opposition to high literary culture, which is, again, figured through the foreign. Lehmann, in fact, explicitly uses the novel as an illustration of the contrast between the contemporaneous experimental school of French writing (led by Alain Robbe-Grillet and Michel Butor) and what he considers the moribund aesthetic of the Movement writers, observing: "*I Like it Here* would seem to have no claims whatsoever to the label of *avant-garde;* it is conventional and undistinguished in its prose means, conventional too in its comic effects" ("Foreword," [1958]). The novel centers on a journey abroad by a writer who thinks of the trip as a "deportation" (7) and spends much time bemoaning "the foreign" generally. Its protagonist, Garnet Bowen, a quasi-autobiographical stand-in for Amis himself, is immediately introduced not as a serious writer, but as someone mistaken for such by others: "Until a couple of years ago Bowen had been supposed to be a novelist who was keeping himself and his family going on the proceeds of journalism, wireless talks and a bit of lecturing. In the last six months or so he had started being supposed to be a dramatist who was keeping himself and his family going by the same means" (8). The falsity and economic insignificance of being an artistic writer are stressed from the outset, and even the literary assignment that catalyzes the novel's plot—a trip to Portugal to solve a mystery—is the product of a literary opinion that Bowen had inebriatedly "pretended to think desirable" (7) being taken up by "some misinformed, progressive and well-intentioned fathead" (7). The novel begins, then, with a description that humorously discounts any notions of meaningful literary endeavor on the part of Bowen.[38] Subsequently, the only scene of Bowen practicing his "craft" is a ridiculous one in which he writes one line of dramatic dialogue—going through three versions of a sentence that means roughly "you must be kidding"—and feels sabotaged by "the reputed rule that none but aesthetic considerations must dictate the shaping of a work of art" (98). This rule satirizes modernist writing as ethereal and divorced from the reality of everyday life, to which, implicitly, the author is cleverly saying, "you must be kidding." After the line of dialogue, Bowen "experimentally" writes a lengthy paragraph of "negative stage directions" so that actors and directors will not misunderstand the sentence as other than a purely ordinary, mundane one. In this way, Amis's parody intimates both the silliness of literary experimentation and the histrionic, overly sublime, and congenitally disingenuous tendencies the novel identifies with the "serious" artistic sphere in general.

The sphere of high literary culture is embodied, of course, by the foreigner Bowen calls Buckmaster: the plot hinges on Bowen's attempt to determine for his publisher whether Buckmaster is or is not the celebrated highbrow author Wulfstan Strether. The contrast between Bowen's folksy nickname and the obviously foreign name of the author is pointed, and this contrast is central to the element of mystery at the heart of the plot. As it happens, none of the editors or publishers can tell whether a submitted manuscript was written by the internationally renowned author or somebody "with the kind of mind that wins the literary competitions in the weeklies" (17). Amis inserts a sample of the writing in question, which Lodge deems "a very creditable parody of bad [Henry] James" (351), and then follows with a judgment by Bowen that echoes the everyday, down-to-earth, positivistic literary attitude that Amis himself promulgated: "He wanted to put the man who had written that in the stocks and stand in front of him with a peck, or better a bushel, of ripe tomatoes and throw one at him for each time he failed to justify any phrase in the Frescobaldi-Yelisaveta scene on grounds of clarity, common sense, emotional decency and general morality" (102). The choice of characters' names is part of the derision, and in this brief but central episode, the novel's contempt for the modernist/symbolist tradition of literature—and its foreignness—is made exceptionally clear.

Beyond the consistent presence of scornful asides regarding *Finnegans Wake* (23), "a poetic kind of revolutionary style" (99), and Bowen's "gross betrayal into non-ironical cultural discussion" (144), the novel's final damning critique of the old international, intellectual literary world is contained within Bowen's reasons for deciding that Buckmaster is actually Strether. The first reason is the fact that in conveying his own belief that he is a better writer than Henry Fielding (one of Amis's favorite authors due to his comic ability and lack of literary pretension), Strether reveals himself, to Bowen's mind, as a "prancing, posturing phoney" (180). Bowen postulates that being "of the great-writer period" (180), now defunct, Strether could not possibly have even realized that he was perceived as such, thereby proving by his own literary arrogance and lack of understanding that he was a "great" writer. The second reason is more subtly revealed, but it hinges on Bowen's interactions with Emilia, a Portuguese woman with whom he has a brief encounter. Amis goes out of his way to illustrate the narrative significance of this encounter, noting that for Bowen "something was nagging at his mind, something to do with Buckmaster, something that Emilia had said" (155). This something is not revealed until the end of the novel, at which point it emerges as decisive to Bowen's verdict on Buckmaster. What Bowen recalls is the fact that Emilia had spoken in English to him. From this, Bowen concludes that since Buckmaster knew only that Emilia did not speak *much* English, he must be who he says he is: if he had been a fake, even that small amount of English would have convinced him not to leave them alone for fear of her revealing too much. The underlying point in Bowen's reasoning is a strong disavowal of complex literary monuments. It suggests that in order to reveal important truths about the world—the only important truth as far as the novel is concerned—no sophisticated, literary language is necessary, only the simplified pidgin English of Emilia. As Bowen reasons, not speaking much English "is a pretty wide concept" (181), and more than wide enough to contain any number of mechanisms for communicating the essential truth of the world.

This view of language efficiency and adornment is furthered by the prominence of another piece of text reproduced in the novel, Bowen's wife's letter. Although he criticizes it for some of its simple and predictable syntactical structures, Bowen ultimately attests to his spouse's communicative power via the ingenuous "closing phrases and interjections of her letter. No part of his nature could resist them or put reservations on what they stood for" (162). Thus, again, the simplest and "most honest" language is deemed the best. Amis's novel, of course, self-consciously holds itself up as a more legitimate alternative—a more straightforward, earthy, "pidgin" form of art—to the international aesthetic that Strether, as a fictional stand-in for writers like Conrad, Joyce, and Lawrence (all alluded to in the book), represents. Thus, *I Like It Here* embodies what Bradbury describes as the era's regnant literary ethos, "one that spoke not for romantic experimentalism but for sense and realism" and "moved toward a more popular and plainer tone" (*Modern British Novel*, 317).[39] Via both form and content, Amis's third novel confidently declares the outmoded irrelevance, even pitiableness of the modernist "great writer period" (180), emphatically locating any value it might have outside the borders of both England proper and proper English.

For Windrush writers, of course, there are a variety of reasons why the consciously English aesthetic found in Amis's novels might not be attractive. For one thing, certainly, in early postwar Britain their racial status immediately marked them as other. Instead of being welcomed into the postwar British welfare state, the Windrush migrants were seen as strange, foreign intruders.[40] Donald Hinds has described the common attitudes toward the newcomers among England's working-class population: "There were many things which they believed about the West Indies which produced 'instant social prejudice.' For instance . . . the people lived in trees . . . they wore no more than a piece of cloth around their waists, the old loin-cloth, you know. . . . The women nursed their babies in public" (*Journey to an Illusion*, 174). A 1960 report by the Family Welfare Assocation, *The West Indian Comes to England*, sketches a similar picture, noting with disapproval that on "several occasions even reputable journals carried feature articles in which were quoted imaginary statistics on the number of migrants, which resulted in creating the general impression that 'Jamaicans' were proceeding to the United Kingdom at an enormous rate for the specific purpose of making an easy living through the facilities of the Welfare Services—that they were introducing strange and previously unheard-of tropical diseases, setting up and managing brothels, and encouraging organized prostitution" (Ruck, *West Indian Comes*, 66). Ruth Glass warns in her 1960 study of West Indian immigration that British social prejudice manifests itself more profoundly for West Indian migrants than for other immigrant groups since "in the case of the West Indians, all difficulties—general or personal, major or minor—are complicated by the inescapable question of colour prejudice" (*London's Newcomers*, 44). Racial discrimination is a common strain running through both fictional and historical accounts of the arrival of the Windrush generation in Britain, and its prevalence—manifested most explosively in the riotous racial violence in Nottingham and Notting Hill in 1958—would seem to prevent any inclusion in the unproblematically ethnonational community Amis's work imagines. In such a light, the cosmopolitan internationalism associated with modernism—characterized by a desire to transcend or at least complicate the strict segregation of national borders— seems a promising alternative.

Moreover, in contrast to the simplicity and plainness advocated by Amis, the complexity of modernism coded as "intellectual"—no small consideration for writers who belonged to a group of people widely perceived to be primitive and unthinking. An affiliation with modernism in the British context, then, could also be seen to help counteract the British populace's general perception of West Indian primitivism and difference. Such attitudes certainly found their way into the literary discussion. For example, Spender, who admired Lamming's poetry and took some interest in the emerging West Indian literature, might be expected to be a sympathetic and fair-minded critic. However, his comments on *Caribbean Voices* betray how deeply the British prejudice toward the character and capacity of West Indians extended.[41] While generally quite complimentary in his evaluation of West Indian poetry, Spender gives some familiar reasons for liking it, opining that "it isn't originality of form that impresses me so much, as the fact that I really do feel something of the colour and the heat and the passion of that part of the world in reading this poetry" (*CV*, 5 Aug. 1951). Evoking the perceived exoticism of Caribbean poetry—"like a breath of bright and fresh air from another part of the world"—Spender then devalues any intellectual quality to the work by observing "a tendency to not thinking carefully enough about technique" before once again praising the "highly colourful and passionate" work of West Indian poets.[42] While the criticism regarding attention to form is conceivably valid, in the context of Spender's repetition of color and passion, it hints at a somewhat less salutary set of assumptions about the abilities and intellect of the poets he otherwise praises. Wyndham, another prominent advocate for the importance of these early West Indian writers, betrays traces of such an attitude as well. At the end of his article "The New West Indian Writers," he suggests that West Indian writers should avoid writing about educated, middle-class characters and concentrate on the more appropriate subject matter of the underprivileged peasant classes, with the implication that West Indian society offers no legitimate experience with anything or anybody educated or middle class.

The tendency to devalue the potential intellectualism of West Indian writers appears even more clearly in an anonymous review of West Indian novels that appeared in the *Times Literary Supplement* (*TLS*) in 1955.[43] The article discusses Lamming, Mittelholzer, and Selvon, labeling them as the best known of the West Indian writers. The review praises Mittelholzer's *A Morning at the Office* for "stating something fundamental to the West Indies at the present time" (Marshall, "Caribbean Voices," xvi). This important truth is that Caribbean people "are not conscious that the present is largely determined by what has happened in the past or that the future will be determined by what is done to-day. They live far more in the moment than Europeans do, their lack of historic sense depriving them alike of the benefits of past experience and the burdens of over-anxiety. West Indian life is emotional rather than ratiocinative, spontaneous in its gaiety and its anger, but not closely connected with outside reality" (xvi). This litany of stereotypical claims sets up a clear trajectory for the rest of the review's criticism. Discussing Lamming, the article questions "how conscious the author was of what he was doing" in shifting from first to third person in *In the Castle of My Skin* and goes on to criticize his second novel because of the evidence it betrays that once in London, the author has "got himself a philosophy and an aesthetic which do not fit him" and has "abandoned the intuition" to which he is much more suited (xvii). Selvon, similarly, is criticized for his second novel, *An Island Is a World,* because it "is muddied by the same intellectualism" (xvii) as Lamming's novels. The article solemnly implies that all three authors should resort to "intuition" in order to better capture the (imagined) Caribbean experience, in short, to be not so much authors as unthinking conduits for exotic sociological description. Such evidence of the critical suppositions and expectations regarding Caribbean writers suggests a milieu in which a less literalist, self-consciously experimental style becomes a clear political statement aimed at frustrating, disrupting, and calling into question British perceptions of West Indians as primitive and incapable of higher intellectual pursuits.

Although it would be irresponsible to assert a direct, unchanging correlation between particular aesthetic and political choices, one can, in a specific context, make determinant, historicized connections between such choices. Thus, it would seem fair to say that, within the literary world of postwar London, Amis's rejection of modernist practice was enmeshed with a certain "Little England" politics. The dismissal of modernism clearly figured as a rejection of the foreign and the international in favor of the cultivation of a properly British identity and cultural practice. This identity, in turn, was associated with a straightforward simplicity that, while potentially similar to racialized notions of the quaintly primitive customs of West Indians, nevertheless resisted assimilation to cultural practices removed from the British Isles. In the postwar era, as Alan Sinfield suggests, "an element of national consciousness, a preoccupation with Englishness, fuelled hostility to Modernism" (*Literature, Politics,* 184) in the decade's writers. For example, Wain, arguing in "How It Strikes a Contemporary," positions the ideal contemporary role of culture as being "directed towards the recovery of a national character" (235), and Donald Davie in essays on poetry throughout the 1950s consistently makes parallels between the Movement's emphasis on ordinary syntax and semantic clarity and the broader notion of a traditional English social order and national continuity (Morrison, *Movement*, 212). In Bergonzi's view, Amis's "attachment to a central thread of English insular nonconformism and his distaste for cosmopolitan modernism" (*Situation of the Novel*, 164) are both pronounced and importantly related. It is within these local, historical conditions that the Windrush embrace of modernism becomes most legible.

Such an embrace makes even more sense when one looks at the narrowing, quietist implications of the Movement's special mode of politics, which reflected a particularly resigned disposition to the world and any hopes of changing it. If on the surface, the Windrush writers might share a common "outsider," antiestablishment, vocally resistant position with writers like Amis and Wain, the structure and focus of the Movement writers' political vision combined uneasily with the more fundamentally transformative politics of Caribbean dissent that the West Indian writers generally sought to advance. That the Movement writers positioned themselves—and were critically accepted— as outsiders cannot be disputed. Both Wain's aggressively new radio magazine and the foundational collection of Movement poetry edited by Robert Conquest, *New Lines*, explicitly labeled themselves as challenges to the staid, comfortable status quo of the literary world. Based in the provincial universities, the Movement initially gloried in the lower-middle-class status implied by that institutional affiliation, attacking the old Oxbridge elite that was concentrated in London. Noting their urge to overthrow the establishment, Blake Morrison describes them as the "'coming' class . . . identified with a spirit of change in post-war British society . . . felt to be representative of shifts in power and social structure" (*Movement*, 57). J. D. Scott's "In the Movement"—the article from which the Movement got its name (and this chapter its epigraph)—explicitly makes this connection as well, arguing for the rising young writers as the literary incarnation of British social change. Morrison notes that many of these writers "identified with a viewpoint hostile to the 'old order'" (74): they wrote about and listened to jazz music as a gesture toward participating in unsanctified culture, while Amis and Conquest both put out critical work praising science fiction, thus pointedly demonstrating their antiestablishment credentials.

In the end, however, the accumulating success of the Movement revealed its "politics" to be based less on a deep-seated commitment to social change than on a frustrated and largely individualized attempt to assimilate into British society. As Peter Lewis archly notes, the anger that animated these writers "evaporated in the affluence that increasingly blurred the class barriers which had provoked it" (*Fifties*, 186). Echoing almost precisely Lamming's critique of Amis, Morrison's account of Movement politics is quite emphatic regarding the underlying complacency of its social complaint: "Comparison of the treatment of social class in the work of the Movement with its treatment in the fiction and non-fiction of later writers . . . reveals the high priority which the Movement placed upon 'adjustment' and 'compromise.' Though conscious and at times resentful of class distinction and privilege, the work of the Movement never seriously challenges their right to exist. There is little sense that the social structure could be altered; the more common enquiry is whether individuals can succeed in 'fitting in'" (73).[44] Sinfield also notes the somewhat paradoxical relationship of outward disgruntlement and inward respect toward traditional values and distinctions, dubbing the Movement's actual political stance that of "the anti-bourgeois bourgeois" (*Literature, Politics*, 190). Thus, while perceived as outsiders, especially in a self-consciously cultural sense, these writers seem ultimately much more insiders than their rhetorical stances indicate. For a group of dissident writers such as arrived from the Caribbean at this time, the Movement's rather sanguinely modest and assimilative goal—to be just "normal chaps" in a normative England—did nothing to address the more urgent political, social, and economic issues that dominated the first West Indian novels.[45] As one critic noted perspicaciously, the real literary outsiders of the era could perhaps only be found in "the Dominions, especially those, like Nigeria, where the writers in English are black" (Heppenstall, "Divided We Stand," 45).[46]

In fact, the politics of the major literati was mostly one of disaffection from politics, so much so that Randall Stevenson's study of the contemporary British novel condemns 1950s fiction as "limited by an anger which is largely self-indulgent rather than—as was often supposed at the time—politically motivated" (*British Novel*, 129). With the revelations about the nature of the Stalinist state tainting the Sartrean notion of the engaged writer, the apparent entrenchment of policies of domestic social equality, and the comfortable impression of what the Tories styled "the affluent society" of 1950s Britain, one of the most quoted and accepted sentiments of the time was Jimmy Porter's supremely disaffected complaint in John Osborne's seminal 1956 play *Look*

Back in Anger: "there aren't any good, brave causes left" (89). For West Indian writers, whose home polities were still struggling to gain national independence and redress generations of economic exploitation, such a sentiment
could only seem egregiously self-satisfied and quietist.

Amis provides a blueprint for this detached ambivalence of Movement
politics in a pamphlet he wrote for the Fabian Society in 1957, entitled *Socialism and the Intellectuals.* Although slippery with irony and vaguely supportive
of causes such as the Welfare State and even, without much hope of success,
the drive "to pull African and Asian workers up the ladder after" their British
counterparts (11), Amis postulates that intellectuals in fact can have no real
political interests, though they should, in the interests of self-preservation,
keep wary of fascism. His pamphlet dismisses what he terms "romanticism" in
politics, which he characterizes as the state of being engaged in interests that
have no bearing on one's own personal situation. Instead, Amis advocates his
evaluation of "political writing and other activity as a kind of self-administered
therapy for personal difficulties rather than as a contribution towards the reform of society" (4). Amis finishes his long assessment of the ideal worthiness
but practical worthlessness of a politically engaged intellectualism with a claim
that the most reliable political motive is self-interest and in the last line of the
essay cynically muses, "how agreeable it must be to have a respectable motive
for being politically active" (13). The politics advanced by Amis here—self-pre-
serving quietism and cynicism—find support in other contemporary cultural
figures such as Conquest, who echoes Amis's diagnosis of political activity as
a symptom of psychological problems. Conquest flatly states, to start his essay
in the 1958 *International Literary Annual,* that "English writers are not at
present very concerned with politics" ("Commitment and the Writer," 13) and
goes on to remark that writers who write about great public issues are, "not to
put too fine a point on it, crackpots" (19). A critical survey of views published
the same year on new novelists notes that "behind their work lies neither the
wish nor the capacity to bring about major changes in the lives of their readers"
(Quinton et al., "New Novelists," 14) and also that the "tendency is to handle
all subjects lightly [and] to ignore national and international politics" (19).
J. D. Scott also observes the insistently humble political goals of the new generation of writers, who appear "prepared to be as comfortable as possible in
a wicked, commercial, threatened world which doesn't look, anyway, as if it's
going to be changed much by a couple of handfuls of young English writers"
("In the Movement," 400). Thus, an apolitical preference is professed openly

by novelists and identified by their contemporaries as a salient (if not always wholesome) trait, leaving later critics to conclude that "it seems remarkable that supposedly responsible intellectuals found nothing before Suez to command their political attention" (Morrison, *Movement,* 96).[47] The writers of the period seemed not only to be, in Orwell's terminology, inside the whale, but after a bit of fuss over precisely where they could take up position, quite content to be there. Writers from outside these relatively comfortable confines, as Salman Rushdie suggests, could be forgiven for failing generally to see the wisdom in such a sanguine approach.[48]

The world-weary complacency characteristic of Movement political thought also allowed, conveniently enough, for a general disconnecting from global (and, of course, imperial) affairs. Indeed, the world outside of England did not seem to engage the Movement writers in any serious manner, the Commonwealth hinterlands presumably being the province of the insufferable "old, sloppy internationalism" derided by Wain in a letter to *London Magazine* ("Correspondence," 55). Doris Lessing, in a vehement contemporaneous critique of the provincial attitudes of the decade's writing, advances a complaint—very telling in the context of Windrush writing—about this widespread literary evacuation from international concerns: "Do the British people know that all over what is politely referred to as the Commonwealth, millions of people continually discuss and speculate about their probable reactions to this or that event? No, and if they did, they would not care" ("Small Personal Voice," 198).[49] Defending the complacent disposition of the age, W. J. Harvey replies to Lessing's condemnation of British authors as "bounded by their immediate experience of British life and standards" ("Have You Anything," 53) by hypothetically asking what on earth could be wrong with such a practice. Moreover, the prominent writers' tradition-bound view of England surely did not encourage engagement with the increasing numbers of immigrants pouring in from the Commonwealth countries and the subsequent racial tensions, except perhaps for the inclusion in a later university novel by Bradbury, *Eating People Is Wrong,* of a pathetic, caricatured African exchange student named Mr. Eborebelosa. He, however, is a figure of fun for his linguistic solecisms and his clichéd cultural baggage, including his five wives, his bumbling attempts to seduce white women, and a predilection for carrying his grandfather's skull around with him.[50] Thus, in important ways, the form of Movement politics led to an inward focus on (white) social-class struggle within Britain. This largely quietist agenda was not nearly broad enough to encompass the concerns of the early West Indian writers coming to London from much more geographically, politically, economically, and racially marginalized positions.

In the literary world of postwar Britain, then, the Movement's aesthetics of earthy literalism were easily (and often explicitly) associated with a nationalist-leaning, conciliatory, and largely disengaged politics. Such associations made realism an unpromising aesthetic mechanism for West Indian authors to use in launching the social critiques they typically wished to advance. For these authors, the state of England was of much less concern than that country's influence on and interactions with the Commonwealth, while conciliation and a total withdrawal from political concerns—the relatively modest goal, in Wain's view, for artists "to keep their heads" ("Along the Tightrope," 78) and not commit one way or another to any belief or political view—could hardly be an attractive option for any but the most self-concerned Caribbean artist.

Positioning Caribbean Modernism

It is clear, then, that the Windrush generation of writers, making their "voyage in" to the metropolitan capital, had vastly different concerns than did the British novelists who were becoming influential during the postwar years. While the latter were focused quite narrowly on England and their own place in it, with little concern for politics or psychological self-questionings, the newly arrived Caribbean writers struggled to have their mere humanity recognized. Agonizing over their British cultural inheritance in the face of racist resistance from the purportedly tolerant British populace, they were intensely concerned with questions of identity and ideology, and the economic and political situations from which they had come gave clear cause for their desire that the British recognize their Commonwealth connections and culpability and then approach these issues through an international frame.[51] Instead of anxious consolidation of a tradition and culture taken more or less for granted, the Windrush novelists were, in the words of Lamming, seeking to help West Indians "change the very structure, the very basis of [their] values" (*Pleasures of Exile*, 36). Given this outlook, neither the complacent "politics" nor the (in some senses) related and equally complacent return to a simpler, traditionalist view of language and literature of the Movement aligned with Windrush interests.

In fact, if it is true that Amis and the Movement were considered the voice of "contemporary common sense" (McEwan, *Survival of the Novel,*

78), then they represent precisely the commonsense notions—about British fair-mindedness, the childishness of colonized peoples, the universality of the British worldview, the timeless and sacred value of British tradition—that the Windrush writers sought to contest. The type of ontological certainty expressed by Amis when he scoffs, "it would be hard to attach any meaning, except as an expression of lunacy or amnesia, to [the question] 'who am I?'" ("Legion of the Lost," 831), is incompatible with a colonial subjectivity steeped in the colonizer's culture and ideology and only grudgingly acknowledged as a sentient member of the human race. Indeed, nearly contemporaneous with Amis's dismissal of such self-questioning is Frantz Fanon's pointed explanation of why such a question *is* meaningful for colonized peoples: "Because it is a systematic negation of the other person and a furious determination to deny the other person all the attributes of humanity, colonialism forces the people it dominates to ask themselves the question constantly: 'In reality, who am I?'" (*Wretched of the Earth,* 250). Further, the type of unwavering British tradition circa 1765 propounded by many in the Movement contains a distinctly different resonance to people whose ancestors were likely considered chattel at the time. Thus, within this nexus of political and literary affiliations, the realist mode of fiction that grew to predominate in the literary field of postwar Britain does not appear particularly well suited to West Indian desires for a contestatory ideological critique that extends beyond national borders and seeks to inspire a reconsideration of common assumptions about race, equality, and the residual effects of empire. If on the linguistic level it seems that these emergent postcolonial novelists might have embraced the truth in Lodge's assertion that the hermeneutic instability of language ultimately "returns to sabotage the positivist, commonsense epistemology at the center" ("Modern, the Contemporary," 349) of Movement work, it seems that the political valences of the Movement would also serve to sabotage any urge for these Commonwealth outsiders to fall in step with the literary fashion of the day.[52]

Returning to Lamming's critique of Amis in *The Pleasures of Exile,* it is clear that, although modernism had not been decisively defined at that time, its general cultural valence was far more amenable to the needs and practices of Windrush novelists than the Movement's preferred modes. Modernism's alliance with internationalism and exile—at the root of the Movement's nationalistic rejection of it—was by then a well-known trademark, available to complicate Amis's complacent sense of English normalcy (and, implicitly, superiority). The contestatory, oppositional impulse of modernism is also a definitive feature, and its focus on interpretation, subjective experience, and the operations of language and ideology strongly impugns the ontological, hermeneutical, and epistemological certainty of the Movement writers. Moreover, its considered approach to tradition provides a much more sophisticated and flexible model for thinking about cultural inheritance and production than the largely backward-looking, tradition-bound thrust that Amis and others promulgated. Thus, the particular lineaments of the literary field in postwar London suggest the potential attraction and utility an alignment with modernism might hold for authors like Lamming, Mais, Mittelholzer, and Selvon.

What follows focuses on the novels themselves, tracing the specific ways in which Windrush authors engaged with modernist forms in generating their own complicated, counterconventional, and sometimes contradictory literary output. Emerging in dynamic interaction with the metropolitan heart of empire, the fiction of the Windrush generation strove to interrogate the culturally and geographically narrow boundaries of British fiction. The following chapters, in turn, seek to preserve this originary openness by keeping the British dimension of West Indian fiction firmly in view, exhuming the purpose and meaning behind these paradigmatic Caribbean novelists' embrace of modernist practice.

2 "Child of Ferment"
Edgar Mittelholzer's Contrary Tradition

> Or let us go to our ignominious ends knowing that we have strained
> at the cords, that we have spent our strength in trying to pave the way
> for a new sort of poetic art—it is not a new sort but an old sort—but
> let us know that we have tried to make it more nearly possible for our
> successors to recapture this art.
>
> —Ezra Pound, "The Serious Artist"

Guyanese author Edgar Mittelholzer is a largely overlooked figure in the contemporary annals of Anglophone Caribbean literature. Despite the fact that
during his life he was identified as "the doyen of the new school of West Indian
writers" (Rickards, "Tribute," 98) and considered to be foremost among West
Indian novelists (Amis, "Fresh Winds from the West," 565), his literary output
is only rarely read or seriously considered today. While he is frequently mentioned, widely known, and often discussed in general terms as an important
novelist within Caribbean literature, the amount of focused engagement with
his work—let alone the availability of his novels—is decidedly incommensurate with his clear preeminence during the 1950s.[1] Undoubtedly, some of this
critical neglect stems from the difficulty of completely coming to terms with
the contradictory aesthetic and political impulses animating Mitteholzer's
work. Aptly dubbed by W. Adolphe Roberts a "child of ferment" (foreword,
vii), Mittelholzer was a cantankerous, contrarian figure, whose strident, calculatedly provocative views align uncomfortably with the prerogatives of cultural
nationalism and egalitarian political and economic reform that underwrite
most twentieth-century Anglophone Caribbean literary criticism. Notorious
for his acerbic dismissal of the possibility of a cohesive West Indian culture,
his nearly eugenicist theories of behavioral heredity, and his increasingly strident calls for the harsh enforcement of social discipline and order, Mittelholzer has been condemned by some critics—not without justice—as fascist, a
label that can be used to ignore his oeuvre as too compromised politically to
merit serious critical attention.[2] On the other hand, in content and, especially,

in form, Mittelholzer's writing displays a concomitant, contrary impulse of liberal iconoclasm, expressing a preference for individual rights of expression and belief and a vigorous opposition to calcified forms of social oppression. Emblematic of this contradictoriness, a column Mittelholzer wrote for the *Barbados Advocate* in 1954 passionately critiques the persecution of Oscar Wilde at the hands of the "Victorians, in the narrowness of their fanatical morality," while at the same time defending authoritarian rule and remarking how "one can almost feel a sneaking sympathy for Nero" ("Malicious Morality").

The disjunction in these tendencies can be perplexing. However, for critics of modernism, such ideological antinomy is a familiar, animating characteristic of the works of T. S. Eliot, Wyndham Lewis, Ezra Pound, and W. B. Yeats.[3] The seeming irreconcilability contained in the work of what Stephen Spender fittingly terms modernism's "revolutionary traditionalists" (*Struggle of the Modern*, 222)—contradictorily combining a longing for radical aesthetic change with an emphatic allegiance to antiquated (and romantically imagined) modes of being—finds striking correspondences in Mittelholzer's writing. While the contextual and historical differences between Mittelholzer and such putative literary forefathers are considerable, there is nevertheless an intriguing strain of similitude in the uneasy mixture of aesthetic avant gardism and political reaction characteristic to both sets of texts. Indeed, viewed through the lens of the Poundian call to arms of "make it new," with all its rich ironies— as Peter Nicholls gleefully notes, Pound ostentatiously adopted the phrase from an ancient Chinese emperor (*Modernisms*, 178), and Pound's *Make It New* consists of studies of past poetic traditions and techniques—a case can be made that there resides some recognizable method in Mittelholzer's apparent literary madness. In such a reading, Mittelholzer's vehement project of literary experimentation—a consistent, restless program of counterconventional provocation intended to unsettle cultural and intellectual verities—can be seen to take up modernism's agonized, agonistic relationship to tradition in a peculiarly West Indian key.

As Mark McWatt has suggested, a hallmark of Mittelholzer's literary production is its "variety and sense of experimentation" ("Critical Introduction," viii). The variegated nature of Mittelholzer's prolific literary output— including twenty-three novels, his autobiographical *A Swarthy Boy*, and the travel narrative *With a Carib Eye*, along with numerous short stories and essays—attests to his embrace of an experimental aesthetic in the widest sense. Indeed, Mittelholzer's novelistic oeuvre stretches across improbably wide terrain, including the multiperspectival social critique of *A Morning at the Office*, the utopian political fantasy of *Shadows Move Among Them*, the carefully researched historical fiction of the Kaywana trilogy, the suspenseful murder mystery/love story of *The Weather in Middenshot*, the allegorical fable *The Adding Machine*, the ghost-story horror novel *My Bones and My Flute*, the psychic supernatural thriller *A Twinkling in the Twilight*, and the domestic drama interspersed with Wagnerian leitmotivs in *Latticed Echoes* and *Thunder Returning*, among others. His body of work suggests a dedicated program of constant and far-ranging literary permutation. A diary entry of Mittelholzer's, published in a reminiscence by his second wife, Jacqueline, shows this tendency as an almost mundane feature of his early writerly life: "Another novel and another novel. Experiment in one kind of technique and in another. Satire, realism, humour" ("Idyll and the Warrior," 81).[4] Jacqueline herself observes that at the end of his career, her husband was still trying out new techniques: "Throughout his later novels . . . Edgar was experimenting with a style of writing in which he eschewed 'stream of consciousness.' . . . The effect was to be of the story unfolding objectively, as it would be seen through the eyes of a perceptive observer" ("Idyll and the Warrior," 35). Although certain thematic concerns do consistently appear in Mittelholzer's writing—an immense fascination with place and landscape, an interest in strength versus weakness, a dissection of race and family relations, an attraction to psychic phenomena and spirituality, an examination of the interplay of heredity and personal responsibility—they are presented via remarkably different generic and technical features, indicating Mittelholzer's strong impulse to experiment extensively with narrative voice, style, subject, technique, and genre in his own writing.

For his contemporary critics, Mittelholzer's broader tendency toward neoteric creativity was a conspicuous feature of his writing. As Colin Rickards observes in his tribute to Mittelholzer just after the author's death in 1965: "'Original' was the word most used about his work by reviewers. The plots were original, the writing original, the characters original" ("Tribute," 102).[5] Certainly, many of Mittelholzer's novels garnered critical notice for being unique in some way. John Raymond introduces his review of *Shadows Move Among Them* by observing that "while it occasionally reminds one of several modern novels, [it] remains sovereignly itself" (573), and finishes by calling it "a bizarre and disturbing book with moments of great beauty" (574). Similarly, Marghanita Laski, in a review of the same novel in the *Observer*, enthusiastically sums the novel up as "a book owing nothing to contemporary literary fashion . . . the stimulating product of an original and astoundingly fertile mind." *My Bones and My Flute* is supportively summarized in the *Times Literary Supplement* with a recognition of Mittelholzer's ability to write effectively in multiple modes: "*My Bones and My Flute* is in the nature of an experiment, but, as well as showing its author's versatility, it is genuinely exciting" (Ross, "Struggle for Existence"). In a related vein, Pamela Hansford Johnson's review of *Kaywana Blood* in the *New Statesman* begins with the assertion that "Mr. Mittelholzer is such an odd fish among writers that no book of his can be devoid of interest." Johnson notes Mittelholzer's predilection for writing "eccentric works" and judges *Kaywana Blood* surprisingly conventional. However, she then goes on to acknowledge that for Mittelholzer, if this novel "is as near as he can get to the commonplace . . . that isn't near enough to put him in any real danger as yet." A *Times Literary Supplement* review expresses its disappointment with *A Tale of Three Places* with similar, if nostalgically wistful, appreciation for the appeal of Mittelholzer's literary uniqueness: "Mr. Mittelholzer has often been erratically imaginative and even whimsical: but before this, one would have found it difficult to believe he could be dull" (Symons, "Caught in the Trap"). This last review hints at Mittelholzer's increasingly negative treatment at the hands of British reviewers, especially in the early 1960s, as his unpopular political views were presented with intensifying repetition and earnestness. Nevertheless, reviewers consistently returned to the fact that, if nothing else, his writing was certainly not standardized, boring, or predictable. Even at the embattled end of his writing career, Mittelholzer was recognized as a writer dedicated to experimenting with the manifold possibilities of literary composition, an artist determined to produce something new and uniquely its own.[6]

In addition to its overarching exploratory impulse toward novelty and difference, an important part of Mittelholzer's work clearly fell within a more narrow, postwar conception of literary experimentalism, loosely understood as a category of writing—now called modernist—that was explicitly opposed to the conventions of literary realism. The most obviously "modernist" of Mittelholzer's novels (as McWatt, among others, suggests) are *A Morning at the Office* and the first two installments of a never-completed trilogy of novels, *Latticed Echoes* and *Thunder Returning*. Most influential, of course, is *A Morning at the Office*, Mittelholzer's second novel, published in 1950 by Hogarth Press in what is generally considered the watershed moment for

Windrush writing.[7] The book's most noticeable features—the intricate focus on the events of a single morning in an office, the narrative voice's constant shifting from one character's perspective to another, and the odd interruptions of the human narrative in favor of detailed descriptions of the histories of inanimate objects in the office (called "telescopic objectivity" in the novel itself)—worked to signal a clear affiliation with prewar modernist practice, furthered, no doubt, by the longstanding associations of the Hogarth Press with the avant-garde aspirations of owners Virginia and Leonard Woolf.[8] The later novels—*Latticed Echoes* and *Thunder Returning*, published in 1960 and 1961, respectively, by Secker and Warburg, Mittelholzer's longtime publisher—employ a conspicuous technique involving the verbal equivalent of Wagnerian leitmotivs interspersed with (and suggestively commenting upon) the novel's more conventionally rendered dialogue and action. Beyond these prominent examples, however, other elements of Mittelholzer's literary output can also be seen to fit into a more narrow understanding of experimental writing. For example, his story "The Sibilant and the Lost," which began the month-long program of "experimental pieces" on *Caribbean Voices* in June of 1950 (*CV*, 4 June 1950), rather showily avoids all *s* sounds until the very last sentence of the story, while stories from *BIM*, such as "Something Fishy," with its stream-of-consciousness narration by a (surprisingly, at the end, murderous) rector, and "Amiable Mr. Britten," an impressionistic first-person character sketch that ends by discussing its own fictionality, also fit easily into the contemporary notion of self-consciously experimental literary practice.[9] Discrete elements of many of Mittelholzer's other novels, too, evince signs of a modernist inclination, such as the increased tempo of different individual stream-of-consciousness portrayals merging into a frantic, climactic crescendo found in *The Weather in Middenshot* and *Of Trees and the Sea;* the strongly marked attempts at affective, onomatopoeic representation of place and atmosphere in, especially, *A Tale of Three Places;* or the telling tendency—highlighted by a conversation between characters in the novel itself—of the narration to refer to Peter's neighbor, Charles Pruthick, in alternately formal and informal terms, depending on context and intent, in *The Piling of Clouds.* Thus, a considerable portion of Mittelholzer's writing lent itself to being read into a prewar lineage of self-conscious experimentalism more narrowly construed.

The widespread critical reaction to Mittelholzer's most influential novel, *A Morning at the Office,* firmly established his reputation as an author with a modernist bent, albeit with varying levels of approval. The *Times Literary*

Supplement provides a quite glowing review of *A Morning at the Office,* calling it "a distinguished piece of work" and allying Mittelholzer with European modernism by praising it as "an almost Proustian analysis of the different relationships" between the characters (Powell, "Caribbean Melting-Pot").[10] In the *Observer,* Francis Wyndham also voices appreciation for the novel's "detailed picture of a complicated society" but is uneasy with the technique to which Mittelholzer "gives the absurdly pretentious name of 'telescopic objectivity,'" and instead lauds the more realistic aspect of the text, which "gives a vivid impression of an unfamiliar background." The *New Statesman and Nation* review has a similar outlook, finding satisfaction in the novel's social realism while critiquing its self-reflexive turn: "aloof and amused, determined to keep his animalculae well under the microscope, Mr. Mittelholzer unwisely slips the book itself on the slide" (White). Arthur Calder Marshall enthuses about *A Morning at the Office* on *Caribbean Voices,* saying the novel "seems to me to be one of the most exciting novels to have come out of the West Indies. It is exciting, because the author, as well as having something to say, is very interested in the manner of saying it. A pre-occupation with technique can be a dangerous thing; it has sterilised a number of our English writers; but it is a welcome sign among West Indian writers, who have too frequently been concerned with writing just the way they feel" (*CV,* 4 June 1950).[11] Marshall's response, containing both approval for Mittelholzer's interest in technique and opprobrium for what is figured as a British overindulgence in the same interest, perfectly registers the contradictory currents of opinion that buffeted modernist-inflected West Indian literature in these postwar years. From whatever perspective, though, critics agreed that Mittelholzer's novel was experimental.

After the novelistic success of *A Morning at the Office,* Mittelholzer's critics seemed to be tolerantly expectant that he would continue to produce experimental prose. Indeed, so pronounced was this expectation that critics largely discounted the political seriousness of Mittelholzer's next novel, *Shadows Move Among Them*—essentially excusing its overt authoritarianism as the product of a somewhat lighthearted thought experiment—and the book even became the basis of a short-lived Broadway production (*The Climate of Eden,* adapted by Moss Hart). On the other hand, Hogarth Press did decline to publish the book, with Leonard Woolf reportedly considering it "off the rails" and offensive in attitude (J. Mittelholzer, "Idyll and the Warrior," 83). In any case, by 1954, Mittelholzer's reputation for experimentation was established such that the *Observer* lauds *The Harrowing of Hubertus* for being "in the old tradition of good story telling," remarking with an air of surprise that "Mr. Mittelholzer for once tells his story straightforwardly" (S. Smith). Reviewing the same novel in the *Spectator*, John Metcalf combines racial and modernist categories to evoke the author's perceived experimental leanings: "There is something of Joyce Cary in Mr. Mittelholzer's writing something of Conrad and something of Faulkner." A few years later John Wain bemoans Mittelholzer's "torrent of wasted words and pretentious stylistic effects" in reviewing *Of Trees and the Sea*, prefiguring the critical revolt that occurs with regard to the introduction of the pronouncedly experimental Wagnerian leitmotiv methods of *Latticed Echoes* and *Thunder Returning*. The *Times Literary Supplement*, for example, betrays impatience with the rather obtrusive technique employed in these two later novels, describing the first one as a misbegotten experiment: "the effect of this musical cross-dressing is to put a severe strain on the reader's staying power" (A. C. Marshall, "Vagaries of the Soul"). The subsequent review of *Thunder Returning* describes its subject distastefully as "an acknowledged experiment in what might be called non-novelism" and compares it unfavorably with the Wagnerian technique that was its inspiration, concluding that "Mr. Mittelholzer's verbal application of it is far more obscure and the result considerably less sublime" (Lejeune, "Without Benefit of Story"). The *London Times* reviewer finds *Latticed Echoes* too demanding on its readers, asserting that the technique unfairly attempts to oblige its readers "to be bludgeoned into sensibility in the manner of Virginia Woolf."[12] Nevertheless, as this last comparison makes clear, regardless of the level of acceptance they achieved in the literary reviews, Mittelholzer's techniques put him solidly in the more specific category of "experimental writer" in the eyes of the British critical establishment.

Thus, experimentation—whether in a larger, ecumenically exploratory sense or in a more narrow understanding of the term as overtly counterconventional—appears as a crucial component of Edgar Mittelholzer's literary aesthetic. Revealingly, however, Mittelholzer's own reflections betray a somewhat uneasy, contradictory relationship to literary innovation. For example, while expressing disdain for an "affected and 'high-brow'" style and what he sees (somewhat anachronistically) as the current vogue for "the primitive, the abstract and the obscure" (*CV*, 11 Nov. 1956) in a *Caribbean Voices* program, a matter of months later on the show Mittelholzer vigorously praises Samuel Selvon's story "My Girl and the City" for its willingness to take technical chances. In this instance, Mittelholzer enthuses that "one of the most promising things about Selvon is that he is not afraid of experimenting. In this story there are even moments of pure sur-realism which, somehow, come off superbly" (*CV*, 6 Oct. 1957).[13] The next year, introducing L. E. Brathwaite's "Rite of Spring," Mittelholzer initially betrays some suspicion of the notion of "Experiment" as it pertains to the fine arts in general but ultimately endorses the poem's experimentation as something valuable and interesting while taking pains to "warn listeners that it isn't the sort of thing everyone will enjoy" (*CV*, 11 May 1958). Mittelholzer's gingerly, equivocal approach to literary experiment in these commentaries is surprising given his notorious outspokenness, and such hesitations point to important tensions circulating (in different ways and with different meanings) through both British and West Indian literary discussions of authenticity and imitativeness, newness and tradition, at the time.[14] Mittelholzer's ultimate response to the issue attempts to acknowledge both sides of the contemporary debate, as he finds literary experiment to be, simultaneously, both an imperative for forging aesthetic originality and a seductive threat to preserving legitimate literary value.[15]

This divided view—in favor of experimentation yet nevertheless suspicious of its potential for faddish appeal or intellectual obfuscation—emerges clearly in Mittelholzer's *Kyk-over-al* appreciation of Roger Mais. In this piece, Mittelholzer praises Mais's first novel, *The Hills Were Joyful Together,* quite highly: "I can say with perfect truth that this novel of Mais's was the first I had read by a West Indian which had held my interest from cover to cover, and which, in my opinion, contained all the ingredients that a good novel should" ("Postscript," 165). Although suspicious of Mais's interest in writing about the working class, Mittelholzer goes on to explain why he finds Mais appealing: "he was no airy, impractical experimenter, and realized that however 'poetic,' however strange and highbrow a novel might be, if it lacks a good story, if the characters don't live, and if the atmosphere is poor, it is a failure" (165). In this formulation, Mittelholzer makes clear his view that experimentation is fine, so long as certain more traditional considerations are also kept in focus. Of course, for Mittelholzer, merely presenting a traditionally compelling narrative is not enough: something new must be offered as well. The importance of newness is emphasized in the discussion specific to Mais's second novel, which Mittelholzer initially dreaded reading as a repetition of Mais's first "proletarian" novel. However, Mittelholzer explains how he "had begun to succumb to Mais's magical manner" (165) after the first chapter and ultimately remarks with great enthusiasm that this novel, *Brother Man,* far from a boring exercise in the commonplaces of pro-working-class literature, is a refreshing "repetition with a difference" (165).

It is this paradoxical simultaneity of repetition and difference—tradition in the guise of the new—that Mittelholzer attempts to articulate in both his literary philosophy and his practice. Thus, in a *Caribbean Voices* essay called "The Torment of Technique" Mittelholzer makes clear that he believes innovation to be a demand necessitated by the individuality of each author, confessing, "every writer, I feel, must in his own fashion find his salvation," and later asserting that "in writing, there are dozens of different ways of overcoming any one difficulty, each way depending upon the individual manner, temperament, whim, or what you will, of the particular writer concerned" (*CV,* 26 Aug. 1956). The emphasis on singularity here is typical of Mittelholzer's libertarian inclinations, but the strictures he later provides for beginning writers—an avoidance of cliché and a striving for "restraint, suggestion and understatement"—point up the more conventional, rule-bound elements of his writing philosophy. Thus, in the same essay propounding an almost infinite artistic individuality, he nevertheless echoes the functionalism of Pound's Imagist dictates, urging his audience of aspiring writers to "try to be as simple and 'uncomplicated' as you can" and to make sure "everything florid and superfluous has been eradicated" (*CV,* 26 Aug. 1956). Mittelholzer was without doubt a fierce proponent of originality, insisting that proper literary writing could not be "a pastiche of half-veiled cribbings from the works of other writers, not a collection of cautious clichés" ("Literary Criticism," 117). Nevertheless, he frequently expresses anxiety that individual creativity could become "airy," mere solipsism or intellectual puzzle, resolutely maintaining that innovation be grounded in the traditional narrative concerns of plot, character, and setting. Ultimately, in Mittelholzer's critical writings, the uneasiness of the relationship between newness and tradition resolves itself into a logic in which experimentation is indeed valorized, but with a careful insistence that it occur only within the boundaries of an already established set of literary criteria. Similarly, in his novels—especially his most overtly modernist ones—this same logic (with all its contradictions) is worked through. The modernist techniques of *A Morning at the Office, Latticed Echoes,* and *Thunder Returning* can be seen to signify, on multiple levels, Mittelholzer's strenuous attempts to imagine, as this chapter's epigraph suggests, a satisfying way of making a new (West Indian) form of literary art via the old (European) forms.

The New Forms of West Indian Literature:
A Morning at the Office

The 1950 publication of Mittelholzer's *A Morning at the Office* is generally regarded as the inaugurating moment of the Windrush generation's literary
efflorescence. As Brathwaite notes in his 1960 survey of West Indian novelists,
it was Mittelholzer "with his novel, *A Morning at the Office,* who gave a voice
and direction to the movement" ("New West Indian Novelists," 205). The
direction in which this novel appeared to point was toward the importance
of formal experiment and innovation, and the experimentation in *A Morning
at the Office* has several discernible functions. The most apparent one, suggested explicitly by the author himself, is to spark a realization in European
audiences that West Indian people are not unthinking, primitive people, but
sentient, intelligent beings who live in a complex society. As A. J. Seymour
observes, Mittelholzer once described the novel as "a mere social document in
the guise of a novel, a grand tract nicely dressed up to debunk certain fallacies
held by people in northern regions about the people in the West Indies (especially the fallacy that makes us out to be a backward, half-civilised people)"
("Introduction to the Novels," 70). The technique of serially presenting (albeit
indirectly) the conscious thoughts of nearly all the employees in the office of
Essential Products Ltd., including, most pointedly, the very human, sympathetic thoughts of the black office boy Horace Xavier, emphasizes the complex
intersubjective negotiations that *all* Trinidadians (not just educated, middle-
class ones) undertake each day. Not incidentally, of course, the presentation of
multiple viewpoints is a familiar modernist practice (exemplified in the work
of Joyce, Woolf, and Faulkner), while the depiction of the mainly mental events
of a quite compact, discrete period of time—a morning in Mittelholzer's novel,
a day in *Ulysses* and *Mrs. Dalloway*—could also be characterized as typically
modernist. In Mittelholzer's case, the detailed portrayal of the ongoing mental
intricacies that make up what is presented as simply the mundane ("another
day at the office") not only provides an index of the sophisticated social strati-
fications of Trinidadian life but also suggests that the ongoing suspicion and
prejudice of the system is based largely in miscommunication and an inability to take into account the motivations and experiential differences of others.
The juxtaposition of different points of view allows Mittelholzer to illustrate
how events are understood in completely different ways by the various characters while establishing at least a partial validity to each one's understanding.

The most explicit example of this egalitarian schema of consciousness is in the depiction of Mr. Jagabir, the East Indian assistant accountant, who is probably the least sympathetic character working in the office. Despite his depiction of Jagabir as a mean-spirited, nosy, and officious sycophant, Mittelholzer nevertheless illustrates that Jagabir's mental life is dominated by his fears that, due to the common Trinidadian conception of all East Indians as "coolies" fit only for agricultural labor, his position in the firm is eternally precarious. In the midst of a minor squabble with Miss Henery, Jagabir's thoughts sketch out precisely these uncertainties: "Fear rose in Mr. Jagabir. He saw Mr. Murrain reporting it to Mr. Waley that his handwriting was illegible. . . . It was causing much inconvenience and annoyance. Several firms were beginning to complain. Mr. Waley reported the matter to Mr. Holmes, the Manager of the Tucurapo estate, and Mr. Holmes came to town for a conference. . . . This coolie, Jagabir, was no good, after all. He was growing grossly inefficient. . . . It would be better to send him back to the estate to some field job instead of dismissing him right off" (86).[16] Without fully excusing Jagabir's rather unsavory behavior toward most of his colleagues, Mittelholzer does provide Jagabir with a plausible chain of reasoning, sensitive to the racialized preconceptions of Trinidadian society, on which his actions are founded. This modernist-influenced presentation of interacting subjectivities, then, serves to advance Mittelholzer's contention that the Caribbean has, contrary to European expectations, a highly sophisticated, emphatically self-conscious social texture.

If Mittelholzer's shifting points of view emphasize the status of Trinidadians as thinking human beings to a European audience, the thrust of his work's social critique can be found largely in the consistent misunderstandings that occur between the characters in the novel. Mittelholzer takes pains to suggest that the socially constructed predispositions of the characters toward ethnic- and class-based suspicion are the major impediments to forging magnanimous human relationships. Narratively speaking, Xavier's attempt to express his love for Mrs. Hinckson is the focal point of the novel: his placing of the love verse on her desk is what begins the narrative, and his overly sensitive response to the results of this endeavor climax at the very end of the novel with his abrupt, tearful resignation. Mittelholzer makes clear that the pathos and insecurity of the situation are informed predominantly by the (racially based) class differential between the two. Xavier is racked by self-doubt just after leaving the note, ruminating that "he should have remembered that he was only a black boy, whereas she was a coloured lady of good family. His complexion was dark brown; hers was a pale olive. His hair was kinky; hers was full of large waves and gleaming" (16). This socio-racial insecurity casts a pall over all of Horace's actions in the book, causing his violent assertion of ownership regarding the copied love poem at the end of the morning. The depth of the effects of Trinidadian racial consciousness on Horace's behavior emerge clearly in the novel's climactic closing scene: seemingly without provocation, Horace stands up and shouts to the office at large, "To hell wid all o' you," followed by, "Because I black? You-all not better dan me!" (216). This emotionally fraught outburst is the first outward expression of the racially guided logic that dominates the thinking of nearly all the characters throughout the course of the novel and, as such, dramatically names the issue as the underlying principle of the office's social interaction. Ultimately, the novel suggests, despite the benevolence of people such as Mr. Reynolds, "the least racially conscious coloured member of the staff" (159), and even Mr. Murrain's attempts to "convince himself that he was above race and class prejudice" (49), the cumulative effects of longstanding social prejudices remain distressingly powerful.

The putative solution to this dilemma offered by the novel appears in an allegorical parable presented in the narrative itself. As William J. Howard has noted, this tale "becomes the functional structure for interpreting" the novel in its entirety ("Edgar Mittelholzer's Tragic Vision," 20), thus highlighting the deeply self-reflexive nature of the novel. Fittingly for Mittelholzer, the solution involves an emphasis on individual responsibility seen within a framework of social and historical weight.[17] The fairy tale "The Jen" is authored by Miss Bisnauth's boyfriend, Arthur Lamby, and involves a Delphic creature, the eponymous Jen, who is interrogated by a little girl named Mooney. Offered explicitly as an allegory, the story largely consists of a conversation in which the five-year-old girl attempts to discover what precisely the Jen—rumored to be a most terrible creature—is. The fairy tale itself appears in the last chapter of the first of two sections in the book; in the corresponding chapter (called "The Jen") of the book's second section, some more light is cast on what Arthur means by his story. In this later section, Miss Bisnauth, in despondent contemplation, describes herself as the Jen:

> She felt completely negative, desperately miserable. And lonely.
> She was the Jen. (212)

This passage reveals the Jen to be an internal state, a negative disposition capable of affecting behavior and outlook. Combined with the enigmatic hints in the story itself, these traits seem to point to the Jen as a causal chain of fear, ignorance, and negativity.[18] In conversation with Mooney, the Jen notes that it consists of "a chain that's always in action," that it itself is a reason "for many things," and that part of its malignity inheres in being misunderstood (124). The moral appears to be that an expansive and optimistic consideration for others—a willingness to assume good faith in the absence of evidence otherwise—is a means of halting the self-perpetuating process of recrimination and prejudice. The key term is "understanding," in both its senses: an epistemological awareness of historical and social forces coupled with an imaginative sympathy for how others may be caught up in them in different ways. In this reading, the Jen is an unhealthy, self-protecting suspicion of others (especially ethno-cultural others) that acts to foreclose the salutary possibility of social connection and transculturation. "The Jen" (and, hence, *A Morning at the Office*) thus proposes to readers a two-pronged means of counteracting the racial suspicion and prejudice endemic to Caribbean society: a greater consciousness of the social and historical forces that structure one's own thinking accompanied by a less suspicious, more tolerant apprehension of the (equally historically conditioned) meanings behind the actions of others.

Part of this formulation, with its stress on tolerant understanding, may seem somewhat rose colored for a self-identified cynic like Mittelholzer, but it is a moral imperative that recurs consistently throughout Mittelholzer's corpus. As the heroic Alfy tells Errol at the end of *A Tale of Three Places:* "Hating and despising people won't do you any good. You've got to be tolerant and sympathetic. You've got to evince a spirit of love. That's the only hope" (344).[19] The other part of *A Morning at the Office*'s moral prescription—with its emphasis on the very material weight of historical circumstances—is more easily reconciled with the bleaker, more deterministic worldview often attributed to Mittelholzer. Moreover, it is strongly accentuated by the most striking experimental feature of the novel: the sections devoted to examining the "backstories" of various objects in the office. The novel's treatment of inanimate objects puts emphasis on the burden of inherited sociocultural conditions—a correlate of Mittelholzer's abiding interest in arguing for the forces of heredity over environment—and problematizes any naive hopes of the tolerant comity to come; ultimately, it functions to underscore the dauntingly pervasive obstacles necessarily circumscribing any attempts to realize a project based in universal love. Indeed, the initial objects focused upon in the first part of the novel, "Persons, Objects, Incidentals," are the key, the door, and the nib, which all have overt connections to colonialism and racism. These objects thus serve to underscore the unhealthy influence of imperialism in even the most insignificant-seeming elements of Trinidadian life. The key is initially described as "one manufactured by Petersen & Jason of Coventry" (12), highlighting the role of British manufacturing in the colonies, while the nib has been carelessly left in the office the night before by a white English overseer meeting with the head of accounting, Mr. Murrain. The door is notable for having a scar that results from a cutlass fight in 1923 caused by a British sailor who insults a Trinidadian by calling him a "bloody nigger" and dismissing "black nytives—every blimed one o' you dusky tropical blokes" (19). These small elements focused on by the narrator connect the surroundings of the characters to a historical chain (recent or otherwise) stretching back to England and its relationship to Trinidad, suggesting a present minutely linked to the colonial past.

In the second half of the book, subtitled "Other Persons, Recapitulations," the stories surrounding all three objects are recapitulated in new events taking place in the narrative present. The owner of the nib, Sidney Whitmer, returns in a drunken stupor to the office to announce his resignation in opposition to the color barrier in Trinidad. Sidney provides a scathing critique of imperialism to his white acquaintances: "The blasted snobbery! The hypocrisy and the *nerve* of you English hounds. You come out to these colonies and squeeze the guts out of 'em—and then you *piss* on the natives" (133). However, the salience of his observations and their implications for a moral awakening are undermined in the chapter by the juxtaposed arrival of Mrs. Murrain, who visits the office and treats the employees with arrogant brusqueness. This unpleasant scene, which effectively overshadows Sidney's visit in the minds of all the employees, is characterized by the mutual snobbery and hatred expressed by both Mrs. Murrain and the employees, who are listening to Syndey's outburst next door. Mrs. Murrain later exclaims that "these coloured people seem to think a fearful lot of themselves" (137), while urging her husband to fire Miss Henery. In turn, Miss Henery cattily dismisses Mrs. Murrain in conversation with Mrs. Hinckson: "And look at the creature! That's what got my goat. I wouldn't be surprised if she was a barmaid in some low pub in the East End of London before she married Murrain. The woman can't even dress. And our black cook at home can give her lessons in walking" (139–40). Although Sidney's outburst seems to suggest a perhaps growing recognition of colonial inequality, and hence some change from the colonial past, the coincident scenes concerning Mrs. Murrain cast doubt on any optimism regarding a new social order devoid of the recurrent hateful divisions.

The chapter "Reminiscent of the Door," too, seems to suggest a continuation of racial misunderstandings rather than any change or progress. The main event of this chapter is the arrival of a shadowy stranger who appears to be the offended Trinidadian in the earlier story about the door, Mungalsingh. He attempts to blackmail the chief clerk, Mr. Benson, over the latter's embezzlement scheme involving petrol invoices, and his appearance serves to catalyze a narration revealing the racism and self-hatred of Benson. The clerk, who "hated coolies as much as he hated niggers" (146), is driven by bitterness about his own status as the son of a black prostitute, a bitterness that leads him to resent just about everyone else in the office. Although in this "recapitulation" of the story of the door there is less overt violence, the insight into Benson's character indicates that the potential for such violence lingers just below the surface: Benson "hated both Miss Henery and Mrs. Murrain" (150) for their color and class status and is bitterly comforted, in looking at his own hand, that "no nigger could show a complexion like this" (153). The recurrence of these two objects in the second part of the book suggests a malignant continuity with the past in which cruelties and hatreds repeat themselves in different forms as time goes on.

The recurrence of the key, however, implies a less depressingly determinate relationship to the past. The dominant figure of this later chapter is the salesman Mr. Reynolds, who, because he is gay, is "the one who was always being sniggered about" in the office (159).[20] Despite being a figure of fun, however, Reynolds is very good-natured and affable, described in the book as someone who "liked helping out and entertaining people in need" (158). In fact, in this chapter, Reynolds deliberately holds a friendly conversation with Mr. Murrain to distract him and make him feel better, and he also obligingly speaks with Horace, whom Reynolds had made "understand that whenever the boy had any worries he was to come to him" (162), and agrees to help him with his entanglement. The key emerges in Reynolds's memory, arising from a story he had been told two years ago about the manufacturing family whose name is on the key. He recalls the details in this chapter: it involves the promising heir of the family "killed in a train smash in France and . . . the young man who was in his company" (162). It is this mysterious young man who fascinates Reynolds, who now dreams "at night of himself sitting in a railway coach beside a young man" (162), a plainly erotic fantasy. Although fantasy and desire are important aspects of the story surrounding the key, the episode can be read in a less private manner as well. The version of the story narrated in the first chapter of the book underscores the notion of disrupted inheritance: the father of the young man killed on the train is worried that his son "showed no signs of marrying and producing an heir" (12), and the train wreck, of course, puts this matter completely to rest. The other important feature of the story is Reynolds's dream of riding on the train with a young man and thus imaginatively inhabiting the role of Thomas Jason. Taken together these elements suggest that Reynolds—undoubtedly, along with Miss Bisnauth, one of the only fully positive characters in the novel—is associated with an imaginative sympathy that somehow subverts and rejects the inheritance of racialized (and homophobic) thinking that surrounds him in the office. Reynolds is approvingly described as someone who is "extremely sensitive to the atmosphere of a crowd—of any group of people" (158), while Miss Bisnauth's "efforts to understand human nature" (156) are also singled out in this part of the novel, underscoring the book's strong advocacy for a disposition of empathy and awareness toward others.

Additionally, Reynolds is shown to be conscious of his mind's relationship with the world around him, as he reflects "how one's private images could be traced back to, and linked with inanimate objects. . . . One shadow behind another, telescoped backwards to infinity" (184). This language precisely echoes the theory of "telescopic objectivity" that Mortimer Barnett relates to Mr. Murrain later in the book. This theory of fiction (obviously reflective of the novel's own practice) is based on the understanding that "behind every human being an innumerable disregarded or forgotten host of event-trails branched away, touching innumerable other lives and innumerable objects. . . . A human being, viewed in entirety, was a coalescence of all the other lives, all the objects and all the events involved with his past" (189–90).[21] The philosophy grounding Barnett's practice of interrupting character-based narrative events with descriptions of relevant objects is thus seen to emphasize a historical awareness that acknowledges the interconnections between the past and the present, as well as an understanding of the interrelations among people, events, and history. An obvious stand-in for Mittelholzer, Barnett believes it is the author's responsibility to make these connections clear. Under questioning, Barnett refutes the idea that these objects are necessarily "static" and only part of an inert past, insisting that "there may be dynamic 'objects' which may well continue to shape the character's life in the present as well as in the future" (192), emphasizing the mutable presentness of the past. Not coincidentally, Barnett uses Murrain's scar, another "object" focused on in the novel itself, as an illustrative example. The scar, from a World War II injury, is the most obvious symbol of the (very material) effects of the past on the present, and the narration has already shown it troubling Murrain's thoughts during the course of the morning. Significantly, the conversation with Barnett "had given him a sudden wild new hope; he had revitalized something in him." After this realization, "Mr. Murrain regarded the scar on his forearm, and it did not make him nervous" (206).

Mittelholzer's own use of "telescopic objectivity" in *A Morning at the Office*, then, can be seen to enact, in both content and form, a very particular vision of tradition and change. The contents of the various episodes of "telescopic objectivity" in the novel illustrate the heavy determining effect of the past and its traditions of behavior and thought yet also point out how acts of empathy and imagination may serve to alter, however minutely, the familiar materials of the past into something better and more humane. For example, the spirit-possessed desk leg, another object highlighted by the novel, allows Miss Henery some fleeting contact with the past. Though the event seems in one sense to be a rather inconsequential authorial joke, Miss Henery concludes by musing that "perhaps this incident, trivial as it seemed, might influence the whole of her future life" (204). Miss Henery (voicing Mittelholzer's own abiding fascination with the possible reality of the supernatural) regards her psychic experience with the desk leg quite seriously, pondering how "she might have produced, by her day-dreaming, the right conditions to precipitate a manifestation" (204). Thus, this episode too underscores the significance of individual acts of consciousness interacting productively with the physical remainders of the past. Similarly, the technique of the novel itself, while laying claim to the status of an experiment, is not conjuring itself out of thin air; indeed, it is merely an intensification of the very familiar practice of novelistic description that results in a seemingly new and innovative form. In this way, the different modes of experimentation within *A Morning at the Office* appear as both an incarnation of the British modernist tradition of "making it new," as well as a prescription for consciousness and change appropriate to a specifically West Indian context.

Tangling with Tradition

On a directly thematic level, *A Morning at the Office* translates its more abstract ideas about newness and convention into a controversial stance on the nature and possibility of a West Indian literary tradition. Tradition was, of course, a contentious topic for Caribbean authors in the 1950s, during which time the main lines of argument generally fell somewhere between the advancement of an utterly new and unique West Indian culture and a reluctant appeal to European (specifically British) models as the basis for literary creation. There was a great deal of highly self-conscious debate about whether a West Indian literary tradition could be said to exist and, if so, of which ethno-cultural elements it might consist. Mittelholzer, in his critical pronouncements, tended to put the most emphasis on the European heritage of Caribbean cultural life, a tendency that, to put it mildly, was not particularly popular in a climate of burgeoning cultural nationalism throughout the region. Mittelholzer makes the case for European influence overtly in *A Morning at the Office* in describing Arthur's writing of "The Jen" as motivated by a desire to rebut the valorization of West Indian folk tales: "He wanted to show that it was a mistaken idea of certain West Indian cultural groups that West Indian literature and art should be based on these primitive tales. West Indians were not primitives. Only a handful of backwoods peasants were familiar with the nancy-stories that featured such characters as Compère Tigre and Compère Lapin" (211). Arthur asserts that there is no natural or historical connection between these supposedly native folk tales and the majority of the West Indian population, and his theory of a predominantly European cultural influence on the islands is advanced as a calculated defense against what Mittelholzer elsewhere characterizes as the program of West Indian neonationalists.[22] On a *Caribbean Voices* program, when asked specifically about whether he agrees with his character Arthur's views in this matter, Mittelholzer responds without equivocation that he does (*CV*, 9 July 1950).

Elsewhere in *A Morning at the Office,* the generally neutral, authoritative third-person narrator expresses a sense of the Europeanized nature of West Indian society even more baldly in describing Miss Yen Tip: "her outlook was the outlook of a westerner. The outlook of all British West Indians" (185). The novel makes a point of emphasizing Miss Yen Tip's Chinese heritage—an "other" to both Western and the preponderance of Caribbean culture—in order to suggest the unmitigated, all-encompassing influence of a European perspective in West Indian society. In his travel narrative *With a Carib Eye*, Mittelholzer reiterates this belief in the longstanding hegemony of European culture in the Caribbean, arguing that West Indian slaves "inbibed [*sic*] the languages and ways of the European" for centuries and thus, upon emancipation in 1838, "were European in outlook; they dressed like their planter masters, ate the same food, and had the same ambitions of possessing land and making their way up in the world" (16). On the surface, such views seem to condemn Caribbean culture to mere mimicry, leaving no room for any assertion of West Indian cultural autonomy or originality. However, the work cited above—*With a Carib Eye*—implies by its very title an idea of differences between Caribbean and European modes of being. Indeed, Mittelholzer's foreword to the book explicitly decries the distortions that he feels result from the presentation of a solely Northern viewpoint of the Caribbean, a viewpoint he criticizes for being prone to an exoticizing emphasis on preconceived and stereotypical elements like "palm-fringed beaches, calypsonians, smiling black girls, and voodoo worshippers" (7). *With a Carib Eye* is expressly intended as an antidote to such misapprehensions: Mittelholzer describes the book as "an attempt to present a picture of the British Caribbean scene as viewed specifically through the eye of one born and bred in the region" (8), so as to provide a more "balanced, authentic picture of the region" (7). In this case, Mittelholzer explicitly articulates the importance of a West Indian viewpoint that is fundamentally different from a European one.

Along these same lines, in a piece in *Kyk-over-al*, Mittelholzer's answer to the question of whether there is a specifically West Indian way of life is in the affirmative (albeit with some characteristically inflammatory reservations): "Yes, there is a West Indian way of life—but it is not as distinctive a way of life as many cranks and faddists, who have West Indian nationhood on the brain, would have us believe" ("West Indian Way of Life?," 200). Later in the response, Mittelholzer expresses doubts about the potential unity of anything called "West Indian culture," since "each island or territory has its own 'way' of speaking, eating, and viewing life, of worshiping and governing its people" (201). Somewhat contradictorily, in the last chapter of *With a Carib Eye*, Mittelholzer describes the "polite dog-fight over the question as to whether such a thing as a definite and recognisable West Indian culture does or does not exist" (186) and allies himself with those who say that it does not. His reasoning, however, depends on the issue he takes with any idea of "West Indian Culture. Note the capital C" (186). By means of this careful orthographic distinction, Mittelholzer suggests it is not that the people of the Caribbean do not have unique cultural traits, only that each island's culture is different, largely the consequence of having been subject to different sorts (and differing levels) of influence over the course of history. Earlier in the book, in a discussion of Trinidad's East Indian population, Mittelholzer belies any outright refusal of a unifying notion of the West Indian, claiming that the "immigrants from India who came between 1845 and 1917 to Trinidad have evolved into Creoles as West Indian in outlook as any negro West Indian" (52). Here, as elsewhere, Mittelholzer seems to suggest his awareness that, despite the irrefutable differences evident *between* separate Caribbean islands, something recognizably different from anything purely European—imperfectly noted as "West Indian"—is important to recognize. While it would no doubt be a stretch to characterize him as a straightforward Caribbean nationalist, Mittelholzer nevertheless endorsed the struggle to articulate a distinct, if epigonal, conception of Caribbean culture and society.[23]

The key to Mittelholzer's views on forming a properly Caribbean culture lies in his belief in struggle: although he accepted, and indeed argued for, the historical facticity of an overwhelmingly European cultural presence in the Caribbean, this tradition was not something that he thought should simply be acceded to with equanimity. In fact, Mittelholzer generally held tradition to be an oppressive force that held back independent development and creativity. For example, in one *Barbados Advocate* column, Mittelholzer associates tradition with superstitious doctrines that occlude perception of the way the world actually is ("Cure for Corruption"), and in another he warns about the tendency for explanatory narratives to be "transmuted by the flexible imaginations of . . . fellow humans into solemn dogma," which is then damagingly "distilled into a thing of tradition and precept" ("Truth and Legend"). Certainly, any number of characters in his fiction come in for ridicule due to their inability to challenge traditional habits of thought and behavior, ranging from the weak-willed and timorous Grace in *The Weather in Middenshot,* who pathetically chooses spinsterhood at home with her elderly parents rather than risking any upheaval that might be caused by her love for Mr. Holmes, to Richard's grandfather in *Latticed Echoes,* whose absurdly rigid patterns of thought prevent almost all sympathy or connection between him and the rest of the (changing) world. In his writing, Mittelholzer's instinctive reaction is almost always iconoclastic, a suspicion of accepted truths and mass patterns of thought: he consistently speaks out against the strictures guarding "the borders . . . of Respectable Thought" and believes that the result of heavily traditional modes of perceiving and acting result in "bigotry and stagnation of thought" ("Spiritual Beyond").[24] Although his resistance to tradition can also take on the characteristics of a reactionary discourse that bemoans the fallen state of the contemporary world divorced from its original goodness, Mittelholzer's most frequent criticism of tradition is its incompatibility with the knowledge and circumstances of the present. Thus, although Mittelholzer understands the European heritage as the predominant tradition in West Indian society, it is a tradition with which, perhaps ineluctably for a contrarian such as he, Mittelholzer advocates conscious contention.

If his cultural politics recognize the need to struggle against a purely dominant European mode of understanding, Mittelholzer nevertheless took great pains to denigrate the more visible projects of West Indian cultural nationalism. Despite being pointedly critical of the predation wrought by colonizing forces, Mittelholzer has little sympathy for what he consistently characterizes as extremists who are "trying to whip into life a spirit of aggressive nationalism" (*Morning at the Office*, 214). For Mittelholzer, who frequently advocates aggression and force, such moderation rings particularly uncharacteristic, but it seems to suggest a view of cultural tradition and human endeavor coincident with the thinking of T. S. Eliot. Like Mittelholzer, Eliot is, in the words of Louis Menand, a figure who "seems at some moments to be the conservator of a certain tradition . . . and at others to be the analyst of their exhaustion" (*Discovering Modernism*, 4), a strange composite of revolutionary urges shadowed by a deep conservatism.[25] Eliot's concept of tradition—articulated most famously in his essay "Tradition and the Individual Talent"—is the site at which some reconciliation between these contradictory urges for radical change and preservation is most readily seen.[26] In this essay, Eliot dismisses a notion of tradition that involves merely "following the ways of the immediate generation before us in a blind or timid adherence to its successes" (4). In its place, Eliot offers an understanding of tradition that depends on a *critical* awareness of past endeavors: for Eliot, a judicious acceptance of the weight and importance of the past is indispensable to any attempt at articulation in the present. Indeed, Eliot suggests that newness consists largely of the old in any poet's work: "we shall often find that not only the best, but the most individual parts of his work may be those in which the dead poets, his ancestors, assert their immortality most vigorously" (4). The point is not that there is no use attempting innovation—conformity to tradition does not make a work of art in this view, indeed quite the opposite—but that the ability to create is far from wholly a matter of freedom and individual caprice. Rather, it occurs only in the context of a hard-won, carefully cultivated sense of cultural history. It is this historical sense, and the recognition of the slow, tectonic shifts by which change can be catalyzed within cultural history, that seems most important to Mittelholzer's understanding of tradition.

Although Mittelholzer generally admitted of almost no positive literary influence or admiration, he refers approvingly to Eliot several times in his writing, most notably in acknowledging "the profound and involved—and often obscure—opinions adduced" by Eliot with regard to aesthetics and criticism in "Literary Criticism and the Creative Writer" (117). On *Caribbean Voices*, Mittelholzer once baldly proclaimed himself "a lover of T. S. Eliot" (*CV*, 27 Jan. 1957), and his second wife, Jacqueline, notes also that Mittelholzer admired Eliot ("My Husband," 309) and frequently quoted his poetry ("Idyll and the Warrior," 58). Moreover, a surprising number of Mittelholzer's characters read or discuss Eliot's works, with *A Tinkling in the Twilight* even taking its epigraph from Eliot's *Burnt Norton*. The opinions of Arthur in *A Morning at the Office* bring out Mittelholzer's Eliotic views about the weight of cultural history quite clearly. Arthur's critique of the idea of a West Indian culture based exclusively on a folkloric tradition derived from Africa seems primarily based in the violence it does to the realities of the last several centuries of Caribbean culture. Arthur asserts that "if the West Indies was to evolve a culture individually West Indian, it could only come out of the whole hotch-potch of racial and national elements of which the West Indies was composed; it could not spring only from the Negro" (214). The emphasis here is on a recognition that the very pronounced cultural mixture of the Caribbean cannot be ignored, while the use of the word "evolve" implies that the creation of any identity known as "West Indian" will be a gradual process of accumulated change, not something summoned out of thin air. Indeed, the unthinking precipitance of the cultural nationalists appears to be Arthur's primary complaint. In attacking "these faddists [who] had awakened one morning with the sudden idea that the West Indies lacked an individual culture and that it was their business to manufacture one without delay" (211), Arthur underscores the rushed qualities of the endeavor, suggesting that the speedy production of a cultural tradition is objectionable not only in its falsity but also in its ill-considered haste.[27] In Arthur's view, a pervasive tradition already exists: "if one had to write fairy tales at all with a West Indian flavour the creatures or characters in them should be very nearly in the European tradition, for weren't the West Indies practically European in manners and customs?" (211). By this account, the historical weight of colonialism cannot simply be shrugged off, despite the political attractions of such an attempt.[28] Elsewhere, Mittelholzer wraps up his opinion on the uniqueness of West Indian culture with a similar recognition of the lengthy process of distilling a definable West Indian way of life: "it will be a long time, I feel, before that way can be charted with clarity on the map of Caribbean mores" ("West Indian Way of Life?" 201). For Mittelholzer, his era's Caribbean literature surely existed as a discrete entity, but it embodied the qualities of "a robust infant," with its mature form as yet indeterminate and its European lineage still clearly discernible (*With a Carib Eye*, 190).

In a symposium on West Indian culture on *Caribbean Voices*, Mittelholzer makes his reasoning about the slow, time-consuming nature of tradition building equally clear. After noting the sundry cultural influences (especially European, but also East Indian, Chinese, and Assyrian in addition to African) that have accrued over many decades in the region, he asks: "How can these influences be thrown overboard overnight and something totally unformed and ill-defined substituted?" (*CV*, 9 July 1950). Similarly, Mittelholzer also asserts in this response his belief that "a culture isn't something you can consciously and deliberately create," implying that culture cannot simply put down roots in virgin territory, but must emerge out of a foundation that has been laid over the course of many years. However, this cultural inheritance does not mean creation or difference is unattainable. As Eliot cautions, the author "must inevitably be judged by the standards of the past" but, significantly, is "not amputated" by them ("Tradition and the Individual Talent," 5).[29] Mittelholzer takes a similarly careful stance toward innovation in the Caribbean context. While he notes that "the West Indian way of life is a way that runs fairly parallel, and very close, to the European way" ("West Indian Way of Life?" 200), Mittelholzer always leaves room for cultural difference: the West Indian way is only "fairly parallel," and its path upon achieving independence from Britain, in Mittelholzer's understanding, has every chance of developing into an increasingly divergent (if never *wholly* autonomous) tradition, into a view of the world that employs something that looks more and more like a distinctly Carib eye. In literary terms, Mittelholzer's careful, Eliotic theory of the role of tradition in a Caribbean context—politically unpopular at the time, not to mention frequently caricatured by his detractors—suggests that, while eager to assert the differences of West Indian literature, he did not believe that such an assertion could be possible or effective outside the contours of understanding already established within the British novelistic tradition.

Same Verse, Different Song:
Latticed Echoes and *Thunder Returning*

A crucial determination in Mittelholzer's discussions of innovation and tradition hinges on the question of individual autonomy. Clearly, in Mittelholzer's view, the world humans inhabit is structured quite prevalently by what it has inherited from its predecessors. In literary terms, this inheritance takes the form of the (primarily, at least) British literary tradition; in more material terms, in much of Mittelholzer's writing, this inheritance is figured along an axis encompassing genetics on one end and environment on the other. In both cases, the dominant factor, to Mitteholzer's mind, is that which is inherited rather than the contingencies produced by individual effort and experience. This view has led to Mittelholzer's reputation as a believer in a deterministic, eugenicist theory of raced behavior and capability. Mittelholzer, for his part, did very little to dispel this impression, declaring in a 1954 column that he "thought environment played no more than a five to ten per cent part in influencing a man's character. The other ninety or ninety-five percent was plain and simple heredity" ("Heredity and Environment"). Numerous characters express similar views about this topic in the novels as well. In *The Piling of the Clouds,* Peter fiercely declaims that "we are each of us *born* with the character we have, and all the environment and traumatic experience in the world won't make us any different from what we are" (212), for example, while in *A Tale of Three Places,* Alfy thinks to himself, "Who could doubt that heredity was the dominant factor in every human life! The psychologists who stressed environment were asses" (270). Nevertheless, although he often appears quite uncompromising in this view, Mittelholzer put more emphasis than is commonly recognized on the small percentage he grants here to the workings of the human will. Even in the above-mentioned column on the subject, there is a grudging acknowledgment that nonhereditary forces in a person's life can "curtail his achievements; it might muffle the development of any possible talents he possesses; it might embitter him up to a point." Although he goes on to assert that "no environment can change the fabric of an individual's personality so as to make him a saint or a rogue," the important distinction, albeit subtle, is between the "fabric" of a person's being and his or her determinate actions: for Mittelholzer, while people have no control over how they have been formed, this by no means predetermines their actions or excuses them from ethical responsibility. For example, an argument for free will structures Mittelholzer's allegorical fairy tale, *The Adding Machine*, in which the protestations of the greedy protagonist Hedge that he is only behaving how he was born to behave (83) are quite evidently meant to appear as craven and self-serving. The story's overt moral about the need for generosity to one's neighbors clearly depends on its author's belief in the possibility of some form of autonomous human behavior.

Many of Mittelholzer's novels advocate similar beliefs, such as *The Harrowing of Hubertus*, which centers on the eponymous protagonist's struggles to act both morally and true to his nature; in this novel, Hubertus himself asserts the importance of human will, declaring that "evil is produced by our deliberate abuse of the talents and abilities bestowed by God upon men" (123). Herbert, an authoritative figure of Mittelholzeresque wisdom in *The Aloneness of Mrs. Chatham*, likewise espouses a notion of individual autonomy (and the consequent spiritual aid that accompanies it): "That is what happened in Mrs. Chatham's case. The moment she resolved to live the life of one dedicated to self-realisation she drew to her side helpers unseen but very much real. We each of us have free-will in everything we do and resolve to do. If we decide to follow the Left Hand Path just as readily beings on that side are attracted to us, and help is offered" (70). Indeed, the strong streak of moralizing apparent in nearly all of Mittelholzer's novels in itself indicates his unwavering devotion to struggling against social ills, a commitment that becomes nonsensical in any purely deterministic philosophy. F. M. Birbalsingh, in examining the moral nature of Mittelholzer's work, rightly concludes that his novels ultimately recognize a fundamental "capacity for moral choice" ("Edgar Mittelholzer," 94). Birbalsingh dismisses any apparent contradictions in Mittelholzer's worldview with the claim that their author's moral platform "represents a cast of thought rather than a systematic philosophy" (94) but intriguingly identifies the author's occasional indignant denial of purpose and value in human life as a reaction to his unrealizable "moralist's wish for definitive placing of live human creatures during their life and growth in relation to a static, preconceived notion of purpose and value" (97). Birbalsingh pinpoints here an important source of Mittelholzer's ever-increasing frustration with the world, yet it is, tellingly, the frustration not of a cynical quietist but of an ardent but bitterly disappointed social reformer. The recognition of the small but important role that free will plays within Mittelholzer's novelistic world points up the strong structural parallels between Mittelholzer's frequently misunderstood views on genetic inheritance and his views of tradition: in both cases, human experience is understood to be powerfully structured a priori by external forces while still being shaped in important ways by an individual's active choices in the present. The leitmotiv experiments of *Latticed Echoes* and *Thunder Returning* can be read as a further elaboration of these views.

The subtitle appended to both novels—"A Novel in the Leitmotiv Manner"—explicitly announces Mittelholzer's intention to use the tools of cultural tradition to establish a new, slightly modified one. On one hand, the impulse to name the "manner" in which the book is written suggests its difference from other novels; on the other hand, the comfortable confidence of the direct article modifying this technique implies a sense that, in fact, the manner in which the novel has been written already has the status of something known and familiar. Mittelholzer's foreword to *Thunder Returning*, written in response to the widespread critical dubiety over the technique of *Latticed Echoes*, reveals his understanding of this experimental dynamic in interesting ways. The crucial starting point of the foreword is an extract from an unnamed review of the first novel that Mittelholzer deemed "solid enough for me to ponder on" (5); in it, the reviewer writes, "Mr. Mittelholzer demands too much of his readers. He neither explains the images, nor shows whether they are in his mind or the characters'; and I confess myself bewildered as I was not by Virginia Woolf's *The Waves*" (5).[30] Mittelholzer's reaction to these claims conveys the contradictory currents into which he had waded. First, he expresses surprise that so few of his readers recognized the lineage, and hence the import, of his technique: "Too optimistically I had hoped that most, if not all, of my readers would be familiar with the Leitmotiv as used in Wagner's operas, especially *The Ring*. Now I realise that this is far from the case" (5). In this way, Mittelholzer lays claim to the tradition of a cultural form (importantly, perhaps, not a literary or British one). His next response is to deny vigorously any connection between his writing and that of Woolf, thus distancing himself from what many critics perceived as his primary literary forebear. Mittelholzer's refusal to acknowledge the legitimacy of any Woolfian parallels is revealingly emphatic: "The technique I use in my trilogy is entirely different and in no way related to that used by Virginia Woolf" (6).[31] Finally, Mittelholzer acknowledges the difficulty the technique poses for his readers—obliging them "to *study* as well as read the books" (6)—and proceeds to describe in detail how the leitmotivs function in the novels. Within this progression are encapsulated the hesitations and paradoxes of Mittelholzer's relationship to tradition, shuttling between acknowledgment and denial of cultural influence, insisting on the comprehensible legibility of the form, and then exhaustively explaining its meanings. The novels themselves both enact and portray his works' difficult positioning between the creatively individual and the inheritably traditional, seeking some space for the former among the pressing presence of the latter.

The overarching plot of *Latticed Echoes* and *Thunder Returning* centers on the disruptive attraction between the two chief protagonists, Richard Lehrer, a light-skinned, British-educated Guyanese architect who has returned home for a three-year government posting in New Amsterdam, and Lindy Rowelson, the German-born wife of a British road engineer who is a university acquaintance of Richard's also working in New Amsterdam. Both characters have British spouses—Richard's wife is Lydia, Lindy's husband is Tommy—and the (ultimately quite conventional) dramatic action thus centers on the tense, complicated domestic relations among these four characters. Similar to *The Harrowing of Hubertus,* the most important struggle in the novel involves Richard's (and to a lesser degree Lindy's) attempt to reconcile his own moral beliefs with what he feels to be a preordained, cosmically fated attraction to somebody outside his marriage. Although Richard consistently and explicitly maintains that he loves his wife, Lydia, both novels suggest that he has a deep-seated yearning for Germanness, concretely realized, it would seem, in his attraction to Lindy. The ineluctable givenness of this attraction is pointed to in a conversation between Richard's aunt Emily and Lindy, in which Richard and his grandfather are both characterized as being predestined to love all things German. Speaking of Richard's grandfather, Emily relates how "it is really deep-sunk in him, this Germanness. It is a hankering that was born in him" (*Thunder Returning,* 128). Emily endorses Lindy's reiteration that such a longing "is deep in his spirit" and goes on to postulate the same ingrained tendency in her nephew: "And especially since seeing something of Richard, I've come to realise this more than ever. Neither of them can help it. It's something they were born with. It was a mistake, their being born in this country—in this continent—so far from Germany. Deep inside, they must both secretly resent the trick Fate has played on them" (128).[32] Earlier in *Thunder Returning* Richard, too, resorts to the language of fate in describing his relations with Lindy as he tries to comfort his wife: "You didn't make the situation. Fate made it"

(77). Lindy also confesses that "something in me compels the action" (124) to reconnect with Richard, despite her moral disapproval of their affair.

Although both novels suggest that something external to Richard and Lindy—variously conceived as fate, blood, or the forces of nature—acts to drive them together, they do not condone complacency as a response. Indeed, at the beginning of *Latticed Echoes,* Richard echoes Mittelholzer's personal belief in constantly struggling against the world's demands, thinking, "I won't get complacent, though. . . . That would be fatal. March and fight" (31). The general narrative arc of each novel, in fact, emphasizes the protagonists' concrete, conscious attempts to avoid surrendering to the attraction. *Latticed Echoes* concludes with an understandably tense discussion between Richard and Lydia, his wife, in which they ultimately agree not to separate; the novel ends with a key word of Richard's leitmotiv—"perpetually" (254)—pointing to his continued need to stay on guard and maintain the balance "between artillery and pensive spaces" (254) that characterizes a stable, ethical life for him. As *Thunder Returning* opens, it emerges that Richard and Lydia have moved to Georgetown, supporting the sense of active agency they employ to avoid Richard's "fateful" attraction. This second novel, too, ends on a note of determined human will, as, after Lydia's suicide, Richard takes responsibility for what has happened, and though Lindy herself has determinedly left her husband, Richard resolves to move back to England despite their apparent freedom finally to be together. Although the lack of a third novel to complete the trilogy leaves the resolution of this romantic narrative permanently inaccessible, it seems fair to say that, despite the persistent echoes and returns suggested by their titles, the two novels' narratives highlight a crucial measure of individual struggle against the otherwise implacable forces in which their characters' lives are entangled.[33]

The leitmotiv technique reinforces the novels' thematic representation of the arduous process of a heavily conditioned individual creativity. Richard's musing description of human existence in *Latticed Echoes* suggests the parallels between the novel's technique and its characters' struggle for agency. Explicitly wondering if a new motiv has entered into his and Lydia's life together, his answer equivocates between newness and uniformity: "Our consciousness is like a kaleidoscope—a kaleidoscope of moods, all built around the central framework of our basic human problems. . . . Moods, moods, moods, love. That's what we are when you come to analyse us. The variations are infinite, but the general pattern keeps repeating itself monotonously. Yesterday's tints and facets merge into to-day's, and to-day's into tomorrow's. In detail, no two combinations are ever alike, but the overall effect is repetitiously the same" (179). While Richard here seems rather pessimistic about meaningful change—his disquisition ends with a vision of stagnation in which "nothing is really changed, nothing fresh really happens" (180)—the insistent reiteration of uniqueness and complexity within the continuity suggests something else as well (as does Lydia's abruptly putting a stop to the monologue, in effect calling Richard out on his self-serving proclamations).[34] Certainly, what Richard describes (and refers to as the working of motivs) matches Mittelholzer's own delineation of his leitmotiv method, in which, he emphasizes, "no word is ever used in a Leitmotiv passage unless it has already been incorporated in some Leitmotiv already stated" (*Thunder Returning*, 9). While Mittelholzer notes that his leitmotiv passages "are intended to mean nothing in so far as their *literal* content is concerned" (7) but are instead "intended to provide a pleasing musical effect, colourful and surrealistic," he also insists they are "not solely for poetic decoration" (6). Inhabiting the role of curmudgeonly schoolmaster, Mittelholzer asserts that "if the reader took the trouble to learn the symbol code he could follow roughly what was happening by reading only the Leitmotivs" (7). This narrative weight can be borne by the leitmotivs, he says, because they are designed to communicate what is happening in a particular scene—including characters, location, and prevalent emotions or conflicts (6–7), as well as, interestingly, the passage of time. Ultimately, then, although it employs a distinctly minimal set of given words for each particular narrative element, the leitmotiv technique embodies an almost infinitely variable set of combinations interacting to create not numbing, repetitious stasis, but the ever-shifting narrative events and outcomes of the novels themselves.

If the technique's expression of recombinatory creativity thus works against Richard's pessimistic vision of a dreary shuffling of ontological certainties with no progress or action, the ways the leitmotivs are used and described likewise belie any complete determinism. For example, it is ambiguous precisely whence each character's leitmotiv words arise. Although it would seem intuitive in a wholly determined world that each character's leitmotiv would simply be given, a conversation between Richard and Lydia early in *Latticed Echoes* implies that it is the characters' own creative imaginations that produce some of the images. The references in the conversation to Richard's leitmotivs are unmistakable. Lydia explains to Richard how his smile "makes

[her] think of bees trapped in a huge basement," and then she notes Richard's own fanciful perceptions of "distant artillery, and a voice that keeps shouting: 'Fight and march! March and fight!'" (10). Richard then explicitly names another key image—"the feather-bed tilting in the dark" (10). These images of course dominate the leitmotiv assigned to Richard in Mittelholzer's schema as it appears in the appendix to *Thunder Returning*, and they function in both novels to signal Richard's presence, such as at the end of the first section of *Latticed Echoes*, as Lydia sleeps and the ship approaches Guyana: "Past the Azores, hovering by day between deck and deck-rail, between past and present, rook-black, swamp-warm, the giant bees tilted and rocked with the illusion of a million images in the perpetual summer sun, and the artillery, bass and distant, sounded mysterious, yet lovely and lonely" (31).[35] In their conversation, Richard and Lydia trace the leitmotiv images back to their own (mutual) artistic capacity—Lydia tells Richard "it's the artistic in you," while Richard replies "you have some of it in you, too" (10). Thus, this important early scene self-reflexively highlights the self-creating aspect of human imagination at the heart of Mittelholzer's structuring leitmotiv technique.

Relatedly, Mittelholzer's foreword to *Thunder Returning* also notes that new leitmotivs take shape in the novels, introduced by narrative events that change characters' emotions, goals, and desires. Discussing a leitmotiv that begins a scene with Lindy and her husband, Tommy, Mittelholzer notes the appearance of some of their key images, as well as the occurrence of "keywords from a new Motiv introduced at the end of the previous chapter—a Motiv indicative of Lindy's secret longing for union with Richard Lehrer" (7). In this way, again, the very technique suggests newness emerging out of recombined elements of the old. Another extremely important leitmotiv—the groaning alligator that appears to signal the actual lovemaking of Richard and Lindy—suggests something similar. Certainly, it functions as a new leitmotiv, emerging in *Latticed Echoes* when the two lovers first consummate their illicit attraction. Interestingly, near the end of the scene, it is counterpoised with another image—the bull frogs quarking—that Mittelholzer identifies with Guyana itself.[36] These two leitmotivs are posed against each other in collocated pairs—"bull-frog or alligator" and "quark or moan" (118)—just as Richard and Lindy's conversation takes them into further passion. Thus, at this eminently crucial moment, the leitmotiv form pointedly blurs the border between external, natural force and human volition, showing the interrelations, or even indistinguishableness, between the natural environment and the new meanings with which the two characters' actions have now endowed it, reinforcing a sense of the creative power inherent in "new combinations" on several levels.[37]

Latticed Echoes and *Thunder Returning,* then, reinforce the purposeful significance of literary experiment that Mittelholzer had pointed to in *A Morning at the Office,* illustrating his cautious negotiations of a familiar postcolonial (and modernist) conundrum: how to make a new, contrary tradition out of the materials of an older, repellant one. In consciously portraying a West Indian social scene that is similar to (but not a precise replica of) a European one, and presenting that portrayal in a way reminiscent of European modernism while nevertheless insisting on its own important differences, Mittelholzer's work enacts the difficult negotiations between a constraining past and an only partially autonomous future with which West Indian fiction of the postwar years had to contend. If Mittelholzer is understood as the pioneering author of the Windrush generation—the first postwar West Indian novelist to attract any critical or scholarly notice in Britain—his writing can be seen as a representative beginning for the period's emergent Caribbean fiction in English. In its modernist forms, it stands as a cogent marker that, for Mittelholzer, despite the urgency felt by his generation to create a distinctively West Indian canon, such creation would never take place uncorrupted by the cultural influence of European colonial society. Mittelholzer's qualified but consistent emphasis on experimentation reveals a belief in the need for West Indian authors to work gradually, and with steady effort, toward new and different ways to represent West Indianness from the foundations of an already established tradition.[38] In this—its own paradoxical, iconoclastic traditionalism—Mittelholzer's work appears as a divergent echo of Eliot and British modernism in general. It insists that, in some sense, literary tradition is kept alive by *not* following in the steps of one's predecessors, yet all the while recognizing that to avoid such steps—to make literature "new" or even to make a new literature—one must still necessarily pay heed to the peregrinations of the literary past.

3   Engaging the Reader
The Difficulties of George Lamming

> Let us never cease from thinking—what is this "civilisation" in which
> we find ourselves?
>
> —Virginia Woolf, *Three Guineas*

Like Mittelholzer, the Barbadian author George Lamming was readily received
in postwar literary London as an experimental "high-art" writer. In contrast
to Mittelholzer's eclectic habits of innovation tout court, however, Lamming's
experimentation was consistently understood as a recognizable species of self-
consciously difficult writing in the tradition of Faulkner, Joyce, and Woolf. In
a *Caribbean Voices* program dedicated exclusively to Lamming's work, broadcast on 4 January 1948, Henry Swanzy's introductory remarks capture this
sense of Lamming's indecipherability, asserting that in his poems "one finds
a strange, oblique, violent, passionate emotion, which I feel, somehow, may
prove of importance to the Caribbean" (*CV*, 4 Jan. 1948).[1] Swanzy's qualifying
"somehow" betrays doubt in his own ability to gauge the precise meaning and
import of Lamming's work, an uncertainty that is explicitly articulated in his
commentary after the first poem is read: "We start with that rather mysterious poem because it seems typical of this writer, who never says, straight out,
exactly what he means." Swanzy thus introduces difficulty as an identifying
characteristic of Lamming's work, while maintaining with cautious imprecision that the work is, somehow, meaningful and important. One year later on
Caribbean Voices, Arthur Calder Marshall reiterates this theme, concluding a
reading of five Lamming poems by commenting, "I wonder what you made of
that. It's not easy stuff, as you heard" (*CV*, 9 Jan. 1949)

Such critical evaluations of Lamming as difficult—many indeed critical
in the sense of negative—appear in more contemporary accounts as well. Ru-
dolf Bader's entry in the encyclopedic *International Literature in English: Es-*

says on the Major Writers begins its discussion of Lamming's works with the caveat that "many readers find George Lamming's novels difficult" ("George Lamming," 143). While Sandra Pouchet Paquet has insightfully suggested that the political concern of Lamming's novels "has a direct bearing not only on his novels' themes, but on their structure and the particular fictional elements he employs" (*Novels of George Lamming*, 10), A. J. Simoes da Silva finds Lamming's complex ambiguity politically constraining, and Supriya Nair's *Caliban's Curse: George Lamming and the Revisioning of History* likewise agonizes over the political implications of Lamming's inaccessibility. For his part, Lamming seems to welcome the critical consensus that he is a "difficult" writer, saying, "this means that I have to be read more slowly than would be the case with some writers, which I think is a good thing" (interview, by Munro and Sander, 11). Immediately after this comment, Lamming signals his awareness of the potential elitism in such a view, an aspect that has animated critiques of Lamming's novels throughout his career. Nevertheless, here and elsewhere, he remains unwavering in his commitment to avoiding simplification.

Lamming's view of the salutary effects of reading more slowly provides a key to the formal aspect of his intentions regarding difficulty—a hallowed modernist effort at "interrupting the 'realistic' processes of habitualized communication" (Eysteinsson, *Concept of Modernism*, 238). The interruptive motivation behind Lamming's prose style has been elegantly articulated by David Scott, who argues in the preface to his interview with Lamming that the latter's novels entail a confrontation with "this obligation: to pause, to doubt, to question, to wonder out loud about the assumptions, the conditions, the terms, the conventions, the values in relation to which, at any given moment, we pursue the projects we pursue" (Lamming, "Sovereignty of the Imagination," 74). In a similar vein, George Steiner has suggested that literary difficulty's most important effects include "forcing us to reach out towards more delicate orderings of perception" and "drawing attention . . . to the inertias in the common routine of discourse" (*On Difficulty*, 40). Fredric Jameson likewise posits the function of difficult, resistant texts as the deliberate frustration of methods of quick reading "intended to speed the reader across a sentence in such a way that he can salute a readymade idea effortlessly in passing" (*Marxism and Form*, xiii). These assessments of literary difficulty speak to a fundamental aim of Lamming's novels: to transform uncritical, passively receptive readers into skeptical, suspicious ones, alert to the cultural, ideological, and political frames within which all narrative is produced and received.

As suggested by the epigraph, this ethical imperative to reexamine, consistently, the very bases of one's own self-conceptions is something that lies at the heart of Woolf's modernist practice as well. In parallel with Lamming, Woolf lauds the "obstinate resistance" of a text as a positive, productive quality, such that readers "must stop, go back, try out this way and that, and proceed at a foot's pace" ("Reading," 32). Bemoaning the current state of writing as "almost servile in the assiduity with which it helps us on our way, making only the standard charge on our attention" (32), Woolf, too, sees literature working properly only if it offers a transformative challenge to a reader's habitual frames of understanding. In observing that "the proper stuff of fiction is a little other than custom would have us believe it" ("Modern Fiction," 106), Woolf asserts her insistence on the counterconventional nature of worthwhile fiction and in another essay presents this dynamic as plainly confrontational. Discussing the value of authors to readers, she notes that "they are only able to help us if we come to them laden with questions and suggestions won honestly in the course of our own reading. They can do nothing for us if we herd ourselves under their authority and lie down like sheep in the shade of a hedge. We can only understand their ruling when it comes in conflict with our own and vanquishes it" ("How Should One Read," 10). In this way, it becomes clear that Lamming and Woolf share a belief in literature's obligation to demystify and restructure habitual patterns of thought and interpretation: for both authors, texts should forcefully resist readers' routines in hopes of directing them somewhere new.

Lamming provides a description of precisely this kind of reordering, epiphanic effect in his first novel, *In the Castle of My Skin,* delivered by the character Boy Blue as part of a long philosophical discussion that the narrator, G., and his friends have on the beach: "You hear something, an' it come to you as a kind of surprise, then it connect up with another something you'd hear long time back, an' what with one thing an' another . . . when they all together you see yourself face to face with something that is true or very very strange. Or it make you remember something that you didn't remember all the time" (133). Boy Blue's sense of transformed apprehension (whether new or theretofore only dimly realized) is valorized in the book as a first, hesitant step toward alleviating what Lamming has called the "tragic innocence" of his first novel's characters (*Conversations,* 49). Elsewhere, Lamming invokes the same experience of newly awakened understanding as the goal of all meaningful literature, which, in Lamming's view, necessarily aims "to create an awareness of society which did not exist before; or to inform and enrich an awareness which was not deeply felt" ("Caribbean Creative Expressions," 3). As Paquet has noted, Lamming clearly sees his "fiction as an instrument of social transformation" (*Novels of George Lamming*, 4), and the complexity of his prose lies at the heart of this vision, aiming to interrupt habitual thought patterns and catalyze a reassessment of the values and goals urged by conventional discourse.

While this assessment of the uses of difficulty sheds important light on the ideal functions of Lamming's opaque literary style (and on ways in which difficulty might converge with postcolonial literature's interests in counterdiscursivity writ large), it is also important to consider the technique's valence in the social and literary milieu in which Lamming's novels were created and received. More recent critical considerations of difficulty have pinpointed its relevance and interpretability less in the work itself than in the intertwined relationships among text, reader, and the publishing and critical arenas. Leonard Diepeveen's *The Difficulties of Modernism*, for example, focuses on how literary difficulty becomes meaningful via the social relationship between author and reader, with cultural and class concerns (expressed particularly by psychological feelings of anxiety and inadequacy in Diepeveen's account) at the foundation of difficulty's effects.[2] This more sociologically sensitive account of literary difficulty suggests something more behind Lamming's perplexing literary technique, emphasizing the sociopolitical thrust of his trademark style.

As noted in chapter 1, Lamming had strong tendencies toward iconoclasm, both literary and political, well before arriving in London in 1950. Like Mittelholzer, he considered disputation both constructive and necessary, and he encouraged opportunities for intellectual contention and debate. Lamming's arrival in England seems to have reinforced these tendencies, especially concerning the issue of race. Lamming's letters to Collymore shortly after arriving grimly register his dismay at the strongly negative British reaction to the incoming thousands of West Indian migrants (as does a contemporaneous poem broadcast on *Caribbean Voices*, "Dedication from Afar: A Song for Marian"), and he briefly muses about moving to the more welcoming cultural climes of Paris as a result. Circumstances prevailed, however, to keep Lamming in London. In the context of this cultural atmosphere, marked by the consolidation of (white) British national character, Lamming's embrace of modernist tactics thus seems calculated to preserve a strong sense of racial and national difference. In addition to the larger aesthetic goal of reawakening critical consciousness in his readers, Lamming's aesthetic choices serve to enunciate his own sociocultural position in a particularly combative way.[3]

Although this combativeness might seem counterintuitive for a young writer from the colonies trying to establish himself, a modernist affiliation nevertheless makes some sense for Lamming in the postwar context. As a black West Indian immigrant, Lamming was already clearly recognized as an outsider in an almost monolithically white postwar England and was thereby seemingly readymade to fit into a category (modernist writer) often associated with difficulty.[4] On the other hand, contemporaneous racial discourses surrounding West Indians insisted on their essential primitiveness, lack of culture, and childlike status, with the implication that high cultural achievement from the Caribbean was simply not in any way conceivable. These poles of "outsider" and "primitive" are crucial, and they find a close conjunction with the twin dangers of assimilation and exoticism Peter Hulme identifies as the main pitfalls in reading (what he terms) Third World literature from the metropolis. The parallels between these sets of terms are provocative, and within them Lamming's modernist difficulty can be read as an assertive literary-political gesture aimed at preserving a West Indian (racial, political, cultural) difference while countering an English exoticism that tended to read West Indians as simple, unthinking (and unworking) residents of a tropical paradise. In this reading, the category of (modernist) outsider functions to allay the threat of assimilation, while the invocation of a highly intellectualized cultural tradition (modernism) strategically disrupts, on several levels, the dismissive reduction of West Indian artists to simple, natural creatures of merely anthropological interest.

In such a light, the modernist difficulty of George Lamming appears as a strategy aimed squarely at *engaging* his readers—in a double sense of both aggressive confrontation as well as attentive interlocution—in an earnest discussion about the legacy of empire. The double valence of engagement echoes the ambivalent activities of the crabs on the beach in *In the Castle of My Skin*, who are represented as either making love, fighting fatally, or both. By putting the crabs, "stuck like things put together" (132), conspicuously contiguous to Boy Blue's description of intellectual epiphany, "the way a thing put itself together" (133), Lamming suggests that engagement, whether of the "clawing wildly" (132) or the "steady, and quiet and sacred" (133) sort, ends in the "twist and shift of quiet and suggestive" (133) understanding. As the works of an anticolonial West Indian writer obliged to publish in postwar London, Lamming's

opaque, resistant texts function as a mechanism for disrupting the unexamined acceptance of a racial hierarchy long naturalized by Britain's imperial
worldview and, subsequently, as an invitation for both colonized and colonizer
to construct a more productive, mutually respectful future.

In a talk commemorating Selvon, Lamming relates an anecdote that underscores the type of interruptive, anticolonial reordering of perception he
sees as necessary. The story involves his querying an Englishwoman about
the arrival of a letter. She responds that no letters have arrived, though she has
been checking carefully for "black stamps." Lamming interprets it thus: "she
meant stamps marked Africa or India, China or the West Indies. One kind,
honest and courteous old woman had fixed almost two thirds of the World's
population with one word. You might say that the woman was a simple example of ignorance but I maintain that ignorant or not it has fundamentally to do
with a particular way of seeing" ("Coldest Spring," 6).[5] Resisting the simple,
dismissive interpretation of the woman as ignorant, Lamming analyzes her
speech as a fundamental effect of her (colonizer's) perception, something *The
Pleasures of Exile* consistently identifies as "an inherited and uncritical way
of seeing" prevalent on both sides of the colonizer/colonized divide (76). It is
against these stubborn, ingrained, and effectively naturalized patterns of colonial perception that Lamming positions his literary difficulty, hoping to oblige
his audience to pay more attention, as Steiner would have it, to the "inertias in
the common routine of [colonial] discourse." Lamming's difficulty—whether
militantly aggressive or passionately encouraging[6]—seems designed, in various ways for various audiences, to instigate the type of defamiliarized, more
broadly synthesized reconsideration of "civilization" (and its implicit other,
"savagery") suggested by Woolf in this chapter's epigraph.[7]

Reading Difficulty between the Lines

Postwar literary critics did not fail to associate Lamming's difficult
texts with what seemed to be their prewar, high modernist predecessors (and
Lamming, unlike Mittelholzer, made no particular efforts to resist such comparisons). The *Times Literary Supplement* review of *In the Castle of My Skin*
muses that "one is tempted to rename this book, 'The Portrait of the Artist as
a young Barbadian.' It recalls James Joyce of the *Portrait* and certain scenes
in *Ulysses*, not by virtue of imitation but in a curious similarity of vision" (A.
C. Marshall, "Youth in Barbados").[8] The same *TLS* reviewer makes a simi-

lar comparison in discussing *The Emigrants,* noting the novel's similarities to *Ulysses* and complaining that "the book is unnecessarily difficult to read" (A. C. Marshall, "In Search"). The *Spectator* reviewer highlights Lamming's unusual technique, again evoking a likeness to Joyce: "Mr. Lamming does not restrict himself to straightforward narrative and description but, at moments of extreme tension, moves into dramatic dialogue, into poetic incantation and into the sort of stream-of-consciousness writing that Joyce has made us familiar with" (Jennings, "Better Break," 411). The *Observer* reviewer, Edwin Muir, brings in the example of Faulkner to elucidate Lamming's prose, while the *London Magazine* decries *The Emigrants* as "deliberately experimental," a novel that has "indulged in innovation at the expense of form," and again (perhaps exasperatingly) brings up a comparison with Joyce (Stern, review, 109). In the end, it seems evident that whether or not they approved (and at the time many did not), Lamming's contemporary British literary commentators identified him as a writer in the old high modernist tradition, someone whose prose was "heavy and dense," "whose style jarred and confused the reader" (A. C. Marshall, "Time and Change").

Critics clearly noted Lamming's efforts to avoid assimilation into the contemporary cadre of British realist writers as well. The *New Statesman* review of *Of Age and Innocence,* penned by V. S. Naipaul, notes that while Lamming "has devised a story which is fundamentally as well-knit and exciting as one by Graham Greene . . . he is not a realistic writer" (827). V. S. Pritchett's review of *In the Castle of My Skin* in an earlier issue is even clearer in making the distinction, arguing that the "book makes our kind of documentary writing look conventional and silly" ("Barbados Village").[9] Since Lamming's style could be comfortably compared to that of older modernist writers, it was not easily allied with his British contemporaries, yet many reviewers also had difficulty assimilating the *meaning* of Lamming's novels, pointing with particular discomfort to his style. The *Observer* review of *The Emigrants* is typical—"The author switches from scene to scene and period to period for no obvious reason, is elliptical without excuse, and obscure where everything is plain" (Muir, "Indirections")—as is the *London Times* when it excoriates *Of Age and Innocence* for being "badly confused by [Lamming's] method of narration which includes extracts from diaries, flashbacks, and other devices which . . . do not provide clear and coherent reading."[10] Of course, it is precisely the British request for coherence and clarity that Lamming's difficulty seeks to resist. Indeed, from Lamming's viewpoint it is the long-established

imperial British narrative itself, purportedly coherent and clear, that has naturalized at an almost unconsciously deep level "the habitual weight of a colonial
relation" that typically equates West Indians with primitive, unthinking children (*Pleasures of Exile*, 25).[11]

Lamming provides a critical demonstration of the expedient and deceptively authoritative workings of the "clear and coherent" colonial narrative in
In the Castle of My Skin. The backdrop to the crucial incident is the landlord
Mr. Creighton's party, during which Trumper, Boy Blue, and the sometime
narrator, G., sneak onto the estate premises and are almost caught after stum-
bling onto a soldier trying to seduce the landlord's daughter in the darkness.
The chapter dealing with the boys' near disaster is a first-person account, and
it is followed immediately by a more traditional, third-person account of Ma
and Pa, the characters representing the archetypal peasant tradition of the island. The focal point of the chapter is Ma's discomfort at relating to Pa the
story she has heard from Mr. Creighton, which emerges eventually as the
landlord's narrative of events the night of the party. It is expressly noted that
the "landlord's story was incredible" (187), that it is one Ma "wouldn't have
believed were not the source of information beyond suspicion" (184). When
the landlord's predictably self-serving narrative does emerge—that the boys
had attempted to rape the young woman—both Ma and Pa placidly accept
its truth, their placidity and its rote nature emphasized by Lamming's presentation of it in dramatic dialogue, with the implication that they are simply
acting out their prescribed roles in accepting an account the reader knows to
be fabricated. An earlier instance of dramatic dialogue in the novel acts similarly: in the conversation of the four schoolboys with the victim of the head
master's beating (a clear evocation of slavery), the rote, repetitive, and circular dialogue of the boys, punctuated by the victim's reiterations of his lack of
knowledge, is rendered in dramatic form, broken up into "normal" narration
only when the victim himself begins to make some analytic connections and
convey to his school friends his interpretation of what has just befallen him.
Elsewhere in the novel, Lamming describes the pervasive logic of uncritical
absorption explicitly, emphasizing its linguistic, literary basis: "The language
of the overseer. The language of the civil servant. The myth had eaten through
their consciousness like moths through the pages of ageing documents" (27).
The image is one of passive decay, suggesting the dissolution of active consciousness through its unthinking accession to accepted ideology. In the novel
this mental inertness extends to encompass the whole village "in a pattern that

remained constant. The flow of its history was undisturbed by any differences in the pieces" (24). The depiction of Ma and Pa's seemingly prescripted relation to the landlord's narration suggests how much "the pattern has absorbed them" (32), rendering them unable to act or believe differently. In its formal features, *In the Castle of My Skin* seems designed to interrupt precisely such behavior, to militate against the complacent submission to discourse it entails. For Lamming, simply presenting the "clear and coherent" tale preferred by the *London Times* would thus be self-defeating: in distinguishing himself from the preponderance of realist authors emerging into prominence in 1950s London, Lamming was not only signaling his own difference but also signaling the importance of a different (ostensibly more difficult) discourse.[12]

In the contemporary reviewers' resistance to Lamming's complexity, another, more racially motivated aspect is also detectable: apparently underlying many of the critiques of Lamming as a type of failed modernist is the supposition that he is better suited to writing intuitively and "more naturally." The most explicit statement of this view occurs in the *Times Literary Supplement*'s 1955 review article "Caribbean Voices," discussed in the first chapter.[13] After describing how Mittelholzer's work attempts to remedy what the reviewer takes for granted as the widespread West Indian inability to think historically in any way outside of the immediate moment, the article introduces Lamming with a distinctly arch appraisal: "The discontinuity of consciousness which Mr. Mittelholzer attempts to eradicate is accepted by Mr. George Lamming, apparently, as normal to the human condition" (xvi). The import of such an assessment is not merely to suggest that Lamming, the naive native, has yet to grasp the sophistication of his European brethren—foolishly mistaking his own culture's condition (of ignorance) for a universal one—but also serves to reduce Lamming's writing process to a largely unconscious representation of his own confusion. The article reiterates this view throughout, asserting, for example, the reviewer's difficulty in establishing whether the book is about the childhood of one boy or about that of a group of boys: "it is also difficult to see how conscious the author was of what he was doing. The reasons for the shift from the first to the third person cannot be perceived by the intellect. It would be hard to justify it by analysis" (xvii).[14] The emphasis on "intellect" and "analysis" reveals an investment in a long-familiar discourse about non-European irrationality, and the review continues in a similar vein, postulating that "Lamming's effects are achieved intuitively" and concluding that "in far too many cases the author becomes self-consciously an 'experimental writer' whose effects are much less original than those he achieved unconsciously when he was not trying" (xvii). Before going on to castigate Selvon for the "same muddied intellectualism" (xvii), the author of the review remarks that Lamming has not quite developed out of his "natural brilliance" into a more controlled, professionalized writer.[15] Even as sensitive a critic as Pritchett, although he clearly if somewhat paradoxically distinguishes Lamming from the portrayal, describes the context of *In the Castle of My Skin* in similarly blithe terms: "We are in the heart of a coloured or half-coloured community, sharing its sudden, unreasonable passions . . . its naïve illusions about the world outside" ("Barbados Village"). Other critics are not so generous. One reviewer of *The Pleasures of Exile* complains about Lamming: "He is no theoretician: his spasmodic attempts to mix Haiti, Hakluyt, *The Tempest,* and Portland Place into a critical synthesis on the British West Indian's position only make lumpy literary porridge. He is best when he just talks on about London and the Caribbean" ("Place in the Sun").[16] Another suggests that Lamming has yet to surmount the inherent difficulty that in the Caribbean the "laws of cause and effect are held in abeyance" (Marshall, "Youth in Barbados"). In the end, it seems that such ethnocultural suppositions, expressed as issues of aesthetic critique, might provide another rationale for Lamming's insistence on difficulty.

Marshall notes Lamming's personal suspicion of "just documentary" writing in the Caribbean context (*CV,* 22 Mar. 1953), and in *The Pleasures of Exile* Lamming himself makes the connection between a sophisticated use of language and the need to fight the degrading assumptions fostered by the discourse of colonialism. Placing the issue into his characteristic Prospero-Caliban trope, Lamming argues that Caliban must order (command) Prospero's attention by ordering (narrating) a new form of history, with the issue of language firmly at the center of the effort: "We shall never explode Prospero's old myth until we christen Language afresh; until we show Language as the product of human endeavour; until we make available to all the result of certain enterprises undertaken by men who are still regarded as the unfortunate descendants of languageless and deformed slaves" (118–19). The modernist echoes of this call to make language new are unmistakable, if differently politicized, as Lamming's emphasis on language as a human endeavor fashions constructivism into an anticolonial strategy.[17] Elsewhere in the book, Lamming praises German scholars who have been taking an interest in West Indian literature, because (as opposed to Kingsley Amis) they are interested in paying earnest attention to what Caribbean writers have to say. Heading off any concerns about European exploitation by these scholars, Lamming emphasizes, "what really matters here is that they are serious readers and the nature of their interest is a good basis for dialogue" (29). In this light, Lamming's overtly challenging literature can be seen as a rejection of any notions of primitive genius or unthinking native intuition. It stands instead as a pointed invitation to consider Caribbean people as intelligent, conscious shapers of language and hence as thinking beings in their own right.

This perception of non-Europeans as primitive, immature, or otherwise not up to Western standards of ratiocination finds its academic apotheosis in the practice of anthropology. Although Jed Esty is persuasive in arguing that as early as the 1930s, with the steadily more evident decline of the British Empire, the English began turning the anthropological lens inward onto their own perceived national culture, his emphasis on emergent British nativism should not obscure the fact that the outward gaze at the "others"—usually objectified and judged lacking—retains a major hold on the British cultural imagination in the postwar years.[18] The special autumn edition of the *Times Literary Supplement* of 1962—"A Language in Common," devoted to writing in English by non-English (including Scottish and Welsh) writers—provides a glimpse of how impermeable these imperially inflected social and cultural categories remained. The section's review of Caribbean writers, "The Caribbean Mixture," begins with a disquisition on the intransigent resistance of cultures to fusion, attributing it to an inherent, disinterested universal law that when two cultures (in the article, also rendered equivalently as "races") are juxtaposed, one, apparently by happenstance, "usually adopts the habits of a master race and imposes its cultural pattern on the other" (Singer, "Caribbean Mixture"). The reviewer, positing this chance capitulation of one culture to another, then asserts that such a relationship may at first lead to diffidence on the part of the subject culture, but then later allows for a sort of minor culture—the example, of course, is West Indian literature—to flourish. The article goes on to connect this minor culture to other objects of anthropological interest: "The emergence of a school of self-assured West Indian writers can thus be related to . . . the continually expanding interest in folk-lore, to the Scottish Renaissance and to that tale of Myles na Gopaleen's where the American recording engineer tapes the grunting of pigs under the impression that it is an authentic Irish story."[19] The far from elevated company in which West Indian literature is grouped—seemingly as a kind of amusing anthropological curiosity—is underscored at the end of the article, whose conclusion unreservedly states that no West Indian writer, "viewed from the highest standards, has yet contributed much to the English language." The concluding sentences of the review find solace for this artistic failure in the purely anthropological function of West Indian literature: "they have given us insights which would otherwise have been denied us into the kinds of life that are lived in the tropics and—what has not been mentioned before because it is so obvious—many wonderful glimpses of the scenery that can be found there." The pronoun usage clearly delineates the contours of the chosen community, as Caribbean writing, outside the pale in several senses, is reduced to the level of a tourist's narrowly ethnographical glimpse of the exotic, denied any possibility of being a truly literary achievement.[20]

Thus, if from a more producer-centered view, Lamming's constructivist highlighting of the Caribbean artist aims at countering claims of West Indian simplicity, a more reception-oriented vantage can espy in Lamming's attempts to disrupt narrative a mechanism designed to short-circuit any easy attempt by readers to process the descriptions of Caribbean characters and situations in an objectivizing, anthropological way.[21] Lamming's technical experimentation functions in this way as a strategy to resist consumption of his novels as, in the phrase singled out by Jeremy MacClancy's discussion of anthropology in early twentieth-century Britain, "the latest form of evening entertainment" ("Latest Form," 78).[22] In discussing the importance of his generation of West Indian writers, Lamming notes the shortcomings of previous efforts to depict Caribbean society, explicitly connecting anthropology with what he characterizes as realistic representation that is merely rudimentary: "We have had the social and economic treatises. The anthropologists have done some exercises there. We have had Government White papers as well as the Black diaries of Governor's wives. But these worked like old-fashioned cameras, catching what they can—which wasn't very much—as best they could, which couldn't be very good, since they never got the camera near enough" (*Pleasures of Exile,* 37–38). The old-fashioned, mechanical apparatus of a distanced anthropological realism, in Lamming's view, must make way for a different, more sophisticated rendering by the West Indian novelist.

Lamming remarks on the deleterious effects of remote, uninvolved observation in *The Emigrants* in a brief disquisition by Tornado, one of the more heroic and politicized of the novel's eponymous characters. In response to the suggestion that the British-Caribbean relationship is one of an unaffectionate parent to child, Tornado takes issue with the metaphor, identifying the prob lem more with knowledge, empathy, and a sense of egalitarian awareness and respect: "Seems to me ... the people here see these things from their side. They know that England got colonies an' all that, an' they hear 'bout the people in these far away places as though it was all a story in a book" (186). This type of removed, distracted perception of an urgently felt and lived human existence is what Tornado sees as most criminal in the English. He goes on to suggest that West Indians would "be nastier to the English than to any one, because we'd be remembering that for generations an' generations we'd been offerin' them a love they never even try to return" (186). For Tornado, it is the personal nature of such a betrayal —the refusal of human reciprocity on the part of the English—that is the most serious crime. In a personal anecdote, Lamming provides a further example of the casual objectification implicit in the English relationship with its colonial subjects, describing a cordial conversation with a Chelsea pensioner that ends with the older man's parting words: "Oh, by the way, there is something I wanted to ask you. Do you *belong* to us or the French?" ("Coldest Spring," 7). Lamming notes the extraordinary naturalness of the man's demeanor in asking such a question, expressing amazement at how casually this man "had turned the person to whom he was speaking into an object, into one of his possessions" (7).

Lamming directly depicts the horrifying effects of such a dispassionate, disinterested approach to others toward the end of *The Emigrants*. Dickson, thinking he has been chosen by his white landlady for seduction on the basis of education—"the common language of a common civilization," as Dickson expresses it (254)—discovers that both she and her sister only want to observe him as a foreign thing: "The women were consumed with curiosity. They devoured his body with their eyes. It disintegrated and dissolved in their stare, gradually regaining its life through the reflection in the mirror" (256). The consequences for Dickson of this anthropological consuming of his objectified body are disintegration, dissolution—indeed, he goes mad—a complete demolition of him as a person; the landlady's mirror—her own racist representations—takes control, providing the only remaining form of his body's existence and giving the lie to Dickson's notions of a civilized commonality. The scene is overtly experimental in form, juxtaposing Dickson's increasingly ragged and disjointed thoughts with a third-person narration, bringing home the stark difference between a (supposedly) objective view, associated with the English ladies, and the hopes, fantasies, and eventually insane disappointment of the human being who is caught in their objectivizing view.[23]

In a later novel, *Season of Adventure,* Lamming also casts doubt on the ability of an analytic, anthropological approach to do justice to its subject. This novel—his fourth and by far his most realistic, least experimental in form—is famously interrupted near its end by the "Author's Note," a direct intrusion into the third-person narration by the authorial voice.[24] The essential thrust of the section is the ultimate unknowability of Powell, the failure of analytic (and poetic) interpretation to adequately contain his motivations and thoughts. The narrator discounts "logical analysis," insisting that "there must be another way to the truth of Powell's defeat" (331). While acknowledging the provisional worth of traditional analytical methods, the "Author's Note" suggests that something nearer and more involved is necessary to recover Powell's truth: what is required is no less than an acceptance of responsibility for Powell's actions. Pointedly removing the reader from immersion in the narrative flow of events, this singular authorial interruption makes clear that it is only with an intimate, deeply felt understanding of Powell's humanity—something anthropology apparently cannot offer—that an appropriately ethical relation can be established. Immediately following the "Author's Note" there is another passage suggesting the illegitimacy of a presumed objective view distanced from empathic understanding. Here the novel forthrightly declares that such a view "can only prove, select and prove, the details of an order which it has assumed; a method of discovery that works in collusion with the very world of things it sets out to discover" (333). The use of "things" underscores the paucity of this kind of scientific method in dealing with people, and "collusion" contains ominous undertones suggesting its unsuitability for accomplishing what the author names as his most critical task: to fight "against the Lie as it distorts the image of my neighbor in his enemy's eyes" (330). As it concludes, the "Author's Note" reveals that in order to recover the truth, the reader cannot simply abstract Powell into an illustration of analytic theory or a mere character in a tale. Instead, the putative author models the type of personal accountability the novel deems necessary, countenancing no excuses and making a plain confession: "I am responsible for what happened to my brother" (332). In forcibly removing the reader from a complete investment in the ethnographic realism of the narration by its intrusion, the "Author's Note" points to the necessity of a deeper commitment, beyond anthropology, as it were, to an idea of Powell's ineffable humanness. Though the *TLS* review may find Lamming's "use of techniques like changing narrators in mid-narrative, and of tricks with space and time . . . pretentious and ineffectual" (Singer, "Caribbean Mixture"), such "tricks" seem to preclude any sheer apprehension of his novels as the wonderous reportage of a particularly observant and literate native informant.

Thus, in the context of the contemporaneous British reception of his novels, the difficulties of George Lamming appear as a strategic effort to navigate a complex literary and social field with a particular political valence: his use of difficulty allows him to maintain a certain distinction from the most popular literary practices of the day while protecting against an often unwitting exoticism that carries such distinction to adverse extremes, steering a careful but combative route between Hulme's poles of assimilation and exoticism. Lamming himself was keenly aware of the paradoxes of his position as a postcolonial intellectual living in the imperial metropole. In analyzing the role of the BBC's *Caribbean Voices* in the creation of a West Indian literature, Lamming articulates the economic, political, and cultural constraints of his position, observing that the BBC "played a role of taking the raw material and sending it back, almost like sugar, which is planted there in the West Indies, cut, sent abroad to be refined, and gets back in the finished form" (interview, by Munro and Sander, 9). In another published interview, with Ian Munro, Lamming acknowledges that the dependence of young West Indian writers "on the verdict of the English publishing houses," even in 1971, "has not substantially changed" ("Writing and Publishing," 19). Such an awareness, perhaps, leads Lamming to note the acceptance of the "new West Indian novel" in England as "deserving if somewhat dubious" (*CV*, 6 July 1958). Given this clear-eyed cognizance of the overbearing realities of the postwar British literary field—still molded by the powerful ideologies of colonialism—Lamming's use of difficulty can be viewed as a pragmatic, militant technique designed, at one level, to prevent his English readers from simply consuming his books without taking pause to consider the historical, human source of the text with which they are confronted.

Difficulty Changing the Subject

Of course, the tactical politics of interruption and distinction within the British literary field—however savvy, strategic, or successful—by no means exhaust the potential meanings of Lamming's difficulty. Beyond signaling the active subjectivity and intellection of West Indians, as well as their principled divergence from mainstream British cultural and political tendencies, Lam-

ming's arduously complex novels also display a more constructive engagement with his readers, exhorting them toward particular ways of analyzing and
engaging with the world around them. Although more focused on the relevant
sociocultural dynamics, even Diepeveen acknowledges the pedagogical impulse at the root of literary difficulty, observing that such texts can inspire a
number of responses, "but the option that the difficult text does not encourage
is that of half-consciously rubbing one's eyes over hundreds of pages of text"
(*Difficulties of Modernism*, 234). If Lamming's aesthetic output positions him,
in his own description, "as a kind of *evangelist*" ("Sovereignty of the Imagination," 197), its primary message would seem to lie largely in this direction:
his works' formal features oblige readers to consider carefully the meanings
created through the linguistic "process of exchange which we take for granted
in all our daily activities" (*Coming, Coming Home*, 29).[25] In this effort, Lamming's difficulty enacts a sophisticated hermeneutical and political project
designed to change the habit of merely instrumental, unengaged reading into
an active practice of reading sensitive to the unavoidable complexity of intersubjective communications.[26]

The question of *whom* Lamming has in mind as readers, however, has
traditionally been a vexed one. On one hand, there can be little doubt that
even though his postwar West Indian audience was limited by socioeconomic
and educational conditions, Lamming wrote with an ideal Caribbean readership firmly in mind. He has noted that his "greatest pleasure would be to
know that the cane-cutters and laboring class [of the West Indies] read and
understood *In the Castle of My Skin*" (interview, by Munro and Sander, 11).
An autobiographical radio manuscript by Selvon recounts a conversation with
Lamming that confirms the importance he attributed to his West Indian audience: "We both agreed one had to be careful not to let the praise [in Britain] go
to one's head—what we were concerned with was how West Indians at home
would greet our work."[27] Early in his career, Lamming saw himself and his
fellow Windrush writers as the progenitors of a critical canon of West Indian
literature on which future work could build: he asserts in *The Pleasures of
Exile* that his generation of West Indian writers "are to the new colonial reader
in the West Indies precisely what Fielding and Smollett and the early English
novelists would be to the readers of their own generation" (38).[28] However, as
he makes clear in 1958 on *Caribbean Voices*, Lamming viewed the building of a
West Indian readership as a long-term, future-oriented process, not something
immediately realizable within the region: reflecting on the hesitant embrace of

West Indian literature by its home audience, he observes that "the creation of this reading public whose elements already exist is a job which remains to be done" (*CV,* 10 Aug. 1958).[29] Beyond this resolutely hopeful focus on a yet-to-be-actualized Caribbean readership, Lamming has also stressed that he thinks his books should be "relevant to intelligent and sensitive reading in any part of the English-speaking world" (interview, by Munro and Sander, 11), considerably broadening the conception of the audience he hoped to reach.

The ecumenicism of this conception is important, and while it surely has a pragmatic basis in the unequal institutional conditions of literary production prevalent then and now, it also suggests Lamming's unwillingness to accede to any straightforward, binary divisions into European and Caribbean. If for Lamming the "inherited and uncritical way of seeing" (*Pleasures of Exile,* 76) against which he works is the foundational postcolonial problem, it is a problem shared by all.[30] Indeed, in a more recent interview Lamming defines "colonized" in an extremely far-reaching manner as simply *any* political position embracing models and texts uncritically ("Sovereignty of the Imagination," 177). Composed amid the growing momentum for decolonization around the globe, Lamming's novels appear to address both sides of the traditional colonizer/colonized divide, seeking to unsettle either side's easy resort to "the safer notion of ethnic or national similitude" (Nair, "'Invented Histories,'" 175), and thus signaling Lamming's effort to keep open the possibility of productive, if necessarily agonistic, communication.[31] In *The Pleasures of Exile,* Lamming pointedly lays claim to Caribbean people's creative political agency, asserting that, at the historical juncture in which he was writing, "the language of modern politics is no longer Prospero's exclusive vocabulary. It is Caliban's as well" (158). The implicit corollary to this situation is provided in a different section of the book, in which Lamming asserts that "the time is ripe—but may go rotten—when masters must learn to read the meaning contained in the signatures of their former slaves" (63). If Lamming was interested in fashioning a future, Caribbean reader, he also directed this activist concern elsewhere, toward a present audience based in Britain. As he insists in *The Pleasures of Exile,* the correct question to ask regarding the Windrush generation of novelists is not what they have contributed to English writing, but "what the West Indian novelists have contributed to English *reading*" (44, emphasis added).[32] Addressing their historical moment, Lamming's difficult novels propose a model of reading aimed at productively defusing the tensions and potential misunderstandings arising from two simultaneous phenomena:

the unprecedented Caribbean immigration to Britain as well as the contentious politics of postwar decolonization.

At the beginning of *The Emigrants*, Lamming provides a portrayal of reading that argues for the act as a crucially generative, if fragile, nexus of knowledge, action, and human meaning. The narrator of the novel, in a recollection of how he got on the ship sailing for England, discusses the turning point in this stage of his life—a realization that the freedom he had been enjoying in Trinidad was a purely private, personal, and contextually limited endowment. At this moment, he comes to realize that his newfound independence "was a child's freedom, the freedom too of some lately emancipated colonials. . . . It was a private and personal acquisition, and I used it as a man uses what is private and personal, like his penis" (13). Directly contiguous to the narrator's epiphany about the boundaries of a solipsistic liberty is his day spent reading a novel entitled *The Living Novel*. His description of this reading reveals it to be emblematic of bad reading practice: he recounts that he "read it as though by habit, page after page for several hours" (14), emphasizing the routine, unengaged, and mechanical nature of such a practice. Immediately after this description, the narration moves on to the fragmented monologue of the narrator to his friend, who, though listening, "nodded keeping his head down as though it made no difference what was said" (14). Like the narrator's reading, his unnamed friend is merely reacting automatically, not truly responding to the words, but instead placidly agreeing with whatever is said. What Lamming presents here is a collocation of juxtaposed events all vividly symbolizing the malaise that leads to his narrator's departure. A lack of engagement and interaction are at the heart of this malaise: the juvenile sense of personal freedom, the disengaged reading, and the hollowly mechanical "dialogue" all appear to be undirected, aimless, ultimately private activities. The narrator underscores the sense of meaningless stasis, saying, "The Novel was alive, though dead. This freedom was simply dead" (14). The book clearly censures this type of mindless unsubstantial activity, and although the novel form seems to hold out some promise of life, a lifeless, habitual, disengaged style of reading—one that does not actively seek understanding or connection—cannot bear this promise out. Lamming's juxtaposition of three apparently unrelated activities in this scene formally conveys the suggestion that the breath of *The Living Novel* can only be provided by a reader's own attentive engagement with the text.

At a climactic moment in *Of Age and Innocence*, Lamming makes a similar, if more overt, claim about what is at stake in the practice of reading, again warning against the dangers of an insensitive consumption of texts. In this scene it is Bill, the somewhat sympathetic British character who has been devastated by the loss of his girlfriend Penelope in the asylum fire, who is depicted as a self-absorbed, inattentive reader. The text in question is a scrap of his friend Mark's diary that Bill discovers, which despite the import of its contents only reconfirms the confused, vengeful thoughts that have already been accumulating in Bill's mind. As he first looks at the paper, Bill "could hear nothing but the silence of the paper spread across his hands and the weight of the gun in his pocket" (305), as both his inability to "hear" what the writing is saying and its link to thoughtless violence are indicated. When he finally reads the paper, he does so in a careless and opportunistically utilitarian manner: "he read a line, skipped angrily over a passage which seemed irrelevant to his need, and then continued . . . waiting for the name of Shephard to increase his frenzy" (307). Lamming makes clear in this passage that Bill is not truly *reading*, but simply using the text as a pretext for confirming his own prejudices. Indeed, it is implied that Bill can hear only himself out of the words on the page, as just before he begins to read, he can "hear nothing but his breathing against the paper which lay across his hands" (306).[33] The effect of Bill's bad reading practice is to harden his own inclinations toward murdering Shephard into a lunatic clarity that the scrap of diary "defined his duty. His mind was free from the slightest fear of consequences, closed to any doubt about the origin of the fire" (307). This narrow, self-serving certitude is, ironically, precisely what the passage from Mark's diary decried (as well as something consistently devalued in Lamming's oeuvre). Mark's thoughts specifically, in fact, postulate that a passion for revenge inevitably leads to self-destruction, such that Bill's actions are directly counter to the clear-cut message of the text he "reads." Although the concreteness of the connection between bad reading and violence may seem a bit heavy-handed—perhaps in part due to being dramatized in a more realist manner rather than formally conveyed—the seriousness of a sensitively engaged reading practice is clearly articulated.[34]

At the root of this seriousness, of course, is a postcolonial variation on a venerable literary dilemma: how to put literary revelations and lessons into operation in the world, as it were, writ large. For Lamming, the poles of the literary and the real find unification in the recurrent need for what could be called semiological estrangement, that is, an approach to the world (and/as text) that consistently reexamines, re-views, and recalibrates. While it would be reductive to claim that Lamming writes difficult novels because the reality he is describing is likewise complex, it nevertheless seems that the engagement that his difficulty aims to generate in his readers would ideally extend well outside the confines of merely reading a book. Parallel to Bill's irresponsible reading habits in *Of Age and Innocence,* an inability to decipher the words, gestures, faces, and facts around them frequently distinguishes the least valorized characters in Lamming's works. The inhumane police chief Crabbe—who serves as that novel's exemplar of authoritarian colonial power—is a noteworthy example. A police officer who goes against Crabbe's orders in aiding the newly emergent political order explains his actions by reference to Crabbe's conscious social alexia: "'An' I was loyal in my fashion,' he said, 'I was loyal. I can do it again, till Crabbe an' all like Crabbe learn not to take this face for granted like some rock you don't care to read. My face hold a meanin' too, an' any stranger here must read me like one man learn to read another he hold in friendship'" (389).

A similar portrayal of human interaction undermined by bad "reading" practices occurs in *The Emigrants* between Mr. Pearson and Collis. In analyzing this scene, Paquet aptly observes that both characters "are trapped by inherited colonial attitudes and postures" (*Novels of George Lamming,* 40). Although the English Mr. Pearson makes efforts to overcome his prejudices and be considerate to his emigré visitor, he ultimately fails in his interactions with Collis. After an unsettling telephone call from his factory dramatically sours the mood (thus suggesting the dehumanizing demands of capital), Pearson enacts his own power-enabled conception of social intercourse as "an encounter between a definition and a response" (139), reducing Collis from someone himself capable of defining and judging to a being acting with pure reflex to the terms already set. At this juncture, "Collis understood that he did not then exist for Mr. Pearson, and he understood too that Mr. Pearson didn't exist for himself" (139). The twofold disintegration of personhood depicted here, in which interlocutors rehearse old prejudices and cease to do justice to the other's subjective consciousness, is once again something Lamming would term "colonial," the easy trap of rote behavior that his fiction seeks to disrupt (and it is no accident that in both examples above, the interaction proceeds along familiar colonial fault lines of race and class). Paquet maintains that such encounters in the novel are "invariably destructive to the emigrant psyche" (40). However, the moments of possibility for connection in this scene, ultimately foreclosed but palpably present before the interruption of the telephone call, point to a potential for stepping beyond these rote roles. In an echo of the ethical dictum of Mittelholzer's *A Morning at the Office,* Lamming suggests here and throughout his work that one must approach others in a spirit of analytic openness, paying the solicitous attention necessary to decipher the rich network of impressions, desires, and historical experience bound within even one person.

Such a stance accounts for the prevalence in Lamming's novels of scenes of long, tortuously uncertain, and conflicted conversations. If the frequency and intensity of politically fraught (and ultimately allegorical) interpersonal encounters increase markedly in Lamming's late novels, *Natives of My Person* and *Water with Berries,* his early novels nevertheless display a similar investment in careful intersubjective congress. As Paquet makes clear, this practice serves, crucially, as an aesthetic insistence "that the worlds of personal relationships and private self are intimately connected with the world of politics" (57). Additionally, it brings Lamming's novels into a noticeable alignment with Woolf's, in that an intricate oscillation between individual consciousness and public interaction characterizes her most prominent experimental works, especially *Mrs. Dalloway* and *To the Lighthouse.* While Woolf's primary focus is certainly more Anglocentric—that is, less obviously anticolonial—than Lamming's, both writers share a concern with the deep, inner complexity of human consciousness. Woolf's well-known description of "an ordinary mind on an ordinary day" bears an obvious affinity with Lamming's interest in portraying the convolutions of everyday thought processes. As she observes: "The mind receives a myriad impressions—trivial, fantastic, evanescent, or engraved with the sharpness of steel. From all sides they come, an incessant shower of innumerable atoms; and as they fall, as they shape themselves into the life of Monday or Tuesday, the accent falls differently from of old; the moment of importance came not here but there" ("Modern Fiction," 106). For Woolf, as for Lamming, the impulse to represent these mental processes with such minute sensitivity is positioned in opposition to "the accepted style" (106), serving as a necessary part of fiction's moral thrust toward disrupting the reflexive simplifications of social intercourse.

A positive statement of this ethical obligation to accord due interpretative attention to others takes place in *The Emigrants* in Lamming's depiction of the basement barbershop, a space offering a comparatively comforting community within the harsh alien environs of England. It is, at least, a location where the men can be secure in the knowledge that "they were not in the wrong place" (127) (though with the litotes, Lamming signals the always partial, tenuous nature of such security).[35] Although Azi—whose language is "a deliberate approximation to the text" (129)—seems to disrupt the communal communication to some degree with a type of stilted, automated response, the general model of attentive, respectful communication holds in this scene. The barber himself embodies this sensitivity most vividly, as he realizes that the men in the room "were his immediate community, and any word, attitude, gesture, was an occasion for thinking" (128). It is this carefully thoughtful approach to otherness that Lamming's difficulty aims to inculcate in his readers, in relation to his books themselves, as well as to words, attitudes, and gestures encountered in the world.

While this implied equivalence between the text and the world is open to a number of critiques, Lamming's view is consonant with Derek Attridge's more recent attempts to argue for a structural parallel between reading an unfamiliar text and encountering "the other." Attridge posits that meaningful reading "involves working against the mind's tendency to assimilate the other to the same, attending to that which can barely be heard, registering what is unique about the shaping of language, thought, and feeling in a particular work" ("Innovation, Literature, Ethics," 25). The language employed here is redolent of the emphasis in *Season of Adventure* on Fola's awakening to the conscious realization of herself as "Fola *and other than*" (174–75), which might serve as a representative figure for this concern in Lamming's work. As in Lamming's portrayal of Fola, Attridge takes care to emphasize that the other thus understood is "a relation or relating rather than an object," an "act-event" that is "not a fixed set of signifiers or signifieds but something like a potential meaning awaiting realization without wholly determining it in advance" (25).[36] Lamming's novels suggest a similar model, aligning sensitivity to textual nuance with an ethical posture toward other people. A simple example of this sensitivity occurs near the end of *The Emigrants*, when the narrator encounters a pensioner in the street. When faced with the elderly man's stereotypical, presumptuous question about whether he is African, the narrator, rather than taking offense or aggressively countering the question, simply replies: "No, but I know what you mean" (225). In doing so, the narrator reveals a tolerant understanding of the ignorance of his interlocutor, without allowing it to remain unchallenged. For Lamming, such hermeneutics of social communication are foundational, and he has consistently held that it is a universal ethical duty—particularly but not exclusively catalyzed by writers and artists—to preserve a space of consideration, to express the obligation to "deal effectively with that gap, that distance which separates one man from another" (*Conversations,* 40). Whether at the level of theme or form—between two characters or between reader and text—the difficulty of Lamming's novels highlights the need for such an attentive interpretive reciprocity, a process at the heart of Lamming's vision of social democracy as a "free community of valid persons" (*Sovereignty of the Imagination,* 1).[37] Far from a coercive, arguably imperial demand for understanding *the* point of his works (a stance frequently, if sometimes unfairly, associated with earlier modernist "genius" figures), Lamming's artistic plea to his audience is simply respectful engagement with the intricacies of ideas and language. The resistance to facile interpretation so prevalent in his works coveys this entreaty, modeling "how extraordinary are the multiple frontiers of behavior we have to explore and negotiate to find ways of entering with courtesy into each other's world" (*Sovereignty of the Imagination,* 54).

The Difficulties of Community

As the intricate, and often failed, attempts at personal interaction in Lamming's work emphasize, however, this epistemologically receptive disposition brings with it no simple guarantees of agreement or commonality. The novels take care to illustrate that any ethics of rigorously open-minded analysis is constantly challenged by the intrusion of mundane, individual concerns that disrupt its efficacy. Lamming has described the travails of an ordinary person seeking to understand the world: "even if the desire for struggle is real, the urgencies of living make it very difficult to sustain his interest: because there is something to be done, something which requires his immediate attention if life is to be liveable. Day-to-day living keeps intruding on that private and solitary world of concerns. It may take the form of the bad-tempered husband who makes trouble when he cannot find something more dramatic to occupy his energy. Or the rent is overdue" (*Conversations,* 42). There is a recognition here of competing demands and responsibilities, the persistent incursion of the outside world—often in the form of other people's needs—into an individual's potential space of reflection and consideration. Moreover, as in the case of Collis and Mr. Pearson in *The Emigrants* (or, even more so, Teeton and the Old Dowager in *Water with Berries*), the historical weight of habit and customary understanding must also be reckoned with.

Even within the nominally cohesive community of the village in *In the Castle of My Skin,* historically conditioned understandings disrupt relationships at the most basic level. Lamming emphasizes this troubling state of affairs via the discursive phenomenon the narrator calls "My People." The capitalization of the phrase underscores its inertly hegemonic presence, and the term describes an all-encompassing colonized mindset, a self-hatred inculcated by racism through the mechanism of the plantation overseer. Everybody is "affected by this image of the enemy which had had its origin in a layer from which many had sprung and through accidents of time and experience forgotten" (26). The internalized racial discrimination against their neighbors, and even friends, affects the villagers everywhere and at all times: "Suspicion, distrust, hostility. These operated in every decision. You never can tell with my people" (27). *The Emigrants,* too, in its painful ending, gives the lie to any straightforwardly utopian conceptions of solidarity resulting from a careful sensitivity to the surrounding world. In the final scene, the Governor is importuned by the Strange Man's recollection of their earlier oaths of communal loyalty, "how de las' time de chaps say how in rain or sun, poor or rich they'd always stick together" (268). However, when confronted with the prospect of offering hospitality to a large group of new arrivants, "the Governor seemed to collapse. He felt no loyalty towards the crowd outside" (268). When he looks to Collis for some confirmation of a requisite group loyalty, Collis flatly denies it, asserting, "I have no people" (270). The private prerogatives and priorities of these characters—in many ways incommunicable to each other—disrupt any easy notions of even the most apparently justifiable solidarities. For Lamming, individual sovereignties (the term he often employs for a person's ability to analyze for themselves) will not unproblematically overlap or agree, and whole communities cannot be expected to cohere magically without tension and struggle.[38]

Thus, the expanded notion of reading revealed in Lamming's novels points to a further iteration of difficulty embodied in the texts' politics of interpretation: a recognition of the complex, contending relations between individuals themselves, and their consequences on notions of community. The difficult relationship between individual and community in Lamming's oeuvre has been noted by critics such as Paquet, whose monograph in fact begins with the perceptive claim that Lamming's novels always center around the relation between individual and community, private and public: "private experience is examined in relation to the larger public events at the centre of every novel" (*Novels of George Lamming,* 1). If the emphasis for Paquet is often on the determinant structuring effects of the colonial system—a unidirectional outlook that risks underplaying Lamming's immense concern with the creative potential within individual subjectivity—the identification of an ongoing, unresolved tension between these two spheres in Lamming's work is irrefutable. The discomfort between Fola and various members of the *tonelle* community (not to mention her own family) is illustrative in this regard: despite her exceptional efforts to understand and act in solidarity, there is palpable and ineradicable tension in Fola's interactions with others throughout the novel, parallel to that expressed in the "Author's Note" vis-à-vis Powell. As Ramchand has suggested in "The Artist in the Balm-Yard," the complexity of *Season of Adventure* arises from the novel's attempts to relate individual to community simultaneously, an uneasy effort whose lack of conclusion conveys a good deal of suspicion about the ease of intracommunal allegiance.

In the Castle of My Skin, of course, traces in great detail this same tension between individual attainment and community responsibility, with narrative resolution eschewed in favor of G.'s uneasy embarkation into exile. In his early review of Paquet's *The Novels of George Lamming,* John Thieme almost offhandedly observes that Lamming's "whole oeuvre to date represents an attempt to reconcile divergent impulses towards individualism and community" (22). Thieme maintains that such an attempt is essayed in Lamming's novels via formal means, "through apparently centrifugal blocks of narrative in which conventional plot interest is surrendered in favour of a mode which gradually reveals how individuals interact and function as parts of a community" (22). Thieme's description is insightful, though the notion of reconciliation in any of Lamming's novels—which famously end in exile, discord, uncertainty, betrayal, uneasy peace, or explosive violence—does not properly capture the combative way in which Lamming's works resist interpretive closure. Thieme's naming of Lamming's "apparently centrifugal blocks of narrative," however, preserves the notion of personal and social contradiction more effectively, hinting at a much more dialectical approach to the world contained within the form of Lamming's work. *In the Castle of My Skin* can illustrate this approach, enlarging as it does from a discrete consciousness to a much broader sociohistorical understanding of what is experienced, what Jameson has described as "a widening out of the sense of the social ground of a text" (*Political Unconscious,* 75).

The entire narrative energy of *In the Castle of My Skin* strains for this widening of the social ground beyond the circumscribed world of G.'s personal subjectivity to Creighton's village and ultimately the political economy of the island itself (while *The Emigrants,* Lamming's subsequent novel, expands its narrative space even further, to the social and political environs of England). In the former, this instructive widening finds thematic expression in the character of the shoemaker, who is approvingly described as thinking for "the first time . . . of Little England [i.e., Barbados] as a part of some gigantic thing called colonial" (99). The formal expression of this principle occurs in the increasing scope of the separate segments of the book, from the students' first early questionings of imperial dogma, to the boys' earnest philosophizing on the beach, on to the revelation of Slime's ties to foreign capital and Trumper's own racial epiphany garnered from his travels in the United States. While Neil ten Kortenaar is right to say that the novel heavily emphasizes the fact that "Trumper has recognized the connections that in the modern world bind human beings together and bind some hand and foot" ("George Lamming's," 53), his mistaken insistence that the novel gives Trumper the last word—and the subsequent weight he (along with other critics) gives to Trumper's somewhat monological understanding of the world—ignores more subtle messages contained within the text as a whole.[39] Indeed, Trumper's invocation of the phrase "My People" (295) duplicates the phrase (also capitalized) used to describe the phenomenon of implacable internecine suspicion that poisons village life earlier in the book. The narrative in fact casts suspicion on Trumper's stance, questioning its rigidity and closed-minded self-certainty: "Whatever he suffered his assurance was astonishing. He had found what he needed and there were no more problems to be worked out. Henceforth his life would be straight, even, uncomplicated" (298). Later, G. confirms the damaging effects of Trumper's self-assurance when he relates that "it was as though [Trumper] knew what I wanted to say and it didn't matter because he knew what was wrong" (301).[40]

Furthermore, contrary to ten Kortenaar's claim, Trumper is not given the last word in the novel: G., as narrator, is, and indeed, G.'s final conversation is not even with Trumper but with Pa, who, like the shoemaker, represents someone constantly seeking new answers. Pa's creative intellect, capable of "using the same raw materials to produce different dreams" (83), stands in sharp contrast to the conceptually moribund future predicted for Trumper. Pa, like Trumper, has been abroad, in his case to Panama: as Lamming notes in his interview with Scott, Pa "has worlds to compare" ("Sovereignty of the

Imagination," 152). The crucial difference seems to be Pa's consistent efforts to question and reexamine his present circumstances, rather than simply relying on past lessons: his multiple "worlds" provoke broader, more diverse horizons than the narrow homogeneity of Trumper's "My People." The narrative drive of the novel, then, works in an ever-expanding scope: it clearly marks the important aspects of Trumper's view—the need for communal action against the forces of socioeconomic oppression and exploitation—but refuses the ideological closure that he advocates. From this important global insight, the novel returns to the singular, particular viewpoint of G., dialectically subsuming the former back into a consideration once again by the latter's skeptical consciousness.

Thus, *In the Castle of My Skin* suggests that the reader Lamming seeks to construct might best be described as a carefully dialectical one. What Thieme calls "centrifugal blocks"—certainly the main component of difficulty blocking transparent, conventional readings of Lamming's earliest novels—formally call forth the necessary analytical traits of making (and reformulating) wider connections and contextualizing (and recontextualizing) in an ever-widening sphere of understanding, which in turn allows for a revised view of one's own personal position. An example of this type of thinking occurs in Lamming's 1956 address to the First International Congress of Black Writers and Artists in Paris, "The Negro Writer and His World," in which Lamming resists the limitations of the particularizing term "negro writer," in lieu of putting emphasis on "his world" and, more particularly, the interlocking relations between that writer and "his world."[41] While acknowledging the overwhelming nature of the suffering inflicted on black people worldwide, Lamming maintains that it is essential that any writer, when writing or thinking about the situation, does not lose sight of "the connection between the disaster which threatens to reduce him and the wider context and condition of which his disaster is but the clearest example" (*Conversations*, 45). In a later essay, *Sovereignty of the Imagination,* Lamming articulates the importance he places on wider contexts, describing his Christian upbringing in Barbados as a form of indoctrination, not due to the moralizing content or even the strictness with which it was enforced, but fundamentally because it did not include any meaningful context. Such training fails, in his view, because it "never provided me with a critique of my relation to where I was born or the social forces shaping my belief" (3). In the same essay, Lamming declares that the exploration of contextual connections is the basis of his artistic and intellectual project:

"I work from the assumption that a mode of perception is not autonomous. It evolves and matures within a specific context, and its function reflects the context from which it is inseparable" (34–35). Critical analysis, he goes on to say, is predicated on the need to "seek to identify, isolate, and define the various components of a particular context" (35). Reflection on wider, systemic circumstances, followed by a return to one's personal experience, thus marks the continuous, shifting, and active cycle of reading that Lamming envisions for his audience. The unremitting nature of this process, however, suggests its inability to provide a permanently stable or predictable basis for community agreement.

A Future They Must Learn

Lamming's work, then, consistently argues that "what a person thinks is very much determined by the way that person sees" (*Pleasures of Exile*, 56)— that is, the way that person interprets the world. As Munro observes, for Lamming political change can only be achieved in conjunction with "a profound change in outlook" ("George Lamming," 168) or, as Imre Szeman describes it, "the politics of consciousness must precede any other politics" (*Zones of Instability*, 79). Lamming's novels thus work to advance a longstanding modernist tenet (by now something of a truism) that the reader has a consequential role in constructing meaning.[42] In Lamming's writing, this view also finds specific resonance with one of the most fundamental of Marx's insights about subjects actively creating, within material limitations, their own consciousnesses and material surroundings.[43] *Properly* reading, for Lamming, thus becomes an intricate process in which one must constantly strive to comprehend sociolinguistic exchange within its broader social and historical determinants. These determinants in Lamming's work are centered on recognizable postcolonial concerns—namely, the historical, psychological, and economic effects of imperialism—but they are, perhaps vexingly, mediated through a complex web of individual experiences and predispositions that resist any simple categorical reduction. As Lamming emphasizes, no individual can depend upon a purely private understanding as accurate; for the writer, as for everybody, self-understanding is "modified, even made possible, by the world in which he moves among other men. Much as he might like to think it otherwise, it is through the presence of others that his own presence is given meaning" (*Conversations*, 44). Lamming's work is thus designed to create a reader who recognizes this interdependence and subsequently understands that "knowledge is therefore social in character" (*Sovereignty of the Imagination,* 35). However, Lamming also acknowledges the limits to creative human freedom by signaling the presence of power within social relations, such that the role of humanistic pursuit is limited to one that "helps us to understand, what is the context of power, the character of that social reality within which those individual personal relationships take place, because those personal relationships cannot be regarded as having an autonomy. Those individual personal relationships have got to be in some way a reflection of another reality which is social" (*Conversations,* 204). The act of reading imagined in and demanded by Lamming's novels thus involves intense self-critical perception, "an unending process of thinking of how one has always to rework the ways in which one claims and exercises the power and the authority of an individual and subjective perspective" ("Sovereignty of the Imagination," 123). His work, in however utopian a way, seeks to inculcate these tendencies in its readers, contemporary and future, Caribbean and Euro-American, directly confronting them with the need to take into account the responsibilities of interpretation and its subsequent ramifications in the material and political spheres.[44]

The notions of engagement that the difficulty of Lamming's work solicits, then, encompass several distinct but overlapping meanings. In the context of a postwar British audience steeped in a racially hierarchical worldview, this engagement appears initially in a more militant vein, seeking to confront and disrupt dominant reading practices that would either overlook the important differences between Lamming's writing and that of his British contemporaries—simply assimilate it, in other words—or treat it as an exoticized, primitive, "natural" object of merely anthropological interest. This combative element also has unmistakable utility in the Caribbean context as a foundational step in the process of what Lamming sees as mental decolonization by questioning and undermining the easy certainties inherited from colonial rule. However, the engagement that Lamming's texts seem to invite from readers also takes on a slightly more constructive, conciliatory tint appropriate to the tense situations resulting from Great Britain's postwar imperial decline. In this context, the difficult structures of Lamming's novels first of all encourage a careful opening out of the reader's consideration from the detailed, intricate negotiations of an individual consciousness—certainly never given short shrift in any of Lamming's novels—to the complicated, often contending relationships such consciousness inevitably provokes with both other individuals and larger social, economic, and political currents. The novels' challenging techniques—such as the persistent juxtaposition of the competing views and aspirations of the different characters in *The Emigrants* or the abrupt alternation between characters' intense internal ruminations and occurrences in the external, political realm in *Of Age and Innocence*—oblige the reader to provide connections in an ever-expanding, ever-changing context, to reconcile disparate, even contradictory elements into a meaningful whole. In this sense, Lamming's novels oblige the reader to enact a specific ethic of reading, making visible in the process that the interpretive act is an intersubjective negotiation. Placing particular emphasis on the mutual creation of meaning, Lamming thereby suggests the subject's potentially powerful role in creating his or her own material and cultural surroundings. With the literary as the primary example, Lamming parallels communication with simply being in the world, arguing that neither can properly be undertaken unless one consistently operates with a reciprocally agreed recognition of others as thinking, feeling subjects.

In the passionate belief that language "is always at the heart of our response to conduct" (interview, by Munro and Sander, 15), Lamming's novels—echoing Woolf's—seem designed to question, challenge, and oblige reconsideration of the uses to which language has been and continues to be put. His adoption of modernism's difficult, counterconventional forms, not to mention its utopian energies, operates on several levels, articulating a forcefully distinct Caribbean worldview while simultaneously addressing, with both assertiveness and sympathy, a wider metropolitan audience. For Lamming, the difficulty of modernist style provides a forceful mechanism for conveying his insistence that Caribbean people be treated as creative, thinking human beings, as well as his adamant belief that, for all people, ethical interchange necessitates a skeptical and supremely sensitive epistemological disposition.

4 A Commoner Cosmopolitanism
Sam Selvon's Literary Forms

> Nationality (if it really is not a convenient fiction like so many others
> to which the scalpels of present-day scientists have given the coup de
> grâce) must find its reason for being rooted in something that
> surpasses and transcends and informs changing things like blood and
> the human word.
>
> —James Joyce, "Ireland, Island of Saints and Sages"

Although both Mittelholzer and Lamming were readily associated with a serious, high intellectual tradition of experimental writing, the work of Samuel
Selvon (who famously traveled to Britain in 1950 on the same boat as Lamming) is often understood in much different terms. Noted especially for its
skillful use of creole language forms and its comedic vivacity, Selvon's writing has conventionally been read as colorful, intuitive, light-hearted reportage,
rather than an artful product of thoughtful literary construction—a perception that remains active in present-day Caribbean criticism. Interestingly, it is
Lamming himself who serves as an authoritative source for the idea of Selvon
as a simple, naturally endowed folk writer. In *The Pleasures of Exile,* Lamming describes Selvon's writing as "essentially peasant" and characterizes this
quality as something unattributable to anything but its author's spontaneous,
natural genius: "no artifice of technique, no sophisticated gimmicks leading
to the mutilation of form, can achieve the specific taste and sound of Selvon's
prose" (45). Taking Lamming's cue in a 1977 article, Frank Birbalsingh, in one
of the first scholarly arguments for Selvon's importance as a founding figure
of West Indian literature, classifies Selvon as a writer who "lacked the firm,
intellectual underpinning" necessary for what Birbalsingh considers genuine
literary greatness. However, the critic concedes, Selvon is nevertheless important, since "what one misses of intellectual interest and technical control
in Selvon's work, one gains in humour, compassion and ultimately pathos"
("Samuel Selvon," 20). Such early, influential Caribbean commentary falls
within a line of argument that in fact echoes the tendency of early British liter-

ary reviewers to perceive of Selvon as an effortlessly talented, almost primitive artist.[1] If, as Louis James observes, "Selvon in the 1950s and 1960s was himself largely disregarded as a serious writer" ("Writing the Ballad," 104), a form of this ambiguously condescending attitude has dogged Selvon's reputation into more contemporary literary debates.[2]

Subsequent critical discussion has at times positioned itself against this influential view of Selvon as the unselfconscious embodiment of folk genius. For instance, Susheila Nasta presents her 1988 compilation, *Critical Perspectives on Sam Selvon,* as in part an effort to circumvent the "obvious limitations in a strictly 'peasant' approach to Selvon's fiction" (9), asserting that Selvon's writing is "clearly the result of a conscious and sophisticated craft" (8). Nasta includes an article by Harold Barratt—"Dialect, Maturity, and the Land in Sam Selvon's *A Brighter Sun:* A Reply"—that explicitly articulates this view. In response to Birbalsingh's seminal assessment of Selvon, Barratt argues instead for the author's craftsmanship, asserting that Birbalsingh's comments "tend to reduce Selvon to the status of, say, a mediocre painter who reproduces a West Indian beach scene with such photographic accuracy that it becomes a cliché with no character of its own" (331).[3] One of the most prominent and polemical examples of criticism opposed to the characterization of Selvon as an intuitive, untutored author is Kenneth Ramchand's introduction to the Longman Caribbean Writers Series 1985 reissue of *The Lonely Londoners.* In this introduction (a reworking of his pointedly named 1982 article "*The Lonely Londoners* as a Literary Work"), Ramchand takes great care to argue for the novel as a consciously composed text, seeking to redress a situation in which "it has become usual to speak of the narrator's stance in *The Lonely Londoners* as being similar to that of a calypsonian" ("Introduction to This Novel," 10). For Ramchand, such a view is harmful in that it has "been accompanied by a willingness to concede that this book is loose or episodic" (10). Accordingly, he focuses on delineating the novel's narrative technique such that "we are drawn to recognize in Selvon's literary artefact a tightness of structure . . . subtlety in the development and revelation of theme; linguistic cunning; and an appropriateness in the presentation and deployment of characters" (10). In characterizing the novel as an "artefact," Ramchand makes clear that Selvon's work should be appreciated not as an arbitrary series of humorous sketches but as a complex and sophisticated piece of literary art. Ramchand likewise makes clear his views regarding the political valence of these readings, observing in the competing, calypsonian interpretation a subtext of purist cultural nationalism: "beware, the implied argument seems to run, beware of using Eurocentric critical tools to assess our literature" (10).

Ramchand's assessment brings out with unusual clarity the antinomy that structures much critical reception of Selvon's work by both the postwar London commentariat and his more contemporary critics: an often absolute choice between championing Selvon as a true West Indian folk artist or recognizing his achievements within a system of traditional British literary values. This antinomy, of course, lies at the foundation of a stubborn postcolonial debate about cultural singularity and difference, in which a localized cultural nationalism, purportedly free of any European taint and frequently associated with "the folk," is juxtaposed with an insistence on the values of a definition of high culture coded as European.[4] The scholarly debate surrounding Selvon indeed has the contours of just such an uneasy opposition, oscillating between contentions that his novels are best read either as articulations of simple, yet valuable West Indian folk customs or as something more worldly and consciously crafted and, hence, more conversant with European literary tradition. One irony of such a debate, of course, is that critics who insist too strongly on Selvon's innate, natural peasant style of writing risk duplicating the early, racially tinged British characterization of his novels as the amusing products of a primitive prodigy uncorrupted by European cultural norms (as well as the dismissal of Selvon's attempts to write more philosophical novels engaged with urban, international themes). A deeper irony emerges if one examines Selvon's first three novels—*A Brighter Sun* (1952), *An Island Is a World* (1953), and *The Lonely Londoners* (1956)—as an accumulating series of formal literary experiments in the modernist vein. Seen through such a lens, these three novels (and, indeed, almost all of Selvon's writings) take shape as literary-formal arguments designed to counteract and ideally overcome the stubborn disjunction between the terms "Caribbean" and "cosmopolitan." In this way, as the epigraph to this chapter intimates, both the aims and the execution of Selvon's work hold subtle resonances with that of his modernist forebear James Joyce. Despite their obvious differences, both authors employed a marked variety of linguistic and narrative experimentation as a means of gesturing toward the need for a complex, nonreified understanding of cultural and political identity, an identity that might be "rooted in something that surpasses and transcends and informs changing things like blood and the human word." Vincent Cheng's postcolonially inflected characterization of Joyce's texts argues that they "advocate and allow for a simultaneous acceptance of (on the one hand) heterogeneity and difference, and (on the other) a potential sameness and solidarity of similarities-in-difference shared by different peoples, within an intercultural, inter-national perspective" (*Joyce, Race, and Empire*, 293).[5] As this chapter hopes to show, Selvon's novels embark on much the same task in—appropriately enough—both parallel and divergent ways.

Peasant Problematic: Representing Humanity

Selvon's first novel, *A Brighter Sun,* poignantly advances a message of interethnic equality and understanding. Deceptively simple (perhaps similar in this way to Joyce's debut book, *Dubliners*), the novel generally presents itself as a conventional bildungsroman, detailing the maturation and increasing consciousness of its young Indo-Trinidadian protagonist, Tiger. On its face, *A Brighter Sun* contains little that would counteract a reader's understanding of it as a straightforwardly descriptive realist narrative, and its central thematic concern—Tiger's recognition of the underlying humanity of all people—is thus difficult to overlook. Tiger's ruminations following his extended family's prejudiced behavior toward his African-Trinidadian neighbors, Joe and Rita, indicate the beginning of this recognition. Responding to his relatives' insistence that he find some Indo-Trinidadian friends, Tiger thinks, "Why I should only look for Indian friend? . . . Is true I used to play with Indian friend in the estate, but that ain't no reason why I must shut my heart to other people. Ain't a man is a man, don't mind if he skin not white, or if he hair curl?" (48). Tiger confirms this slowly consolidating ecumenical outlook near the end of the novel when he remarks to Joe, "it look to me as if everybody is the same," proposing that instead of emphasizing his Indian ancestry by wearing a dhoti, he should "think of all of we as a whole, living in one country, fighting for we rights" (195). This conversation caps Tiger and Joe's halting but ultimately successful efforts to forge a friendship despite their differing ethnic and racial backgrounds, candidly signaling the novel's affirmative views on intra-island solidarity.[6] The book's emphasis on Tiger's deeply philosophical musings on society and the significance of human life, coupled with his painstaking sloughing off of prejudice, marks Selvon's attempts to portray Tiger as a complex human being who comes to a hard-won conclusion about the necessity of recognizing and cultivating the foundational links between people of all kinds.

There is only one formally unorthodox feature in the novel: many of the chapters begin with factual descriptions of international events that gradu-

ally telescope down into local Trinidadian happenings. This feature serves
to underscore the book's primary concern, discussed above, with linkage
and belonging. Though Simon Gikandi's *Writing in Limbo* interprets these
"newsreel" openings (which some reviewers compared to John Dos Passos's
manipulation of journalistic accounts) as essentially comic juxtapositions illustrating the remoteness and relative unimportance of Trinidad, they can also
be read as narrative mechanisms connecting Tiger's circumscribed but ever-
expanding world with the world as such. While it is true that Tiger (along
with Selvon himself) expresses doubts about the meaningfulness of so small
a country as Trinidad within the global context, the profound role that the
American road and base construction has on everybody in the novel certainly
indicates the connection between Trinidad and larger historical events: jobs
proliferate, new cultural forces appear, rivalries between soldiers and local
men come to a head. The chapter beginnings increasingly interweave international developments with more serious local effects, and the last occurrence of
the news listings, in the final chapter of the novel, describes significant local
changes directly resulting from the end of the war:

> V-E and V-J Day celebrations were marked by patriotic demonstrations and
> wild merriment; steel bands, growing in the war years, took to the streets
> for the first time, and pandemonium reigned as Trinidadians were allowed
> to indulge in two days of Carnival. . . . Censorship was stopped altogether,
> motorcar zoning abolished, and restaurants were allowed to serve meals late
> in the evening. In the sugar and oil industries wage agreements were signed,
> but many people were still out of work, and labourers marched in the street
> with placards, and a delegation visited the Governor, seeking relief. (210)

This passage, while emphasizing in some ways the overwhelming control the
Trinidadian colonial government exercised during wartime, also pointedly
notes postwar ramifications at the very heart of modern Trinidad's self-conception—labor struggle and the music of Carnival. In doing so, Selvon would
seem to suggest not simply a comedic dismissal of Trinidad's negligible status
vis-à-vis the wider world, but an insistence on its intimate connection, however unacknowledged or overlooked, with international affairs. Indeed, Tiger's final worries about stasis in Trinidad express frustration with the way in
which his fellow islanders seem oblivious to the fact that they exist in a wider
world: "there was too much of this sameness, all over, in the gardens, in the
shops, in the village streets. What difference did anything make? It seemed

no one knew that a battle had been won" (214). This portrayal suggests not the lack of an important connection with the wider world, but the lack of *an awareness* of such a connection on the part of most Trinidadians.[7] The "news-reel" passages, then, can be seen to address this shortcoming, reinforcing the book's claims about the need to recognize meaningful linkages across cultural and geographical boundaries.

Although Selvon's first novel thus attempts to underscore Tiger's fundamental humanity and his connections to people throughout the world, the vast bulk of the critical reception of *A Brighter Sun* tended to read the novel in a much less inclusive way. The British response consistently obscured the book's apparent message of a unified humanity by distancing both the novel's characters and its author as guilelessly primitive natives who come from an unalterably foreign, exotic part of the world. In the *Manchester Guardian,* for example, Elizabeth Jenkins emphasizes the strange and the simple in her two-sentence review of the novel, describing it as "a very touching and attractive picture of native life in Trinidad and the marriage of two young West Indians, Tiger and Urmilla, who in Europe would be still at school." A notice in *New Commonwealth* treats the work as mainly of anthropological interest, suggesting that the "novel thus has documentary value, in addition to the appeal of its unusual setting."[8] Naipaul, in the *New Statesman,* looking back at *A Brighter Sun* in 1958 (upon Selvon's publication of a sequel, *Turn Again, Tiger*), also emphasizes the uncomplicated charm of Selvon's first novel, describing it in familiar terms as a "simple, lyrical and moving book" (826).

In addition to the characters and the setting, Selvon himself gets characterized in a faintly condescending, unflattering light.[9] The *Times Literary Supplement,* for example, praises *A Brighter Sun* quite highly, calling it "a first novel of quite remarkable quality" and complimenting Selvon on "his handling of the picturesque native idiom." However, it finishes with a somewhat backhanded bit of praise, comparing the novel to Douglas Firbank's *Prancing Nigger* and remarking how unusual it is to find a writer who can describe "the quality of native colonial life so dispassionately and with such literary skill when he himself has been a member of a similar community to that which he describes." Although this review implies in some sense that it is the book's disinterested portrayal that is so remarkable, there lurks beneath this a palpable surprise at how talented the "native" writer actually is (Ross, "Struggle for Existence"). Lionel Hale's review in the *Sunday Observer* also compliments Selvon's realistic portrayal, but Hale, too, suggests that the book's "natural and dramatic rhythms" are largely a product of simple mimetic reflection. Even the *Times Literary Supplement*'s 1972 review of the paperback reissue of *A Brighter Sun* describes the novel as "a simple account of life in a Trinidadian village" and, echoing the "calpysonian" account of *The Lonely Londoners*, contends that "it is not so much a novel as a series of portraits loosely strung together" ("Storm-Tossed").[10] Citing Lamming's depiction of Selvon as a folk poet, the reviewer opines that the latter is not so much a novelist as a precocious recorder of mundane facts who "recreates with an impressive accuracy the feel of the place, and the passage of the seasons." Although frequently positive, the reviews of *A Brighter Sun* are characterized by a resolute refusal to apply the book's overt message of equality to their own literary reflections, insisting instead on seeing Selvon largely as a recorder of tropical customs and native simpletons who somehow managed to put together, without much forethought, some writing that reflects its surroundings.[11]

In this context, the characteristics of Selvon's second novel, *An Island Is a World*, can be read as a concerted attempt to advance a similar message of universality while circumventing any dismissals of Trinidad or Trinidadians (and, of course, novels written by Trinidadians) as simple, primitive, or merely amusing oddities.[12] The very title seems to signal a shift from the folksy, tropical image of *A Brighter Sun* to a more overtly philosophical expression linking specific place and the world as a whole.[13] The protagonists, too, offer a much different picture of Trinidad's inhabitants: the story centers around two brothers, Rufus and Foster, who have been raised in a middle-class home in Trinidad's second city, San Fernando.[14] Finally, the settings of the novel are considerably more international, as during the course of the novel Rufus emigrates to the United States and Foster to England, and their father-in-law, Johnny, the lower-class object of much comedy, eventually departs for India. Indeed, the novel announces its departure from the limited awareness of the characters in *A Brighter Sun* in its first lines, which make a point of showing Foster's global consciousness and Trinidad's concrete place as (a small) part of the world:

> Every morning when Foster awoke, it was the same thing. The world spun in his brain.
>
> The world spun in his brain, and he imagined the island of Trinidad, eleven and a half degrees north of the equator. He saw it on a globe, with the Americas sprawled like giant shadows above and below, and the endless Atlantic lapping the coastlines of the continents and the green islands of the

Caribbean. The globe spun and he saw Great Britain and Europe, and Africa. The eastern countries, Australia. (1)

The beginning of the novel thus palpably portrays its main character as an educated, self-aware man ruminating on the geographical space he occupies—a stark contrast with Tiger's initial status as a wide-eyed, illiterate peasant farmer. Perhaps most important, the style of the book is pointedly different from *A Brighter Sun:* the novel eschews (via its prologue) a strict historical chronology; narrates with a variable mix of dialogue, third-person observation, letters, and introspective internal monologue; and, most noticeably, engages in disorienting, abrupt, and unannounced shifts of scene that serve to illustrate its major theme. Thus, *An Island Is a World* advances a similar message to its predecessor while, in both content and form, seeking to sidestep the simplistic stereotypes of West Indian guilelessness that characterized the previous novel's reception.

As Salick observes, there is a definite thematic continuity between Selvon's first two novels: both novels focus on "the depiction of the hero, struggling to find knowledge and meaning, expressed through the archetype of the journey" (*Novels of Samuel Selvon,* 77).[15] Indeed, the prologue to *An Island Is a World* makes this continuity quite apparent, focusing as it does on Foster's daily ruminating (similar in its general subject matter to Tiger's in *A Brighter Sun*) about the meaning of his life and his place in the world. Moreover, *A Brighter Sun*'s overarching moral—the necessity to acknowledge common ties between people—appears almost immediately as well. In the prologue, Foster is depicted riding a bus to work in Port of Spain, consciously articulating his connection to everybody else: "he sat down, feeling sorry for all the passengers. It was a humble sorrow, like if he had said, 'We are all in the same boat, I am sorry'" (4). Just as Tiger's reflections on the world and his place in it lead to an understanding of the foundational commonality in everyday human living, Foster's own vexed philosophizing—his restless movements between abstract thought and unselfconscious absorption in the mundane rhythms of his life—enables him to realize a similar fundamental truth: that by embodying the local on his island home in the Caribbean he also genuinely becomes a part of the wider world.

With regard to Selvon's first two novels, however, it is not the thematic continuities but rather the discontinuities (also noted by Salick) that are most illustrative. While Foster is implicitly paralleled with Tiger in his questioning consciousness of the world around him, the circumstances in which he is introduced are considerably different from the rural Chaguanas cane fields of Tiger's upbringing.[16] Foster's thoughts occur, significantly, on a crowded bus driving to the capital, Port of Spain, which is described as "a city with emotion and life and radios and a modern sewerage system" (4), thus emphasizing Trinidad's modernity. He is depicted glancing at another passenger's newspaper, reflecting that its contents involve "New York, London, the Middle East," and "things happening all over the world" (4), offering a further suggestion of Trinidad's modernity and its (modern, newspaper-informed) awareness of events around the globe. The settings of the novel encompass much of this world as well: while Tiger and Urmilla's move from Chaguanas to Barataria can be read as a spatial emblem of an increasingly urbanizing creolization within Trinidad proper, the main characters of *An Island Is a World* move back and forth from Trinidad to England, the United States, Venezuela, and India, in a conspicuous insistence on the island's global interconnectedness. If Tiger's preoccupations are generally limited to a national stage, Foster and his friends are engaged in activities spanning much further afield. Thus, in thematic terms, *An Island Is a World* demonstrates an interest in topics of a more urban and international nature than the easily romanticized and exoticized peasant setting of its predecessor.

These tendencies toward expansion and more explicit global interrelation are mirrored in the book's techniques, which differ considerably from *A Brighter Sun*. The most noticeably nontraditional technique Selvon employs in the novel is a series of abrupt, intentionally confusing transitions into different scenes involving different characters and locations. The nature of these shifts is first hinted at in the transformation between the prologue, describing Foster, and the beginning of part 1, which centers around Johnny, Foster's eventual father-in-law. The prologue ends with the trailing off of Foster's interior thoughts, followed by part 1, which jumps immediately into a description of Johnny, a completely new and unknown character: "Every morning when Johnny awoke in the largest room of his house, he used to feel for his wife, though he knew she had risen long ago to prepare breakfast. But he did it all the same, out of habit, because Mary was a big ball of soft flesh, and he liked when could throw his legs over her, and his arms" (8). This second beginning to the novel provides a complete and sudden break. Not only is the audience thrust into the thoughts and habits of an unfamiliar character, but that character's concerns are noticeably different from Foster's solitary philosophical meditations. Johnny's thinking here is concerned with physical sensations—his wife, breakfast, and the pleasurable feelings of lying in bed with her—and it quickly emerges that Johnny, a lower-class, comically drunken jeweler who rarely thinks about more than money and alcohol, seems to have almost nothing in common with Foster, whether temperamentally, intellectually, or in terms of social class. However, despite this sudden, seemingly interruptive introduction to a character who seems completely remote from Foster, Selvon also suggests that they are somehow similar. The prologue begins with the words "every morning when Foster awoke" (1), while part 1 begins with a precise echo, only changing the name—"every morning when Johnny awoke" (8). In abruptly juxtaposing character and scene with almost no introduction or preparation, Selvon emphasizes the considerable differences between Foster and Johnny, while also subtly suggesting their similarity via an exact repetition of the phrases that introduce them. Although Michel Fabre has dismissed this "contrastive device" as "clever but sometimes artificial" ("Samuel Selvon," 154), the technique, continued throughout *An Island Is a World,* formally enacts the novel's advocacy of a worldview that recognizes a type of negotiated similarity within difference as the basic human condition.[17]

The book's sudden, unannounced juxtapositions initially act to catalyze confusion, in that names or details do not seem to make sense. This feeling is succeeded by a reorganization of assumptions and expectations occasioned by the recognition that the novel has changed its subject from one character to another. For instance, chapter 8 begins with an account of Foster's brother Rufus's first days in America and a transcription of his first letter home to Rena, his wife. After a precisely detailed episode in a bar, the narrative describes how Rufus sneaks home to bed, then specifies that "the next day he got a letter from Rena asking him for a divorce" (94). With no break, the narrative continues with a letter, beginning with the salutation "Dear Dog" (94). The reader naturally expects this letter to be the one from Rena to Rufus asking for a divorce, and the greeting does little to challenge this expectation.[18] However, the very first line of the letter—"here I am, little man in big country, and though I hadn't intended writing many letters, I have a feeling I will" (94)—reveals that the writer is certainly not Rena. By the next paragraph of the letter, it emerges that the writer has to be Foster, but the disorienting effect is palpable and generates important effects. Most notably, perhaps, it draws attention to the friendly irony of Foster's address: expecting the use of "dog" as an insulting dismissal of Rufus, the reader is forced to reinterpret the greeting as humorous, underscoring the context-dependent status of textual interpretation and bringing attention to the very different valences that can attach to one, very simple word. The initial notion of a little man in a big country brings out the similarity of the immigrant situation shared by Foster and Rufus, while the long, detailed, and very introspective nature of Foster's letter appears as a highly noticeable contrast to Rufus's earlier letter to Rena (91), which is concerned almost exclusively with mundane material details regarding travel and the weather. In all these effects, Selvon makes clear to the reader that there exist important parallels between these situations, even though they occur in very different parts of the world between people involved in two very different types of relationship. He makes equally clear that crucial differences—especially in tone, affection, and level of personal concern—must likewise be kept in mind.

Other prominently abrupt transitions provoke the same awareness of basic similarity underlying only apparently irreconcilable differences. When Foster's best friend, Andrews, proposes marriage to his girlfriend Marleen in chapter 10, the chapter ends with his simple, hesitant question: "Marleen, darling, will you—will you marry me?" (124). Chapter 11 begins with another line of dialogue, "How can I marry you?" (125), though the text goes on to relate that it is Rufus, not Marleen, who is speaking. This is a clear manipulation of the reader's expectations and again encourages a consideration of how the situations between the two couples—Andrews and Marleen, as well as Rufus and his American girlfriend Sylvia—are similar in certain ways, yet also markedly different. Indeed, Andrews's earnest, shy, and humbly honest approach to his relationship with Marleen contrasts strikingly with Rufus's approach, which employs devious excuses meant to avoid revealing that he is already married. However, not long after this, Selvon provides another juxtaposition that underscores the crucial similarities between the two couples. In this instance, at the end of chapter 11, Andrews and Marleen are depicted having a heartfelt discussion about their marriage and its potential to disrupt Andrews's political and social advance due to Marleen's lower-class status. Andrews ultimately convinces Marleen that she matters more to him than any other concerns, they agree to marry, and the chapter ends on this promising note:

> They stayed a long time on the hill, and when the sun sank and darkness fell they were still there, locked in each other's arms.
> The new car shone in the darkness. (139)

Chapter 12 begins with a conventional narrative marker of passing time—"two weeks later" (140)—as if the novel is continuing on with the tale of Marleen and Andrews. However, the focus of the action is in fact Sylvia, and the time marker apparently refers to the abortion that she and Rufus arranged for her to have. Despite the unromantic, potentially traumatic implications of the event, the novel concentrates on what the event has done to improve their relationship. Indeed, the result seems to be similar to the heartfelt discussion against which these events are juxtaposed: "Sylvia was back at work, and she and Rufus were talking about what had happened as people do after their experiences, examining themselves to find out why it was that it didn't matter as much as it did at the time" (140). The abortion and the subsequent reflection it inspires in fact strengthen their relationship: "instead of drifting them apart, the incident drew them even closer together. Passion hadn't gone its natural course and died. . . . Now it was deeper, smoother, like after a happy honeymoon" (140). Thus, although the circumstances are utterly different in most ways, the intense personal interaction, reinforced by the invocation of a honeymoon, draws the depictions of the two couples together, implying that they in fact have much more in common than the superficial distinctions originally suggested. Again, Selvon implies, one should not lose track of either the differences or the similarities between the situations.

The novel's technical portrayal of this subtle interlinking of universality and particularity emerges most visibly in the treatment of the two brothers, Rufus and Foster. The inherent configuration of brotherhood, of course, provides a convenient mechanism for indexing the notion of similarity and difference: the two brothers share a very close genetic bond, yet their physical and emotional attributes are patently distinct. As Ramchand observes in his introduction to the novel in its 1993 reissue: "the initial contrast between Rufus's positiveness and Foster's hesitancy, between Rufus's pursuit of love and achievement and Foster's entanglement in thought and speculation does not prevent us from recognising the parallels between the two brothers' lives" (xviii). The novel's abrupt transitions serve to solidify recognition of this complicated symbolic relationship between the two brothers. One such transition occurs in the novel at a moment in which Rufus is in confusion about how to explain his need to go back to Trinidad without revealing that he is already married. Rufus's thoughts work toward justifying his dishonesty to Sylvia, as he thinks, "they had been together so long without her knowing anything and no big catastrophe had happened, that he was led to believe she need never know the whole truth," and then continue with a resolution to tell only as much as is absolutely necessary: "nevertheless, she had to be told that he had to leave the country" (142–43). Similar narrated thoughts continue immediately after, with no indication of any shift in consciousness: "It was not until some time after that he realised the dimensions of the matter. Accepting it had been easy, so that when the realisation came it came like a new problem" (143). This interior monologue continues for several paragraphs before a parenthetical reference to Julia, Foster's English girlfriend, indicates that this second section is not about Rufus distracting himself from his untruthful relationship with Sylvia, but about Foster distracting himself from his own denial concerning Julia. The depiction of self-delusion is startlingly appropriate for either brother's situation. Foster's thoughts on immediacy—"it seemed to him that the heart of the matter was not the important thing, that what was important was the background of the days they lived, the places where they walked, the way she looked" (143)—are equally appropriate for Rufus's dogged devotion to the everyday rhythms of his life with Sylvia. However, when it is finally revealed, the difference between the two situations (especially on an ethical level) appears vast: Rufus is in fact consciously withholding the truth from Sylvia, but Foster is desperately, and more or less unconsciously, trying to convince himself that his relationship with Julia is still viable. Nevertheless, it is suggested, these two situations cannot be too rigidly distinguished, and lying to oneself, or being incognizant of one's own deeply felt reactions, is of a piece with a more obvious type of dishonesty.

Another of these fraternal juxtapositions occurs in chapter 13, which begins by depicting Rufus's reluctant departure from America back to Trinidad to arrange a divorce from Rena. This section ends with a description of Rufus's thoughts: "he wasn't looking forward to Trinidad at all. All his thoughts were on the great continent behind him, not the small Caribbean island he was heading for. . . . It was as if the ship were traveling backwards all the way to Trinidad, the way he kept his mind on America and the life he was leaving behind" (151). These musings are followed immediately by similar deliberations: "if only there were some creed to hold on to, some culture, some doctrine that offered hope, something worth dying for" (152). Such thoughts, couched in a more philosophical terminology, are ultimately identifiable not as a continuation of Rufus's interior monologue, but of Foster's, as he too contemplates returning to Trinidad. Seeking cosmic purpose, Foster looks around and approvingly observes people "going to their jobs, or going home, or seeking to entertain themselves for the evening. . . . They know, they are satisfied, they have little destinations in their minds, little goals and ambitions" (152). These humble pursuits alone, however, do not seem adequate, as the next passage conveys dismay at the inattentive immediacy of Foster's fellow West Indian emigrants: "No sense of gain or loss, no backward glance. No hope of making progress in the old 'Brit'n,' but it was better than living on the 'rock.' Here and there they slouched about the streets, men without future or hope or destiny" (153). Prefiguring the sense of aimlessness portrayed in *The Lonely Londoners,* Selvon here suggests that Foster, like his brother, is struggling to reconcile the everyday features of emigrant life with some bigger significance. Thus, despite their apparently divergent reasons for returning home, both brothers share an exile's longing to anchor their everyday activities in a larger purpose. The differences are surely important as well: Foster is longing for such meaning, while Rufus is at this moment living it, and their decisions about where to live are tellingly distinct. Nevertheless, the outlines of their desires are the same. With this set of complex juxtapositions, the novel again emphasizes a sense of difference coexisting within an underlying sameness.

Although distinctive in its own right, the formal drive of *An Island Is a World* finds similarities in Joyce's work. One of the dominant concepts of *Ulysses,* parallax, is a case in point. Seizing on the astronomic understanding that objects appear differently from different positions on the earth, Joyce's novel emphasizes the need to arrive at "proper" assessment via multiple points of view, enacting this process by illustrating how the radically dissimilar interior monologues of Leopold Bloom and Stephen Dedalus ultimately find common ground in both thought and action over the course of the day. The parallactic technique of *Ulysses*—its famously shifting viewpoints and discourses—"makes concrete Joyce's method of subtly forcing the reader to synthesize . . . shifting perspectives" (Heusel, "Parallax as a Metaphor," 135).[19] The disorienting scene shifts of *An Island Is a World* aspire to an analogous outcome, intertextually extending *A Brighter Sun*'s message of cross-ethnic similarity across an even wider geographical and cultural terrain.

Particularly Cosmopolitan

On the thematic level, *An Island Is a World* closely connects Foster's personal identity crisis with the larger question of national identity, shedding light on the overtly national-political valences of particularity and universality that comprise the novel's major theme. The central image Selvon uses to describe Foster's self-deception while exiled in London is striking. Unhappy and directionless in London, Foster thinks of his situation as one that "was like keeping your shadow behind you, but one day the sun threw it out in front of you and it went and flattened itself against a wall so that as you walked forward it seemed to stride like a live thing and the two of you collided" (143). The figure is compelling, because Selvon himself has referred to his "Trinidadian-ness" in the same terms: discussing Trinidad in 1979, Selvon noted that "this island is my shadow and I carry it with me wherever I go" (*Foreday Morning,* 224–25). The overlap between these images emblematizes the intersection of the personal and political in the novel's thinking.

At first glance, Foster seems to reject any narrowly national identification. Early in the novel, Foster's longing for a communal human togetherness is expressed in a poetic line he relates to Andrews: "Oh kiss me the universal kiss . . . and there's an end to the world's wrangle" (62). Later in the book, observing some Indo-Trinidadians gathered together for passage to India, Andrews asks Foster if he can relate to them, and Foster responds with a similarly antinationalist message, saying, "I see their position the same as I'd see it with any other nationality. They're human beings to me, not Indians or your Trinidadians" (213). When Andrews points out how the European-trained missionary Father Hope's thesis on "a universal religion, a common ground" (236), sounds exactly like Foster's own philosophical goals, Foster initially rejects the comparison but ultimately displays an embarrassed ambiguity that confirms Andrews's observation. In one of his final conversations with Julia, Foster also expresses this desire for the world to transcend narrow identifications, when he complains, "No one thinks of the world. I am an Englishman. I am an American. I am a white man. I am a black man. No one thinks: 'I am a human being, and you are another'" (155). Given these examples, Foster's personal concerns about belonging and responsibility suggest a philosophy of worldwide commonality opposed to any aggressively nationalist sentiment.

On the other hand, the novel also sees the goal of an easy universalism as misguided. One of Foster's letters to Andrews vividly underscores the book's discomfort with a facile belief that "all o' we is one." In discussing the folly of his previous faith in the automatic cosmopolitanism of Trinidadians, Foster makes clear his sense that such unity can only arise from a foundation of particularity:

I used to think that this had merit, that we'd be able to fit in anywhere with anybody, that we wouldn't have prejudices or narrow feelings of loyalty to contract our minds. I used to think we belonged to the world, that a Trinidadian could go to Alaska and fit in, or eat with chopsticks in Hong Kong, and he wouldn't be disturbed by the thought that he belonged somewhere else. I used to think of this philosophy as being the broadest, the most universal, that if it ever came to making a decision on an issue involving humanity itself, we'd have an advantage with this disadvantage, as it were, that we'd be able to see the way clearer, unbounded by any ties to a country or even a race or a creed. (106)[20]

After dismissing his earlier optimism concerning universal brotherhood, Foster proffers his new beliefs, tempered by his international experience: "it isn't like that at all. Other people belong. They are not human beings, they are Englishmen and Frenchmen and Americans, and you've got to have something to fall back on too" (106). Continuing in this vein, Foster asserts the need for some kind of national identification: "So I feel now, that all those idealistic arguments we used to have at home don't mean a thing. You can't belong to the world, because the world won't have you. The world is made up of different nations, and you've got to belong to one of them" (107). As Ramchand notes in the introduction, for Foster "this is a hard lesson to learn, a sad loss of the dream of universal understanding and tolerance" (xxiii), but it leads to an important change of attitude: a recognition that one can arrive at universal goals only through solid grounding in the particular.

Ramchand's view emphasizes cultural nationalism as Foster's response to this crisis—his expressed desire "to build up a national feeling, living as we are in scattered islands with our petty differences" (106)—and goes on to relate this national feeling to Foster's critique of English society, with an implication that the vibrant, young potential culture of the West Indies might supersede the tired, old European version. However, Foster's vision of cultural nationalism in fact has distinctly communal, international aspirations (and the novel seems equally wary of the tired corruption of Trinidadian politics, something that as the narrative ends is about to be addressed, intriguingly, by a British royal commission). Foster's emphasis on Trinidad carefully positions it among other countries: "We never sort of visualized Trinidad as part of the world, a place to build history, a young country which could reap the benefit of the bitter experiences of older countries" (106). Moreover, to ignore the world and focus only on narrow identitarian interests, as Foster explains elsewhere, would be an abdication of responsibility: "it's defeat from the beginning. You talk about the state of the world as if it belonged to somebody else, and we're just renting a room" (155). For Foster, Selvon makes clear, a nationalist sense is fundamentally important, but only when it is rooted firmly in a larger, worldwide context.[21] In this regard, Selvon's view echoes that of Fanon in *The Wretched of the Earth* regarding the imbrication of national and international consciousness, an approach that insists on the need for a strong, confident national identity, but only within the context of the need to participate in an international community, not simply for one's own country's (or indeed one's own) advantage.

This model of actively belonging to the world, of asserting (in distinctive ways) one's own individual membership in constituting a communal relation, is at the core of the novel's politics. In order to belong to the world, Selvon's novel suggests, one must first be aware of it at a local, personal level. One of Foster's meditations names this as a crucial aspect of meaningful human life: "Be forever conscious of living. The world spins, and somewhere on that globe you are, a microscopic dot in a land mass" (129). Importantly, this global perspective is Foster's prescription for preserving uniqueness and avoiding a state in which "each action is mechanical, habit charting a beaten, circular course, criss-crossing over the beaten, circular courses of every man" (128). However, Foster also conceives of such minutely attuned awareness as a necessary first step in any world political process: "We used to think we could put open minds to the world's problems, not mindful of anything particular ourselves. But watch that ochro tree in your own back garden, and see how it is thriving. That post under your house which is rotting, you'd better take it away and put in a new one" (107). Here, Selvon connects a wholly abstract musing on the world's problems to a minutely mundane focus on the everyday, suggesting, as Ramchand expresses it, how the novel "explores not the separation of the private and personal from the public and social, but the necessity for the one to be involved in the other" ("Introduction," xx).[22]

This necessity helps explains the downfall of Father Hope, whose life of sacrifice in helping the poor, rural residents of Veronica is otherwise portrayed in the novel as an almost miraculous exercise in political and moral achievement. Father Hope is indeed, as Salick characterizes him, a heroically "educated, dedicated, and selfless" (84) character whose philosophy provides the novel's title. In conversation with Foster, Father Hope insists that "an island is a world, and everywhere that people live, they create their own worlds" (73).

This message is in keeping with the novel's own views about the importance of the local, and Father Hope's belief that "a man couldn't save the world but perhaps he could save a few souls" (71) resonates with the book's consistent critique of high-minded but totally abstract visions of social belonging. However, there is a suggestion that Father Hope's views are not cosmopolitan enough, notwithstanding his early years of travel and education in Europe. As the book reveals, "Father Hope never left Veronica to go and preach elsewhere. He had come back to the valley to be alone. And he remained alone, out of touch with the world or even the local happenings in the island" (71). His solitary withdrawal from the world is reiterated just before his mysterious death when he happens on Foster at the edge of the village and remarks that he has "never been this far out of the village yet" (228). Ultimately, however, the outside world—in the form of the British policeman Johnson—does intrude, leading directly to Father Hope's death, suggesting that while an island may be *a* world, it should not be misapprehended as *the* world. Selvon's second novel thus intimates that a solipsistic attitude such as Father Hope's, however locally effective, cannot in the end remain viable—a more consciously expansive engagement with the world is needed.

In this way, *An Island Is a World* both continues and critiques *A Brighter Sun*. Selvon, when asked by Fabre in an interview about the shift between his first and second novels, observes that he "did not consider it a shift" ("Samuel Selvon," 68). Indeed, the second novel's depiction of a meditative central character and its careful insistence on an underlying, all-encompassing human commonality coincide convincingly with its predecessor. However, *An Island Is a World* is nevertheless a departure, notably in its different settings, the variation in social class of its characters, and its much more pronounced experimentalism. It is thus possible to read the change in form and content between the two novels as an intertextual instance of the abrupt, juxtaposed transitions that *An Island Is a World* employs in its narrative technique, a gesture designed to raise awareness of differences without obstructing or disallowing a recognition of underlying similarities. Importantly moving its predecessor's frame of reference from the intranational to the international level, the novel's form and themes argue for a cosmopolitanism that remains attentive to local specificity. The disposition suggested by Selvon's work is perhaps best captured in Walter Mignolo's concept of critical cosmopolitanism. For Mignolo, the term connotes a process that counteracts the centrifugal, Eurocentric movement toward an abstract universal by emphasizing the dialogic, centripetal influence of diversity as constituted in the colonial "periphery."[23]

Read from the metropolitan center, however, *An Island Is a World*'s attempt to outmaneuver the exoticizing reception of *A Brighter Sun* by making the same arguments in a noticeably different manner met resistance. In fact, the novel's reception within London periodicals is marked by the same patronizing suppositions about Caribbean culture and intellect that greeted *A Brighter Sun,* only this time with a much more direct focus on the author himself. Perhaps the most blatant example of this ad hominem dismissal occurs in the *Spectator* review by Isabel Quigly. In a transition from discussing W. L. Heath's *Violent Saturday* into her review of Selvon's novel, Quigly succinctly expresses her assessment of Selvon's writing skill: "Mr. Heath knows where he is going: almost too neat-footed, he skirts the dangers of novel-writing with the air of a prim-nosed cat. Mr. Selvon, in *An Island is a World,* does not." Quigly goes on to reveal her dismay at the lack of a clearly Caribbean quality to the novel, noting that "apart from the conscious passages of description and local colour, this novel might just as well have been written by an Englishman."[24] Although her observations imply some type of potential parity between the English and the West Indian, Quigly quickly dispels any impressions of egalitarianism by expressing her sense that Selvon is simply not "developed" enough to handle a serious, philosophical novel: "It is absurd to complain that Mr. Selvon has got away, as undoubtedly he has, from his island; absurd to expect the vision of a primitive from one who is at least half sophisticated. But Mr. Selvon at this stage has lost the directness of the one before acquiring the complexity of the other, a common occurrence in a world where the eye of innocence is given spectacles at the earliest age and in the remotest places." The language of the review reveals a familiar discourse of the West Indian as innocent and childlike, not yet sophisticated enough to write a properly civilized novel like the British.

Like Quigly, the *Times Literary Supplement* reviewer, Arthur Calder Marshall, identifies Selvon as suffering from the strain of a too-rapid process of civilization: "all novelists have trouble with their second books: the West Indian has rather more trouble than others, if he has transferred from the Caribbean to Europe" ("Caribbean Voices," xvii). For Marshall, Selvon's migration has dimmed his ability to render bright local color and caused his writing to be "muddied by . . . intellectualism" unbefitting such a natural talent (xvii).[25] Another *Times Literary Supplement* reviewer, Geoffrey Rudolph Elton, takes a similar view, dismissing the "tedious and rather shallow philosophy" in the novel and expressing disappointment that "though Mr. Selvon is himself an Indian and a native of Trinidad he does not succeed in bringing either his characters or his setting entirely to life" ("Various Pursuits"). Other reviewers likewise seem to prefer Selvon in his earlier incarnation as purveyor of exotic realism, such as Maurice Richardson, who notes that "the island parts are the best" and celebrates Selvon's handling of dialect, or a reviewer from an unidentified source in Selvon's own papers, who asserts that *An Island Is a World* is not as successful as *A Brighter Sun* in such a way as to make clear the critical expectations of Selvon (and other West Indian authors): "it lacks the spontaneity and freshness of the previous [novel]. In this book his main characters are not naïve and simple; they have some knowledge of the society they are in and an awareness of the world and what goes on in it."[26] Thus, it seems, in trying to escape the distancing category of primitive that haunted his first novel despite its message of a common humanity, Selvon's attempts to convey the same message in a manner presumably less likely to be read as primitive end up, by and large, perversely reinforcing precisely that category and his own "natural" place in it.

Communicating in Tongues:
The Lonely Londoners

Selvon's third novel, *The Lonely Londoners,* can be seen to take up the problem of simultaneously articulating West Indian difference from and similarity to the British people with yet another experimental innovation. This novel, published in 1956, is almost certainly Selvon's most popular, best-known work. In critical discussions of West Indian and postcolonial literature, *The Lonely Londoners* is consistently invoked as a seminal work, with primary attention falling on its experimental use of a modified vernacular narration.[27] The novel's treatment of West Indian immigrant life and its employment of demotic English are so well known, in fact, that during his lifetime Selvon was "concerned that the preoccupation of many readers and critics with these two features of his writing led them to neglect others of equal importance" (Ramraj, "Samuel Dickson Selvon," 7). In spite of this possibly overabundant critical attention, the narration of *The Lonely Londoners* clearly merits recognition as a watershed moment in West Indian literature that provides symbolic legitimacy to a pointedly Caribbean way of thinking and speaking. As Birbalsingh observes, one of

Selvon's main legacies is that "attitudes and speech habits which our colonial environment led us to believe were not respectable—he made respectable" (Clarke et al., "Sam Selvon," 63). Judging by their British reception, Selvon's earlier two novels do not necessarily manage to subvert "the conventional associations of dialect with comic characters or with characters on the periphery" (Ramchand, *West Indian Novel*, 96). However, in his third novel, Selvon's use of an unidentified third-person narrator speaking in a modified West Indian vernacular assertively makes claims for such a language to be recognized as legitimately literary.[28] Selvon himself seems to have embraced the notion of his linguistic creole as a means, once again, of articulating a distinctly West Indian consciousness within a mutually understood (among English-speaking audiences) idiom. In one interview, Selvon emphasizes how he strives "to keep the essence, the music" of the way Caribbean people actually speak, while at the same time trying "to avoid some words or phrases which ... would be very difficult for an audience outside of the Caribbean to follow" ("Interview with Sam Selvon," by Dasenbrock and Jussawalla, 115). In conversation with Fabre, Selvon reiterates his desire to somehow portray West Indianness in a language comprehensibly British, claiming that he "wrote a modified dialect which could be understood by European readers, yet retain[ing] the flavour and essence of Trinidadian speech" ("Samuel Selvon," 66). Thus, *The Lonely Londoners* appears to share a similar goal to its predecessors, enacting on both a linguistic and a thematic register a sense of (potential) unity-within-difference.

The novel's language does indeed seem to act as "a deliberate subversion of the colonizer's language" (Joseph, *Caliban in Exile*, 85), a display of linguistic dissonance indicating opposition to the standards of conventional English (and thus, metonymically, of conventional British society). Numerous incidents in the novel underscore this dissonance as a necessary gesture motivated by the ignorance and racism of the British populace. Early in the novel, the narrator describes one of Moses's first experiences with discrimination at work, relating how "all the people in the place say they go strike unless the boss fire Moses" (29), and this incident sets the tone for the novel's consistent if somewhat understated limning of the racist outlines of postwar British society. From the "color-coded" employment office records, to the outright racism of Bart's girlfriend's father, to the prejudiced Polish restaurateur, to the British child's loudly expressed shock upon seeing Galahad's black skin, the novel relates a continuous stream of incidents indicating the validity of one of Moses's early observations to Galahad about the British: "they just don't like black people" (39). As many critics have noted, the novel unmistakably conveys the sense that "under the kiff-kiff laughter" of the novel's characters there is a great deal of unrest and unhappiness (141) caused by a racism deeply embedded in British social patterns.[29] Thus, the novel does mark difference quite consciously and, in addition to a frequently jubilant celebration of West Indian moxie, creativity, and resilience, also offers an illustration of the suffering that difference entails, giving the choice of narrative dialect a pointed political valence.

The pain that results from the immigrants' clearly marked distance from the native population of London seems to preclude any purely celebratory reading of West Indian difference in the novel. The very title communicates some of this ambiguous unease: naming the characters in the novel "Londoners" is a strong claim for West Indian belonging in the British capital city, but the modifier "Lonely" surely signals that a sense of community is missing. Indeed, as Moses envisions the aimless wanderings of the boys in London during the contemplative conclusion of the novel—"he could see the black faces bobbing up and down in the millions of white, strained faces, everybody hustling along the Strand, the spades jostling in the crowd, bewildered, hopeless" (141)—their racial separateness is emphasized, as if to underscore the misery of still not belonging. Thus, while in one sense staking a claim to the validity of a distinct West Indian idiom, the novel is also deeply concerned with reconciliation: like its predecessors, *The Lonely Londoners* expresses a desire that West Indians be accepted as equal contributors in the social and cultural world. This novel, while certainly gesturing in both language and content toward an articulation of something distinctly West Indian, also takes considerable steps to indicate the need for rapprochement, for a recognition of the efforts necessary for a mutually achieved understanding between "the boys" of the novel and the other inhabitants of their newly adopted home.[30]

Even at the level of language—so widely celebrated by critics as distinctly, even aggressively Caribbean—the novel asks for such acceptance. Galahad's famous reply to an English woman who complains about his language can be read as the novel's own plea for understanding: "What wrong with it? . . . Is English we speaking" (93). Moreover, the novel is not solely a critique of British ignorance and prejudice: it does not separate out the responsibility for understanding onto one group or the other. The expectations of British women are certainly not lauded, as revealed in Moses's long, unpunctuated "summer-is-hearts" reminiscence: "but the cruder you are the more the girls

like you you can't put on any English accent for them or play ladeda or tell
them you studying medicine in Oxford or try to be polite and civilise they
don't want that sort of thing at all they want you to live up to the films and stories they hear about black people living primitive in the jungles of the world"
(108). However, Moses makes clear that the immigrants choose to go along
with these expectations as well: "that is why you will see so many of them
African fellars in the city with their hair high up on the head like they ain't had
a trim for years and with scar on their face and a ferocious expression" (108).
Indeed, there is a sense that the "great restless, swaying movement that leaving
[everybody] standing in the same spot" (141) diagnosed by Moses at the end of
the novel is a product of *both* sides continuing on in the same bifurcated roles.
British ignorance is one side of the equation, but Selvon hints at the need for
West Indian responsibility in the novel as well.

On a formal level, the famous passage about summer enacts what most
of the novel's characters seem unable to do. In its breathless, unpunctuated,
stream-of-consciousness style, this passage is strikingly reminiscent of Molly
Bloom's monologue to end Joyce's *Ulysses* and thus stands as the most direct textual instance of the Joycean in Selvon's work. Indeed, several reviewers
picked up on this parallel, including Gwendolen Freeman in the *Times Literary Supplement* and Isabel Quigly in the *Spectator*. In openly paying homage
to what was then perceived to be an established part of British literary tradition, while nevertheless narrating in the novel's distinct West Indian demotic,
the passage makes a point that aligns with Mittelholzer's Eliotic vision: it man-
ages to signal its affiliation with a recognizably British model at the same time
as it advances an unmistakable West Indian difference. It bears mentioning
that the Dublin-born Joyce, of course, emphatically resisted identification as
an Englishman. Nevertheless, although his texts are now understood to express a sophisticated anticolonial politics, in the postwar years (as the many
reviews cited in these pages help illustrate) Joyce was often straightforwardly
accepted as one of the foremost representatives of the British literary canon.
Clearly, his work, like Selvon's, recognizes the linguistic alienation of colonized subjects. Most famously, in *A Portrait of the Artist as a Young Man*, Stephen Dedalus thinks, as he converses with his English dean of studies, "The
language in which we are speaking is his before it is mine. . . . His language,
so familiar and so foreign, will always be for me an acquired speech" (189).
Although implicitly accepting the English claim to linguistic primacy here,
Joyce's later works explicitly seek to upend the power dynamics inhering in

Stephen's uncanny relationship to words: the demystifying counterdiscursive drive of *Ulysses* (focused most directly on language in the "Oxen of the Sun" chapter) and the multilingual verbal exuberance of *Finnegans Wake* both work to make the allegedly natural, dominant language of English simultaneously familiar and foreign to readers. The long, *Ulysses*-like passage in *The Lonely Londoners* works in a similar way, formally conveying a disposition that both recognizes and productively alters the set modes of communication and thus suggesting a framework within which the immigrant and the native-born might be able to converse.

A crucial instance of the novel's advocacy of the need for this type of mutually reciprocal cultural recognition occurs during Harris's party near the end of the novel. The reader's introduction to Harris is as someone snobbishly resistant to his own West Indian roots: "Harris is a fellar who like to play ladeda, and he like English customs and thing. . . . When he dress, you think is some Englishman going to work in the city, bowler and umbrella, and briefcase tuck under the arm, with *The Times* fold up in the pocket so the name would show" (111). The suggestion is that Harris is someone who wants to appear English, but, as the narrator wryly notes, "only thing, Harris face black" (111). Despite what are read as pretensions to Englishness, however, Harris clearly has some redeeming qualities that in fact take him outside the category of British identity: "he does be polite and say thank you and he does get up in the bus and the tube to let woman sit down, which is a thing even them Englishmen don't do" (111). Moreover, his linguistic skills are deemed impressive by the narrator: "man, when Harris start to spout English for you, you realise that you don't really know the language" (111).[31] While Harris does in many respects strike the reader as a deracinated "Afro-Saxon," he is also seen to have positive qualities and indeed has much more contact with the white world of London than anybody else in the group. Depicted as primly censuring the more outrageous antics of Five at his fetes, Harris is also, tellingly, responsible for bringing the boys all together (along with some of the few West Indian women depicted in the novel) for a big party at which sympathetic whites are present.[32]

The most subtle point Selvon makes is when he depicts Harris talking for the first and only time in dialect, urging the boys to be respectful when the band is playing "God Save the Queen" at the end of the evening: "some of you have a habit of walking about as if the fete still going on, and you, Five, the last time you come to one of my dances you was even jocking waist when everybody else was standing at attention" (122). By slipping into dialect, Harris's words serve to signal respect for the boys' style of communication in his own plea for them to respect others, highlighting the performative nature of his own (and, by implication, everybody else's) speech habits.[33] Via this linguistic shift, Selvon suggests that for the boys, adjusting their behavior in accordance with context is not only perfectly plausible but also a productive social strategy. Foster makes a similar point about language use in *An Island Is a World,* hypothesizing that he and his friends slip into dialect as a strategy of defensiveness, a paradoxical way of communicating an unwillingness to communicate: "Whenever we're talking and we find ourselves losing ground, we fall back on broken English" (66). Similarly, via Harris, Selvon suggests that the boys' unruly behavior at the party is in some sense a lazily one-sided view of social interaction, making no allowances for the customs or expectations of others.

The same refusal of seriousness criticized by Harris is shown earlier in the novel as well, when Big City convinces a man discussing the color problem at the Orator's Corner near Marble Arch to let Galahad speak on the issue. Instead of letting Galahad speak, however, Big City heckles him until "all the people looking at the two of them and laughing" (99). By depicting such a scene—the most pronounced chance offered the characters for some kind of public discourse about the racism on which the novel concentrates—Selvon suggests that it is not only the ignorance and misplaced fear of the white British population that are at fault. The refusal of the boys to engage seriously with socially sanctioned mechanisms for contact with the native population also contributes to the disunity so prominent in the city. Despite his comic reputation, Selvon also criticized what he saw as a too-prevalent West Indian tendency toward disavowing laughter: "you want to start a serious discussion, and there again, this laughter comes out very clearly. Maybe the laughter started to jar on me and I said, what the hell? Why should we laugh at a serious discussion? Let's rather come to grips with it" ("Interview with Sam Selvon," by Nazareth, 82). As Ramchand has observed in his introduction to the novel, Moses's final ruminations also point to a need to step back from the reflexive patterns of laughter and forgetting that characterize the boys' behavior throughout the novel. Indeed, the novel's exhortation to reconsider one's assumptions—"sometimes you does have to start thinking all over again when you feel you have things down the right way" (61)—could be seen to address not only the prejudiced views of white England but the equally stubborn, exclusionary behavior of the boys themselves.[34] Selvon's review in the *Evening Standard* of Joyce Eggington's *They Seek a Living,* a study of recent migration to Britain, articulates precisely this viewpoint of reciprocal adjustment and engagement: "it is time now for the English people to understand and accept us, for most West Indians are here to stay. But it is vital that we migrants remember that ours is the greater effort towards that understanding" ("Place Out of the Sun"). Such a sentiment directly expresses what is subtly suggested in *The Lonely Londoners:* if it is in fact true, as the narrator states, that "people in this world don't know how other people does affect their lives" (76), then all are in need of an education.

However, reviewers and critics of *The Lonely Londoners* generally overlooked this message of universality and reciprocal compromise.[35] The contemporaneous reviews of the novel are largely complimentary (as they were for *A Brighter Sun*), but in a way that reinforces perceptions of difference and incompatibility. Most reviewers greeted the novel with what seems like collective relief that the "natural exuberance overlaid by a rather obtrusive literariness" present in *An Island Is a World* is no longer discernible (Quigly). Quigly praises the "liveliness" of the novel and its "exotic themes," and many other critics applaud its curious language, characteristically described by the *Evening Standard* as "the racy, lively idiom the West Indians use among themselves."[36] The newspaper's characterization of Selvon's linguistic style is accompanied by an apprehension of his characters as pleasant oddities—"those happy-go-lucky people from the sunshine of the West Indies"—and such a pattern is consistent through most of the reviews. *The Lonely Londoners* was, like *A Brighter Sun,* generally received as an authentic insider's picture of strangely simple people, with the naturalistic language a further proof of authenticity and artlessness.[37] Just as John Lehmann (an early, enthusiastic supporter of West Indian literature) sees *The Lonely Londoners*'s dialect as an immature, not yet self-conscious linguistic expression in his 1957 "Foreword" to *London Magazine* (11), other critics saw the novel's characters as "feckless and innocent and trusting" (Shrapnel, review). The reviewer for the *Surrey Comet* concludes, after reading the novel, that there are only three options for viewing the immigrant characters of *The Lonely Londoners:* with disinterest, pity, or distaste.[38] While this view is unusually harsh, it does serve to underscore the general sense that in trying to depict both the humor and the pain of the recent West Indian sojourn in the metropolis, Selvon's novel was almost universally unsuccessful in convincing metropolitan critics to see the book's characters or its language as anything but fascinating in their unalterable difference. In many reviewers' eyes, the novel was "fresh and original" and "strikingly vivid" (Richardson, review), but not of any real political, social, or cultural concern to a British audience.

Coupled with this perception of the novel and its characters as refreshingly unsophisticated was, again, a similar perception of Selvon himself. For example, the *Surrey Comet* reviewer refuses to consider the book a novel at all, complaining that the book's author "makes no attempt to analyze the position" of his characters, while John Betjeman's *Daily Telegraph* review takes pains to suggest that Selvon is capable not of "connected narrative," but rather only of "significant reportage."[39] The *Times Literary Supplement* likewise seems to conflate Selvon with his characters, as a somewhat simpleminded, good-natured West Indian. Identifying Selvon with "his countrymen" in the novel, the review goes on to assert that "the book is in the form of a novel, but there is no plot" (Freeman, review). The events depicted are seen to "give an effect of simpleness and helplessness," and the review ultimately concludes that Selvon's "tone is humorous and with a tolerance that is perhaps characteristic of the race." Although she notes the parallel with *Ulysses* in passing, the reviewer's final observation assesses the novel as a harmlessly amusing insider's account of "rich comic humanity, unhappy most of the time but with moments of uninhibited pleasure beyond the experience of the white man." The novel thus seems to have strengthened the sense of perceived difference between English and West Indian people, perhaps even reinforcing British expectations of "natural" and "simple" writing and a childlike immigrant people.[40]

Interestingly, just as British critics generally read the novel as a marker of West Indian difference, critics of Caribbean literature frequently valorize the novel for the same reason, reading the same difference positively. John Thieme, though cautious about its ultimate political efficacy, assesses the language of Selvon's third novel as a carnivalesque subversion of a Western imposition of order, a manifestation of "the kinetic, antiauthoritarian spirit" of West Indian resistance ("World Turn Upside Down," 201). Margaret Paul Joseph's *Caliban in Exile* makes the claim that "Selvon's use of the calypsonian's dialect and form, therefore, is itself a proclamation of independence from the colonizer's mode of narrative" (87), using a strongly political metaphor to indicate her perception of the aggressive difference encoded in the novel's language. Salick asserts that Selvon's vernacular usage "liberates the West Indian novel from the strictures of standard English, the language of the colonial master" (*Novels of Samuel Selvon*, 5), and Fabre, too, emphasizes the sovereign distinction implied by Selvon's linguistic experiment. Although Fabre notionally advances the idea of dialect as a gesture of negotiation between two different but mutually comprehensible linguistic systems—observing that Selvon's language is aimed at "bridging the gap between local Creole and accepted standard English" ("From Trinidad to London," 222)—he predominantly emphasizes Selvon's linguistic originality as a force acting to "liberate Trinidadian fiction" (221) and to "explode" and "subvert" European mainstream traditions (220). Thus, critics of Caribbean literature often proclaim Selvon's work as a bold announcement of West Indian difference and cultural autonomy. Although their evaluations of the difference between West Indian and English culture are emphatically positive, these critics' delineations of a pronounced difference partake of the same structural separation as the early British reviewers' resolutely racialized views of the novel.

Selvon himself seems to emphasize not difference but similarity, and his view of his own literary vernacular coincides with the assertion by F. G. Cassidy endorsed by Ramchand in *The West Indian Novel and Its Background* that West Indian Creole "coexists with English and the two have more in common than apart" (92). Indeed, in an interview with Fabre, Selvon confesses that he is uncomfortable with the West Indian language in Austin Clarke's novels because it "sets them apart from Canadians. This is not a good thing" (Selvon, "Samuel Selvon," 75). In contrast, Selvon reveals his own unifying linguistic politics, suggesting what he would do if writing about West Indians in Canada: "build the writing into the society . . . build their language in as I did in *The Lonely Londoners*" (75). Selvon does not elaborate on this point, but it is clear that he views the purpose of creole in his writing as a sign of active efforts at mitigating, not enhancing, a sense of segregation.[41] Selvon's review of Colin MacInnes's *City of Spades*, a problematically sympathetic novel about London's new black migrants, also emphasizes this impulse toward incorporation and belonging. Selvon bemoans the fact that the novel accentuates its black characters' inaccessibility to a white audience by never representing their point of view in the narrative.[42] He expresses disappointment at the resolute separation of the black characters the novel seems to support, noting that "it ends on the disconsolate note that 'civilised' love cannot touch their enigmatic hearts, and to tolerate them is much more possible than to understand them." For Selvon, such separation lies at the root of the social strife his novels seek to address.

In this light, the trajectory of Selvon's first three novels can be read as a series of strategic gestures designed to outmaneuver the consistent reception of his universalist message as confirmation of the incontrovertible otherness of West Indians. Certainly, Selvon's work can seem, even to this day, to be trapped in the perverse logic adumbrated by Michael North in *The Dialect of Modernism* in his discussion of another Caribbean author, Claude McKay, and his use of dialect writing. For McKay, North observes, dialect is already immovably established as a sign of "black Jamaicans as natural, childlike, and full of tomfoolery" (110), such that "language a writer like McKay might use against the standard English . . . has already been turned into a harmless curiosity before he can get to it" (110). In North's formulation, a writer such as McKay or Selvon can either confirm his audience's primitivist stereotypes by writing in dialect or write standard English in an apparent capitulation to the dominant culture, but both options have been defined in advance on British terms. Derek Walcott has described the two-sided nature of creole language use by Caribbean authors similarly: reviewing one of Selvon's later vernacular novels, *The Housing Lark*, he notes that such language can "both protect him from and accuse him of being, if not ignorant, then naïve" ("Selvon Has Returned"). In the face of such a bind, Selvon's works execute a strategy of alternation and juxtaposition, attempting to illustrate the simultaneous validity (and context dependence) of identities on both sides of the divide. In this view, Selvon's calculatedly demotic modernist experimentations with language and form point to a way of representing the cosmopolitan without being elitist, of signaling the universal without wholly subsuming the local in the former's abstracting force.

In a postcolonial critical context, these literary articulations of a type of universal human identification can be vulnerable to the critique that they erase racial and ethnic identity and thus elide the damage colonialism instigated in the name of such identities. Certainly, as Elizabeth Ingrams points out, "in his lifetime Selvon suffered for his outspoken refusal to ally himself with any one political cause" ("*Lonely Londoners*," 35), and Selvon's evocations of universalism cause critics such as Michael Thorpe to view him as a "nonideological writer" ("Sam Selvon," 87). Lamming, too, calls his fellow author "the least political of us all" (*Pleasures of Exile*, 43). However, Selvon's conceptions of the universal always arrive *through* a more local identification, and his work could hardly be said to overlook the implications of race or imperial domination.[43] Selvon's interviews consistently establish his outright West Indian allegiances while preserving a universal frame, such as when he defends his dependence on Caribbean characters to Alessandra Dotti: "But, you see, I am a Caribbean man myself and it is the psyche that I know best, so that other characters from other cultures would really be superficial to some extent. . . . It isn't my culture and in that sense I would always try to stay with what I know best. This is why, wherever I go, I think I would be writing in a universal way to have my characters be universal too" ("Oldtalk," 131). What Ken McGoogan characterizes as Selvon's "expansive, inclusive, and welcoming frame of mind" ("Saying Goodbye," 73) is surely apparent in his early novels, which emphasize the pitfalls of a merely exclusivist, oppositional version of identity. As Gikandi argues, Selvon's writing is expressly concerned to expose the danger that a complacent acceptance of tradition-bound images of self-sufficiency and separatism "entails the imprisonment of the subject in the economy of the other" (*Writing in Limbo,* 129). However, as Gikandi also notes, Selvon's works simultaneously seek "to penetrate the totality that official discourse promotes" (118), emphasizing Caribbean difference and distinction as a way to counteract the homogeneity upon which empire depends. Combining both impulses, Selvon's novels attempt a careful balancing of the particular and the universal: they advance the notion that differences, while never concretely effaced, can at times—and to great political purpose—be subsumed under a larger category of similarity.[44]

Perhaps inevitably, the paradoxical nature of Selvon's literary vernacular language itself stands as an apt analogy of his aesthetic attempts to articulate his philosophy of cosmopolitan belonging. The use of dialect, as North describes it, obliges an author to perform a delicate linguistic process of making language distinctively "communal without making it metaphysical or politically exclusive" (*Dialect of Modernism,* 194), or, as Ramchand characterizes it, enacting the necessity for "dialect to cease to be a secret language and become an open language" ("Sam Selvon Talking," 99). It is this paradoxical difference—existing precariously under an overarching if not always predominant unity—that the overtly experimental modes of Selvon's first three novels attempt to communicate.[45] Although the British propensity to view West Indian fiction in a culturally separate frame seems largely to have drowned out their message, Selvon's early novels—"rooted in Trinidad Creole dialectal perceptions . . . also open to English experience" (Dickinson, "Sam Selvon's 'Harlequin Costume,'" 71)—take shape as formal arguments for an ideal, open-ended community without exclusionary closure. In these postwar years, Selvon employs modernist forms to convey his insistence on Caribbean people as particular—and particularly well equipped, in light of the enforced cosmopolitanism of the region—examples of a world citizenry.

5 The Lyrical Enchantments of Roger Mais

> If we can't hear the cries far down in our own forests of dark veins, we can look in the real novels, and there listen in. Not listen to the didactic statements of the author, but to the low, calling cries of the characters, as they wander in the dark woods of their destiny.
>
> —D. H. Lawrence, "The Novel and the Feelings"

Jamaican novelist Roger Mais, although he arrived in London not long after Lamming, Mittelholzer, and Selvon, took a rather different path toward metropolitan literary success. Comparatively isolated from the eastern Caribbean cultural scene, and evidently disliked by Cedric and Gladys Lindo, the Jamaica-based editorial gatekeepers for *Caribbean Voices,* Mais was already well established as a journalist, writer, painter, dramatist, and cultural commentator on his home island before he left for Britain.[1] With two subscription-based short story collections—*Face, and Other Stories,* along with *And Most of All Man*—under his belt and a long list of stories, poems, and articles published in Jamaica's establishment newspaper, the *Daily Gleaner,* and Norman Manley's nationalist organ, *Public Opinion,* Mais departed for London only after securing a contract for the publication of his first novel by Jonathan Cape in the summer of 1952. This novel, *The Hills Were Joyful Together*, appeared in 1953 and was followed in quick succession by two more, *Brother Man* and *Black Lightning,* a prolific and promising beginning that was cut short by Mais's untimely death in 1955. Despite the brevity of his overseas publishing career, Mais captured a fair amount of attention in the British literary scene, sitting for an interview for *John O'London's Weekly* in 1953 and garnering a prominent obituary in the *London Times* (as well as a letter to the editor from his publisher in response to the obituary, ruing the loss and reminding people of the recent publication of *Black Lightning*).[2] In the Anglophone Caribbean critical tradition, Mais has generally been grouped with Selvon as something of a populist-oriented, vernacular writer, albeit one with more overtly nationalist credentials. However, in Britain Mais's novels were initially received as experimental literature, helping him achieve some measure of fame.

Critical discussion of Mais has tended to cluster around the categories of the political and the literary. Mais's deep involvement in nationalist politics—he was an early and active figure in Norman Manley's People's National Movement—has often led to the characterizing of his work as politically driven "social protest" literature. Manley himself helped establish this view in his introduction to Sangster's 1966 reissue of Mais's three novels in a single volume, praising Mais for his realistic, anticolonial portrayal of "raw humanity and how it suffers in the framework of hardship and in the face of authority" (viii).[3] In this short introduction, Manley claims the national independence movement as the very essence of Mais's aesthetic, asserting that "Roger was a product of that moment of history and drew from it the direction and power and purpose which his writings reveal" ("Introduction," vi). L. E. (Kamau) Brathwaite, one of the most prolific and sensitively attuned critics of Mais's work, has been a formidable force in establishing Mais's critical reputation as a primarily political author. Although Brathwaite treats Mais's aesthetic complexity with careful attention, his readings are unerringly intent on redeeming the novels' diasporic African credentials, displaying deep discomfort with Mais's "remarkably conservative" Eurocentric aesthetic tendencies ("Unborn Body," 14) and casting suspicion on *Black Lightning* for its move away from an overt commitment to community. Overall, his ingenious readings of Mais affirm only those qualities—unevenly present in the novels, as even Brathwaite acknowledges—that he considers politically appropriate to authentic Caribbean literature. For example, despite his intricately observed delineation of *Brother Man*'s jazz stylings in "Jazz and the West Indian Novel," Brathwaite can only account for the climactic moment of the novel—the vicious beating the protagonist suffers at the hands of the community—in terms of aesthetic failure, since it undermines the valorization of community Brathwaite sees as the novel's primary achievement.[4] Brathwaite, along with other important critics like Sylvia Wynter and Jean D'Costa, has helped establish a strong critical tradition that sees Mais as a nationalist author with a predominantly political orientation.

Alternatively, other foundational Mais critics—notably Bill Carr and Kenneth Ramchand—have consciously steered attention away from the political content of Mais's work, emphasizing instead its literary craftsmanship.[5] Carr, for example, baldly states his interpretive agenda near the beginning of

"Roger Mais: Design from a Legend": "Mais was not a political novelist; his significance cannot be understood in terms of the impressively original social content of his two published Kingston novels (original, that is, on first appearance); and finally he is not to be ultimately associated with something known as 1938 and the movement for independence" (5). Ramchand, although considerably more nuanced in his approach, nevertheless expresses discomfort with ideological readings of Mais. He seizes on the lyrical aspects of *The Hills Were Joyful Together* to insist that the book is "something more than Jamaican social protest" and lauds Mais's third novel for finally escaping the dread trap of localized race and politics, enthusing that Mais "had learnt that to be truly native is to be truly universal" ("Black Lightning"). A more recent commentator, Evelyn Hawthorne, has joined in questioning the understanding of Mais as a purely nationalist writer in *The Writer in Transition: Roger Mais and the Decolonization of Caribbean Culture.* In this book, Hawthorne delineates what she describes as Mais's "Romantic" qualities—which to her, on their very face, are incompatible with nationalist consciousness—and ultimately advances a generational argument, suggesting that Mais (born in 1905) was caught between old (Romantic) and new (nationalist) values.[6] Thus, although Hawthorne's book usefully complicates an understanding of Mais's work, its structuring antithesis nevertheless reinforces the traditional opposition between the literary and the political that characterizes Mais criticism.

The contemporaneous British reviews of Mais display a similarly bifurcated structure, albeit from markedly different ideological ground. The seamy social realism of *The Hills Were Joyful Together* certainly caught the attention of British reviewers, who duly reiterated the familiar exotic stereotypes of the Caribbean. R. D. Charques's review in the *Spectator* is typical in this regard, stressing how the novel's characters and setting "pullulate with sex, animal high spirits and poverty." Similarly, Hugh Skies Davies employs the book to demarcate a careful line between British and Caribbean life, observing that the latter is "in itself, more primitive than our own, and the books it makes are bound to assault our tamer minds, as this one does, with uncomfortable primitive violence."[7] With a bit more adjectival gusto, Andrew Dakers likewise emphasizes the primitiveness of the book's Jamaican characters: "naïve and savage, generous and cunning, sensitive and gross, violent and tender victims of their muddled bloods, they move through the story high-spirited and gay, singing and dancing, loving and lusting, with outbreaks of primitive barbarity that evoke pity and terror" ("Novelist from Jamaica"). Left at this level,

Mais's stated purpose in writing the novel—"to give the world a true picture of the real Jamaica, and the dreadful conditions of the working classes" (Dakers, "Novelist from Jamaica")—would appear to be a rather dubious political achievement, allowing as it does for a distinct disidentification between "civilized" British critic and "savage" Caribbean subject.

Many British reviewers of Mais's first novel, however, also registered its more plainly aesthetic aims, thus modulating a matter-of-fact acceptance of the book's naturalistic portrayals. The reviewer for the *Sussex Daily News* (identified only as W.J.C.), for example, pays admiring attention to Mais's "impressionist technique," which is characterized as an artful alternation of the lyrical and the realist.[8] In the *Manchester Guardian,* Paul Bloomfield is unequivocal in his praise of the novel, naming it as "among the strongest and best new novels" of the last few years because of its display of technical virtuosity— "the masterly touch of a writer who knows how to present, significantly, any amount of vice, misery, disease, and madness" (review). While acknowledging that *The Hills Were Joyful Together* is in one sense an attempt to portray the brute realities of unromanticized island poverty, the *Manchester Evening News* also enthuses over the artistry of the novel, exclaiming that "at times the writing is sheer poetry, with all the singing and gold that marks the highest in mankind."[9] Walter Allen's short notice in the *New Statesman* expresses reservations about the novel's overarching structural coherence but nevertheless sees vague promise in the author: "one will be glad to read more of Mr. Mais, for in addition to his skill in rendering colour and violence he has a feeling for human dignity" (review). Even Charques, while also critical of the book's uneven structure, discerns an aesthetic value beyond the immediate flaws, noting that Mais "has his moments of illumination and pathos" even if the novel does not quite manage to "achieve the emotional force it was evidently meant to carry" (review). Charques's perception of an attempt at "emotional force" is perhaps the most apposite formulation of what these critics sensed in Mais's first novel: a lyrical effort, however vaguely defined, to get beyond the simple mimetic presentation of sordid sociological facts.

These perceptions of Mais's first novel are echoed in reviews of *Brother Man.* The *London Times,* for example, though sanguinely observing that in the West Indies "the turns of phrase of local speech are full of natural poetry," takes pains to underscore Mais's achieved aesthetic skill.[10] After remarking on the Caribbean's naturally picturesque linguistic bounty, the reviewer goes on to praise Mais's conscious utilization of it: "Mr. Mais knows how to use these gifts to advantage. He uses words unusually well, maintaining a proper balance between the native idiom and the varying style of his own commentary." This description approvingly presents Mais, not as a naturally talented primitive genius (as Selvon was often seen), but as a writer in full control of his medium, up to and including his "varying style." The reviewer finds Brother Man a somewhat artificially allegorical figure but largely accepts the novel as "very good indeed" and commends Mais for seeing "with the eye of an artist." The significance of such praise in terms of Mais's perceived aesthetic allegiances is crystallized in the *Times Literary Supplement*'s review of the novel. Here, the then-anonymous reviewer, David Tylden-Wright, begins by evoking the apparent duality of Mais's artistic practice, describing him as "both poet and moralist." Tylden-Wright then mentions *Brother Man*'s most well-known feature, the choral sections that precede each of its five chapters, describing them as "very reminiscent of Dylan Thomas's method of poetic description" ("Irreconcilable Worlds"). With the BBC's first production of Thomas's multivoiced play *Under Milk Wood* only six months gone, the comparison with Mais's own quasi-dramatic, dialogic choral passages seems both apt and timely. However, the invocation of Thomas also has implications within the postwar literary debate between the writers of the Movement and their "Mandarin" rivals, as Thomas was a bête noir of the up-and-coming writers, convenient shorthand (similar to Woolf) for the type of allegedly pretentious, consciously artsy writing that the Movement found so distasteful. Certainly, Tylden-Wright writes approvingly of Mais's resemblance to Thomas, and by the end of the review, he has abandoned the initial duality of *Brother Man* with which he began, content to position Mais squarely within an aesthetic of unique artistry (apparently autonomous from politics). Summing up the novel, he observes, "Mr. Mais's drawings, as well as his dialogue, take some time to get used to, but finally blend satisfactorily into his highly individual vision."[11] Less than a year later, the *London Times* obituary for Mais reiterates, almost word for word, the *TLS* comparison with Thomas, using it as an example of the author's "very great advance in technique" and solidifying the sense that Mais was welcomed in London as a poetic, experimental novelist.

The obituary, of course, appeared before *Black Lightning*, which, despite its editors' letter to the *Times*, seems to have gone largely unremarked by the British literary establishment. There is no way of knowing precisely why the novel was so unacclaimed, but its distinct stylistic departure—away from lyrical exuberance into a spare, tightly controlled dramatic form—could be considered part of the equation.[12] Intriguingly, the fault line between the more contemporary critical focus on the literary and the political in Mais's work lies in the perceived difference between the author's first two novels and his third. The social critique implicit in Mais's portrayal of poor Kingstonians in *The Hills Were Joyful Together* and *Brother Man* fits easily into the notion of Mais as a political writer; *Black Lightning*, a much more personal, less sociological consideration of the nature of art and the artist, does not. An example of this disjunction is D'Costa's monograph on Mais, which, in its attempts to claim Mais as a bona fide Jamaican nationalist artist, simply leaves aside any consideration of his third novel. The title of this work, *Roger Mais: "The Hills Were Joyful Together" and "Brother Man,"* succinctly conveys the scope and focus of its critical prerogatives.[13] On the other side, critics like Carr and Ramchand heap praise on *Black Lightning* as Mais's culminating aesthetic achievement. In their view, Mais's first two novels are apprentice work, marred by undignified political polemics, and it is only in his final novel that Mais realizes his true artistic potential. Ramchand, for example, contends that "it is in *Black Lightning* that Mais's art and understanding are in greatest harmony, and that it is upon this his last published novel that his reputation must rest" (*West Indian Novel*, 179). For one group of scholars, then, *Black Lightning* is a puzzling anomaly, difficult to reconcile with a reading of Mais as political firebrand; for another, the novel is the apogee of his literary development, confirmation that Mais had moved beyond mere social concerns into the more rarefied air of true artistry.

This large fissure in Mais's small oeuvre seems primarily the result of critical inclinations to segregate "universal" literariness and local political topicality into opposing, impermeable categories. Sydney Singh's discussion of Mais rightly finds fault with this tendency, asserting that "a concern only with the universal applicability of the theme of the novel is as critically limited an approach to the work as an exclusive concentration on its immediate social relevance" (*"Hills Were Joyful Together,"* 111). If Mais's work is read through the prism of its modernist self-reflexivity, however, a much more unified critical narrative can emerge. Mais's British reviewers were initially attracted to his experimental, incantatory style, which seemed aimed at unlocking a transformative, transporting power of language. In this, Mais finds a lineage not only in Thomas's poetry but perhaps even more so in the prose of D. H. Lawrence, whose experiments in style similarly longed to spark an all but indescribable, redemptive transcendence via an appeal to the emotional register. Mais's early, unpublished book on fiction writing, *Form and Substance in Fiction,* persistently employs Lawrence as example and guide, testifying to their shared interest in experimenting with the suprarational transformative powers of language.[14] This interest in affective language is quite different from the ideological critique that Lamming attempts in his writing—indeed, Lamming himself observes of Mais that "his relation to language and the concerns which that language served were so different from mine" ("Tribute to a Tragic Jamaican," 243). Nevertheless, the reformative impulse of Mais's concern with language cannot, strictly speaking, be labeled apolitical. Indeed, in many ways, Mais's novels strive to transcend any easy aesthetic-political dichotomy, self-consciously taking up Lawrence's exhortation to write effectively affective "real novels" with real political consequence. Although their progression reveals an increasing dissatisfaction with the efficacy of this practice, Mais's novels nevertheless take shape as a Caribbean variation on modernism's bedeviled attempts to match the consciousness-changing potential of high aesthetic production with political ends.

Summoning the Word

At the beginning of *Form and Substance in Fiction,* Mais plainly states his own sense of the writer's political responsibility, asserting that the "real purpose of fiction" is "to make humanity articulate, to make a mouth of every single wound, to give voice to every single human hope and hunger, and aspiration and fear" (1). The bodily imagery employed in this declaration of social duty intimates Mais's close adherence to Lawrence's attempts, as one critic has it, "to use language in ways that would touch the reader's somatic modes of experiencing and responding" (Burack, *D. H. Lawrence's Language,* 2).[15] Indeed, Mais's treatise on fiction refuses to separate intellect and emotion, invoking a passage from Lawrence's *Lady Chatterley's Lover* as illustration of how novels should function (28). The well-known passage gives a clear sense of Lawrence's (and, via its prominent citation, Mais's) aesthetic philosophy:

> It is the way our sympathy flows and recoils that really determines our lives. And here lies the vast importance of the novel, properly handled. It can inform and lead into new places the flow of our sympathetic consciousness, and it can lead our sympathy away in recoil from things gone dead. Therefore, the novel, properly handled, can reveal the most secret places of life: for

> it is in the *passional* secret places of life, above all, that the tide of sensitive
> awareness needs to ebb and flow, cleansing and freshening. (117–18)

This holistic, transformative sense of the novel's proper domain—a complexly aligned phenomenological and epistemological space—emerges in Lawrence's essays as well. For example, in "Why the Novel Matters," Lawrence asserts the body as the foundational instrument of knowing, enthusing, "my body, me alive, *knows,* and knows intensely" (194). Accordingly, he claims, the novel is superior to other methods of imparting knowledge: "the novel as a tremulation *can* make the whole man-alive tremble. Which is more than poetry, philosophy, science or any other book-tremulation can do" (195). Likewise, in "The Novel and the Feelings" (from which this chapter's epigraph is taken), Lawrence complains that "we have no language for the feelings" (203) and proposes the novel as the remedy, "a slow and strange process, that has to be undertaken seriously" (204) in order for human life to be properly redeemed. As *Form and Substance in Fiction* indicates, Mais's thinking followed markedly similar lines, embracing writing as a mechanism for summoning in his readers a complex, embodied consciousness that would, in turn, lead to awareness of the need for deep social and political reform.

Mais's most famous piece of journalism—"Now We Know," published in *Public Opinion* in 1944—demonstrates his belief that the tones and rhythms of highly wrought language could serve important political ends. A response to the wartime British government's refusal to publish the new draft of Jamaica's constitution, the article became grounds for Mais's prosecution for sedition and a six-month prison sentence.[16] A rhetorical exercise in high dudgeon, the article's solemn, incantatory style is used to deliver a fiercely anticolonial message. The article begins with a simple declarative sentence: "Now we know why the draft of the New Constitution has not been published before." This clear statement of discovery is followed—and implicitly contrasted with—three scathingly sarcastic paragraphs delineating the hypocritical, obfuscatory language of British officialdom. Mais pointedly observes that the "real official policy" does not inhere in the suppressed document but is instead "implicit in statements made by the Prime Minister from time to time." Excoriating "that man of brave speeches," the article suggests the slipperiness of his language, maintaining that the government's true intentions, though "avowed in open parliament," have only emerged "in so many words," rather than in definite declarations of intent.

The article then embarks on an anaphoric tour de force delineating precisely what has been revealed about the causes for which the British government is asking Jamaica to sacrifice in World War II, beginning with the following: "That the sun may never set upon aggression and inequality and human degradation." Emphasizing the paradoxical British desire somehow to fight tyranny (in the form of fascism and Nazism) while preserving its own tyrannical empire, Mais lists a succession of condemnatory descriptions of colonial rule, all beginning with the phrase "that the sun may never set" and later intermingling another phrase, "for such things as these," to sustain the piece's rhythmic, incantatory tone. Only at the very end does the anaphora finally relent, with a stark repetition of the article's original words: "For such things as these we are fighting side by side with others in the good cause.... Now we know." The literariness of this polemic seems obvious enough, but it is employed against something to which it bears some resemblance: the deceptive cant of hypocritical politicians. The implications of this opposition—slippery, self-serving rhetoric versus a grander, somehow more honest literary kind—are intriguing, suggesting as they do not a simple dismissal of fine phrasing, but a more finely grained understanding of the potency of verbal expression and the ends to which it can be put. While "Now We Know" clearly believes it has truth and justice on its side, its formal pyrotechnics betray much more interest in summoning the emotive force of words to bring its point home. Mais's novels take up a similar interest in the way aesthetics operate affectively.

The most obvious experimental aspect of *The Hills Were Joyful Together*—sections D'Costa describes as "choric, poetic meditations of the omniscient author" (*Roger Mais*, 13–14)—are strikingly similar in style to "Now We Know." Anaphoric and solemnly rhythmic (and thus bearing resemblances to Mittelholzer's subsequent leitmotiv style) these passages emerge about a quarter of the way through the novel, irregularly interrupting narrative events with lyrical, enigmatic reflections on chance, time, human struggle, life, and death.[17] Critics typically treat these sections as ancillary to the novel's "real" subject. For Ramchand, at different times, they represent either a discomfiting (and ultimately unsuccessful) attempt "to remove the [novel's] issues from a deadly sociological plane" ("Black Lightning") or an inartistic authorial intrusion that interjects a view of cosmic indifference at odds with much of the book's narrative events (*West Indian Novel*, 180). For more sympathetic critics, the sections function largely as a type of cosmic context abstractly conveying a sense that "within and behind this human underworld lies beauty and pattern" (Creary, "Prophet Armed," 53). Both viewpoints have their merits: the lyrical passages are not necessarily successful or consistent with the narrative action, and Mais is clearly gesturing toward a wider, more empathetic understanding of his characters' tragically imprisoning circumstances. However, in parallel with "Now We Know," these odd poetic interludes appear to be something more than nonnarrative excess or cosmic mood music. Indeed, they should be read as integral to the enactment of Mais's particular sense of aesthetic purpose.

A key element of the novel's lyrical passages is when they begin: shortly after the critical fish fry scene. This scene, as has been noted by numerous critics, appears to be the apogee of joy and togetherness in the novel, an almost miraculous moment of communal sustenance in a book otherwise strongly characterized by misery, oppression, and violence.[18] It is initiated by an event—the mysterious appearance of hundreds of fish washed up on the beach—that is itself colored by overtones of divine grace and charity. It begins when Ras, "prodigal with the sense of miracle that invested this phenomenon . . . decided he would take the rest of the fish up to the yard and everybody would have one hell of a feed" (39). Both the less ethereal phrasing at the end of this description and the narrator's careful scientific explanation of why the fish appeared (38), however, maintain the event's focus on the material plane: the true miracle occurs after everyone has eaten their fill and sits around joking, sleeping, and talking for a while.

At this redemptive moment, the novel portrays a dramatized, call-and-response version of a song Mais renders as "Ribber Ben Come Down," comprised of short descriptive passages punctuated by choral verse sections.[19] The effect of the scene's role play—the leader singing a verse and acting out a difficult journey across a river, the crowd clapping and singing and dancing in response—is a brief but deeply mutual happiness. Ras is depicted with "his bearded face split in a grin," just before Euphemia "stood up, smiling, and went across with Zephyr in time to join in with the responses" (50). At one point, Rema is seen to "let out a shriek of laughter" (51), and even Shag has "a little turned-in smile" (50), though he, notably, does not join in either the singing or the dancing. It is not just the occupants of the yard who react either: "Some people passing on the sidewalk stopped, hearing the singing, looked in through the broken fence, grinning to see the people inside merrying-up themselves, and some even clapped their hands too and joined in the responses" (49). The scene's emphasis on communal happiness is pronounced, and it is closely associated with rhythm: the steady alternation of description and chorus mimics the mutual exchange of the participants, who "clapped their hands and swayed their bodies in rhythm" (49), until they ultimately merge their actions with the leader, as they, "acting the spirit of the adventure, teetered with him in a dance movement, patterned, rhythmic, explicit" (50). This group harmony builds to a moving finale, at which time "they all laughed, and bright tears stood in the eyes of some, to witness that they still understood the meaning of miracles" (52). This shared secular miracle is a product of what the novel names, intriguingly, a "simulated *and* real excitement" (52, emphasis added): it represents the actual transfiguration (however brief) of a dismal reality by an act of creative cooperation and performance. Its importance in the novel is difficult to overemphasize, and it is this moment of grace—achieved via an ineffable combination of words, music, imaginative sympathy, and fellow feeling—that suggests the ambitious aims of the novel's subsequent lyrical passages: to enchant the reader into a similar state of attentive, sympathetic consciousness.

The title of the novel is taken from a passage of Psalm 98, which urges the world to sing a joyful song in praise of God. Critics have typically read this ironically, given the suffering that predominates the novel as well as the fact that Rema's madness manifests in delusions of the hills surrounding Kingston clapping and dancing (169) and, eventually, in a fear that they will trample her to death (207). However, this scene suggests an alternative reading, in which the clapping of hands and dancing here is the truly spiritual, joyful activity the title describes (in contrast to the arid, nonparticipatory worship led by the Sisters of Charity, via which the novel actually transcribes the song [272]). Certainly, the subsequent poetic passages, with their patterned repetitions and rich imagery, formally recall the almost mystical moment created in the yard by the performance of "Ribber Ben Come Down," as if longing to recapture a similar inspiriting effect. The first such passage, appearing soon after the fish fry, begins with the line "the sea is an old man babbling his dreams," which is repeated with minor alterations at the end of each of the three paragraphs. It also asks a series of questions, answered by succeeding lines, so that the question-and-answer form echoes the call-and-response pattern of the song, an association that some (but not all) of the subsequent passages also reinforce. This first episode of lyricism, moreover, evokes the spiritual sung at the fish fry, asking "who are they that passed along the weary beachheads and sang their songs before us" (63), suggesting the timeless, mythic nature of the yard's moment of inspired group performance. In all, the tonal progression of this and subsequent poetic passages—from dark trouble to glimpses of hope to clear-eyed wisdom—echoes that performance's general story of tribulation (temporarily) overcome through struggle, establishing a more teleological narrative parallel. Read this way, the apparently digressive lyrical passages of *The Hills Were Joyful Together* resonate importantly with the novel's key scene of joyous creativity, gesturing evocatively back to the transfiguring power of art that occurred there.

The general reference of the passages, while never explicit, seems to track the narrative development of Surjue, who ultimately emerges as the novel's main protagonist and largely sympathetic martyr. Although halting and uneven, Surjue's progression toward a kind of enlightenment is explicitly linked to the effects of both the redemptive spiritual at the fish fry and its subsequent echoes in the novel's own lyrical passages. The chapter immediately following the end of the fish fry celebration, apparently taking place later on the same night, marks some notable changes in Surjue.[20] Although the jauntiness he feels is hardly an alteration from his previous cocky persona, Surjue's first action is uncharacteristically generous. Approached by a small boy begging for money, he immediately puts his hand in his pocket, "and though he remembered with an inward wince that he was pretty nearly broke his hand came up with a flourish and he gave the boy sixpence" (56). Even the fact that Surjue is going out to discuss a business proposition (albeit an illegal one), rather than indolently sitting around the house with Flitters dreaming of making money by gambling, suggests a slight, if ambiguous change for the better in Surjue. Indeed, Mais juxtaposes Surjue's companions explicitly in the chapter, describing Surjue shaking off unpleasant thoughts of Flitters on his way to the meeting: "He was meeting Buju and Crawfish at a place in a lane off the street to discuss a business proposition, and it wasn't a matter of racing tips tonight. Racing tips made him think of Flitters, and he frowned" (56). At this point, an incipient moral awakening in Surjue is identified.

This change is explicitly marked at the end of the chapter as Surjue returns home and is startled by an onrush of desire for his wife, Rema. Although his desire is tinctured with animal lust and the suggestion of violence (generally reserved for negative characters in Mais's writing), this is modulated by Surjue's careful actions and self-examination: "he could have touched her by reaching out his hand, but he didn't; he sat there and thought for a while" (62). Compared to his earlier depiction as somebody so shallow as to be "tricked" by the sunlight on a teapot, "so that he winked back at it without knowing that he did" (26), his thoughtfulness here marks quite a shift, as he contemplates his own feelings of desire by listening intently "to the horned music singing inside him, and underneath it the beating of drums" (62). Significantly, Mais employs the figure of music to portray Surjue's newly awakened sensitivity, representing his character's transformation as attentiveness to a natural harmony and rhythm somehow related to his own thoughts and desires. Immediately after this scene, the first lyrical passage appears, suggesting the novel's own investment in musicality and rhythm. As these passages roughly track Surjue's burgeoning attunement to the world, they simultaneously ask the reader to develop a similar awareness.

The tone in the next few lyrical passages is unquestionably dark, evoking a sense of despair and misery; the corresponding events in Surjue's narrative comprise the least hopeful moments of his imprisonment after his arrest. The second lyrical passage, immediately after Bedosa's grisly death on the railroad tracks, is a stark assertion of the anonymizing inescapability of human mortality, closing with lines expressing an overwhelming fatalism: "death speaks with a thousand whispers, but a single voice" (132). The next such passage continues in similarly gloomy tones, opening with an intimation that "the dark shadows beyond our ken crowd in upon us and stand and wait unseen . . . they wait in silence and drink us up in darkness" (150), while going on to suggest that vaguely malevolent forces of destruction "are always in waiting somewhere against the wall" that encircles human endeavor (150). The imagery constructs a sense of dreary imprisonment, and the two lyrical episodes coincide with the first stages of Surjue's actual imprisonment, in which he is mercilessly beaten by the police and then, afflicted with dysentery, winds up in the grim, overcrowded prison hospital.[21] At this point, although there are hints of grace in his befriending the veteran prisoner Cubano, Surjue is simply bitter, swearing to get revenge on Flitters for betraying him to the police. The hopeless nature of Surjue's initial prison experience mirrors the poetic passages' evocations of grief, fear, and misery.

The next few lyrical interludes suggest a gradual lightening of mood and experience, accompanied by Surjue's slow advance toward self-understanding. If the lyrical passage beginning chapter 4 of book 2 evinces fatalism, it nevertheless moves away from the grim imagery of darkness and destruction of its predecessors. Instead of the unrelenting darkness of night, "the young moon in crescent comes to the gate under the duppy tree" (165), and there is some space "between the wall and the wall" (164) in which the wind blows and admits the possibility of intellectual interrogation: "within the ruin of walls we question the wind and it makes answer unto us" (165). Although answers are not easily forthcoming, there is still at least a suggestion of meaning—and even circumscribed enjoyment in and understanding of human limitations—within the passage. These ambiguous glimmers are echoed in Surjue's experience in prison, in which his seizing of a gun in a struggle with the overbearing and spiteful prison warder Nickoll leads to a nearly fatal standoff against the prison authority. As Mais makes plain, Surjue is redeemed from this situation first by taking sole responsibility for the situation—he wisely orders the other prisoners on the parade ground not to get involved—and then by his cautious extension of trust to the prison's superintendent. This latter gesture, wholly unthinkable to both prisoners and guards in the novel, courageously establishes a mutual respect that allows the incident to end without further violence. Mais emphasizes the calculated but risky nature of Surjue's decision to rely on the superintendent's word of honor by employing the language of gambling, as Surjue compares the negotiations to a card game: "I know what I've got, Super. An' I'm not throwin' it away. I'm playin' this hand meself, see?" (175). When he finally agrees to the proffered deal, Surjue observes, "I'm takin' a hell of a gamble on this" (176). The contrast with Surjue's earlier impulsive, underinformed gambling on horses is plainly made, and the fact that it is a contract of trust with another person is also a noteworthy difference: in this way Mais underscores Surjue's increasingly thoughtful attitude toward his own life and its relation to others.

Shortly after this scene, the next lyrical interlude reinforces the slight, hopeful shift in tone. Although again asserting a fatalist vision of human life and its inevitable suffering, the interlude's final thoughts indicate a value in humanity's involvement in the process of living. Describing a representative man, the passage gravely concludes: "his separate death matters nothing . . . it matters all, that he has turned his back upon life" (184). This assessment, while starkly observing the cosmic unimportance of individuals, also asserts the absolute importance of an active engagement with life. Surjue, by this time, has begun to do just that—to think actively about the world and his role in it. The scene immediately following the lyrical passage centers on an elderly prisoner who is scheduled to receive a flogging. Almost literally pissing himself with fear, the old man attempts to engage the sympathy of Surjue and a few fellow prisoners: "His eyes searched their faces for some sign—some least prop on which to pin his hope. But their faces were blank, and gave nothing; of pity, or anything, there was not the least shred" (185). Immediately after, however, their joking attempts to discuss the matter subside into embarrassed silence: "They curiously avoided each other's gaze, as though they were secretly ashamed about something" (186). Newly sensitized, Surjue chokes down his impatience and eventually helps the incontinent old man back to bed. Unable to sleep himself, Surjue reflects, for what seems like the first time, on the morality of punishment: "They treat prisoners worse'n animals, he thought. . . . Hell, you wouldn't do that to an old mule" (189). Then, in concert with the moonlight, the prison chaplain's words of empathetic humility enter his head—"All of us are guilty . . . equally guilty" (189)—and the chapter ends with Surjue's questioning thought: "Why were there people like him and Cubano and that stupid, blubbering, bladder-weary old man in the world" (190). Both the language and the philosophical disposition of the question resonate deeply with the lyrical passages that have preceded it, again linking the novel's poetic outpourings with Surjue's new, more contemplative disposition toward the world.

This link is solidified after the next lyrical passage, which, in terms of imagery, is the book's most hopeful and optimistic. Rife with positive images of young love, laughter, and the sense that "things turn back to their beginnings again" (200), the passage ends by asserting the possibility of human redemption: "Somewhere in the world something to redeem them . . . resolve their doubts, blot out their deeds . . . resides something . . . like love trembles on a young girl's lips, unspoken . . . waits laughter to lighten, now, and right them . . . redeem them, resolve them . . . redress them . . . somewhere in the world" (201, original ellipses). The insistent optimism evoked in these words can be connected to numerous adjacent episodes in the novel (Surjue's hopes for a parole to see Rema, Wilfie's sympathy for Manny, Manny's newfound tenderness, the gentle generosity of Mass Mose' toward Rema), but the interlude is closely followed by a remarkable moment in the text—the full integration of the novel's lyricism with a depiction of Surjue's thoughts. In this instance, rather than beginning the chapter, the poetic passage comes after a short description of Surjue feeling ill and heading off for some water. The style and imagery of the three-paragraph outpouring are unmistakably similar to the other poetic interludes, beginning, "Walls, walls, and all that passed between them . . . a man un-manned, un-countenanced, given over to the naked stare of self pity . . . society, and the cankering, unyielding sore" (208). Yet the end of this meditative reverie is signaled by another description of Surjue, as he washes his mouth out with water, clearly signaling that it is his, not the narrator's, thoughts being recorded. The straightforward narration continues briefly, delineating Surjue's memory of a murder in the prison, and it is followed by another, shorter poetic vision of "the teeming thousands of lost men who had been processed between these walls" (210). Narrated in the same elliptical, image-laden prose, this passage is even more clearly marked as Surjue's inner vision, confirming that his own thought process has now taken on the characteristics of the novel's poetic lyricism. Although his terrifying vision of the degradation of prison contrasts sharply with the most recent lyrical passage—the lesson of Surjue's vision occurs when "a voice whispered in his ear, '*They make animals without hope of the men who pass through here*'" (211)—the formal characteristics Mais employs to depict it suggest the completion of Surjue's initiation into social and historical consciousness. He recognizes himself among "the generations of lost men that were brought here damned to insensible negation out of sight of the world" (209), and the passage emphasizes that he is, finally, able truly to see where he is and what his situation means. Bringing this point baldly home, Mais marks the end of Surjue's illuminating reverie with the phrase, "Suddenly his eyes went wide" (211).[22] Although the *content* of Surjue's poetic vision is about the relentless dehumanization of prison life, the *fact* that he is having it suggests the full humanization of Surjue himself: Mais intimates that Surjue's newfound sensitivity to the nature of his surroundings allows him a clear new vision of the world and his place in it.

This vision, of course, is hardly an aesthetically or ethically pleasing one—indeed, the graphic degradation and violence of prison life are if anything increased from this point of the novel forward. However, it is in Surjue's newly gained awareness—the product, Mais indicates, of a kind of aesthetic awakening—that the novel's hope seems to lie. Surjue, no longer a callow, boastful, happy-go-lucky youth content to try his luck, has gone through a (resolutely nonreligious) spiritual transformation, allowing him to emerge as the novel's hero. Through his transformation, Surjue has gained understanding of what is truly of value to him—his relationship with Rema—and it is this understanding that redemptively structures the rest of Surjue's actions in the novel. Although ultimately seen to be of little individual use, the assiduous, clear-eyed, and thoughtful resolve that Surjue discovers in prison is affirmed by the novel as the only meaningful human response to the overwhelming destructive power of the Jamaican social system (and the blunt impassivity of the universe).

To this end, Mais goes out of his way to parallel Surjue's two most concrete misfortunes: Surjue's imprisonment results from his being abandoned on the roof by his burglary partner, Flitters, while his death likewise occurs after a climb, as Surjue is shot just as he reaches the top of the prison wall. The contrast, however, is more salient. Surjue's partnership with Flitters is based largely on bravado and ignorance—Surjue ignores Rema's warnings about his partner and blunders blindly into his unfortunate imprisonment. In contrast, Surjue has recently witnessed the brutal punishment meted out to prisoners intent on escaping, and his partner in the escape, Cubano, has proven himself a wise, reliable, and diligent friend. The plans of the escape, too, are carefully laid over a long period of time, and they are the product of purposeful thought. As the escape begins, Surjue notices his own flustered agitation: "He realized it was the excitement before the race. Like a horse jumping off before the flying of the tape. He felt better. Cubano was all right. He was betting on Cubano. He had to" (269). This bet (similar to the one Surjue makes earlier on the superintendent's promise of fairness) is a considered one, unlike the unreasoning nature of Surjue's earlier relation to horseracing. Similarly, Surjue here relates himself to a horse about to race—as a participant in the actual race, rather than a casual observer hoping to get lucky. This distinction is suggestive: Surjue's ill-fated escape attempt can only be dignified, in contrast with his ill-fated burglary attempt, because he is participating fully and knowingly in the action, aware of his choices, the nature of his partner, and the long odds against him. Thus, a very subtle difference—the sensitive awareness that has been summoned in him over the course of the novel—is seen to transform Surjue from farcical clown to martyred hero.

These moments of attentiveness and awareness in Surjue (which find parallels in other residents of the yard, including Zephyr, Lennie, Wilfie, Rema, Mas Mose', and Ras) seem decisive to the novel, and they embody the definition of true thinking Mais provides in *Form and Substance in Fiction:* "a man in his wholeness wholly attending" (34) (a line that originally comes from a Lawrence poem, "Thought"). Mais's high valuation of this holistic Lawrentian thinking helps explain why the remaining lyrical passages appear to convey some optimism and wisdom despite the multiple deaths alongside which they appear. The poetic musing in Jamaican creole, in particular, with its calm, airy confidence that one will "see de livin' clouds o' witness standin' in de sky" (253), is hard to read as even remotely nihilistic, while the final lyrical evocation of an old fisherman sitting by the sea "content, scratching himself, untroubled by any dreams" (262), suggests an amplitude of earthy wisdom gained through experience (the itching is the product of a "shark-tooth scar") and focuses not on darkness but on the light cast by a rising moon. The palm trees, too, evoke some sort of liberation, as they "lean over the water's edge beyond the wall" (262). The positive tenor of the final lyrical passages, even as Surjue, Rema, Shag, and Euphemia meet their doom, suggests that the awakening of Surjue's responsiveness—crystallized when his thinking takes on the lyrical attributes of those passages—is the slight gleam of redemption that can be extracted from the novel's overwhelming carnage. Mais asserts in *Form and Substance in Fiction* that literature should be judged by its effect on readers: it is successful only when it is "calling forth into responsiveness those same attributes of observation, sympathy, and imagination" that an author employs in writing (22). In *The Hills Were Joyful Together,* Surjue serves as the model of just such a successful summoning into responsiveness, and the novel's form urges its readers toward a similar transfiguration. Gesturing back to the artistic miracle wrought in the fish fry scene, the novel's lyricism plies its readers to follow Surjue and awaken their own sympathy and sensitivity in protest at the indignities visited upon their fellow creatures, both fictional and actual.

While there is room to doubt how successful the novel is in finally meeting this ambition, the book provides enough evidence to suggest that Mais is certainly aiming to achieve what the *Spectator* reviewer identifies as an "emotional force" (Charques, review). Various later commentators identify a similarly affective aim in the novel, such as Singh, who enthuses that "very few West Indian novels can equal *The Hills Were Joyful Together* in emotional appeal" ("*Hills Were Joyful Together,*" 119).[23] Emotionally charged words, certainly, are at the center of the novel's project, and it reveals little patience for words that lack this elusive, oracular quality. The prison chaplain, for example, brandishes a copy of *The Universal Declaration of Human Rights* in his argument with the superintendent. Although clearly in agreement with the sentiments it expresses—he approvingly reads part of Article 22—he is disappointed in its worldly ineffectiveness, bemoaning that "already it has come to mean nothing to us but more words in a book" (238). The aesthetic stance conveyed in *The Hills Were Joyful Together* requires words, somehow, to go beyond simply existing dully in a book, and its own efforts at lyricism suggest an attempt to employ words in exactly such a mysterious way, activating emotions in the reader in order to reenchant a lost, disenchanted world. In this way, the formal experimentation of Mais's first novel embodies an aesthetic philosophy (quite Lawrentian in nature) that functions, at its base, as broad sociopolitical critique.

More Than Words Can Say

In a 1952 article for *Public Opinion,* Mais professes a strong belief in an intangible quality in art, something that arises from, but cannot be identified in, the material elements employed. The article, "The Critics Criticised II," is a defense of the Jamaican painter Albert Huie, laying out the reasons Mais thinks the painter's critics are mistaken. Ultimately faulting Huie's critics for failing to appreciate the works on their own terms, Mais summons the words of Ralph Waldo Emerson as his final defense: "Criticism is an art when it does not stop at the words of the poet but looks at the order of his thoughts and the essential quality of his mind . . . 'Tis a question not of talents but of tone; and not particular merits, but the mood of mind into which one and another can bring us." The assertion Mais adopts from Emerson presents problems of analysis, to be sure, in its reliance on a vague, general terminology of tone and mood. However, its emphasis on the affective force of art is typical of Mais's aesthetic views, foretelling some of the difficulties he will be obliged to address in his later novels. For a writer, certainly, the inarticulability Mais sees at the core of successful art poses something of a problem: "mere" words are not enough, though it is only through words that the novelist works. John Hearne's personal memoir of Mais reflects something of this difficulty, proposing that in Mais's case it was in fact painting that "came to almost dominate his life," since it "seemed to fulfil so many of the demands he made of art" ("Roger Mais," 148). F. E. F. Fraser, also a contemporary of Mais, goes even further, advancing his view that Mais's "books are not novels at all—merely sheets of paper pinch-hitting for lengths of canvas." Despite the exaggeration, Fraser's characterization contains a grain of truth about the uncertainty Mais's novels reveal about the reliability of their very medium— language. If *The Hills Were Joyful Together* depends on a (potentially facile) faith in the emotional power of words, Mais's subsequent novels uneasily confront the tensions inherent in an aesthetic that seeks communal salvation in the achievements of an artist acting as a high priest evoking an affective response.

Some of Mais's early stories surely express a suspicion of language. A prominent example is the title story from *Face, and Other Stories,* the climax of which incorporates an insistence that the face the little girl makes after getting off the bus is more eloquent than words, a perfect encapsulation of the unspoken feelings of everyone on the bus.[24] *The Hills Were Joyful Together* betrays a different, more ominous uneasiness about the power of words through the character of Shag. Cuckolded by Euphemia, Shag eventually goes mad and returns to murder her late in the novel. His lack of sanity manifests itself in his thoughts, characterized by Mais as a sinister, self-deluded poetic fluency: "Words flowed and took forms and made into images in his mind . . . and in his hands he held the tokens of them and he sent them forth and they did his bidding and returned like doves to his hand. . . . the words themselves were a shibboleth, and were without meaning other than that which he endowed them with, so that they became the most beautiful, whole, perfect, sheer, excellent words in the world, like the secret names of God" (113). Very little distinguishes Shag's verbal madness from the lyrical flights in the novel discussed above, except perhaps for his focus on personal control and secrecy. At one point he thinks: "some people didn't understand about words. They did not know the meaning that went with the sound. The meaning of the sound of a word like *vulnerable* was like a great anaconda snake coiled around the base of a woman-tree" (180). Although this reverie, in light of the novel's advocacy of aesthetic sensitivity, could be seen as a moment of redemptive verbal creativity, Mais makes clear that Shag's poetic inclinations are horribly flawed. In his final murderous confrontation with Euphemia, Shag continues in a similar vein, fixating on the word "vulnerable" and speaking incomprehensibly to Euphemia about her resemblance to a tree. With this final scene Mais confirms the danger of Shag's way with words—their terrible solipsism. With all its ingenuity and imagistic leaps of thought, without the modulating injunction that it be communally comprehensible, Shag's verbal dexterity descends to idiolect, the ravings of a mad, murderous man. Mais's later writing continues to explore these linguistic difficulties, caught between a fervent desire to capture truth in language and an anxiety that language's emotive power might actually impede the separation of truth from self-serving falsehood.

The choruses of *Brother Man,* in their distinction from the lyrical passages of *The Hills Were Joyful Together,* reveal Mais's concern to ensure the communal intelligibility of poetic language. Specifically labeled as "Chorus of People in the Lane," these sections appear in a much more ordered regularity

—at the beginning of each of the book's five large divisions. While there is clearly a narrative consciousness at work in their descriptive parts, a substantial portion of each chorus is also made up of snippets of conversation of the people living in Brother Man's neighborhood, emphasizing the chorus as a mutual creation. In the book's first chorus the narrator asserts that "all, all are involved in the same chapter of consequences, all are caught up between the covers of the same book of living" (8), underscoring an insistence on (literary) meaning as a shared phenomenon. Although the language of ensnarement can be read as somewhat fatalistic, the notion of consequences moderates this with a suggestion of human agency. The end of the chorus reinforces this latter sense, asserting that the people's tongues "carry their burden of the tale of man's woes" but that in fact "it is their own story over that they tell" (9), implying, despite the graphic parallel of dogs "licking their own ancient scrofulous sores" (9), that the community is ultimately responsible for its own narration. Instead of the haphazard, occasional lyrical outpourings of an unseen and unknowable narrator, the chorus sections of *Brother Man* strive to discipline themselves into predictably periodic, communal communication.

The counterexample of ideal language use in the novel is Papacita, the book's least disciplined, most self-centered character. His smoothly manipulative rhetorical bonhomie is made plain as the narrative opens, when he is attempting to soothe his girlfriend Girlie's anger after he has stayed out all night. The softly coercive style of his blandishments is emphasized in this scene, describing how Papacita encourages Girlie to join him on the bed "softly, throwing the words at her as he might a cushion or one of those big soft indiarubber balls" (11). Momentarily put out by Girlie's resistance a bit later, Papacita's face reveals a trace of frustration, but "then he came all contrite, all treacle and melting butter again" (12). Continuing on his campaign, Papacita again urges Girlie to sit on the bed "in a tone that was like warm butterscotch" (17). The scene's figuration of Papacita's self-serving relationship to Girlie—"like a cat watching a mouse" (22)—makes it clear that his slick rhetorical suasion is functioning as a decorative distraction from his underlying ill intentions. Indeed, when the relation of physical and emotional power is reversed at the end of the novel, as Girlie murders her former lover for his betrayal, the characters' rhetorical characteristics are also reversed. Just before she brutally stabs him to death, Girlie confronts Papacita with similarly deceptive panache, "looking at him sloe-eyed" (187) and speaking "in that soft, silky voice" (188), revealing the terrible menace the novel identifies at the core of its characters' sweet speechmaking.

Another of Papacita's most pronounced traits—his love of riddles—also reveals *Brother Man*'s anxieties about the potential misuses of language. Papacita is depicted telling riddles on three different occasions, and the novel expresses a marked uneasiness with their effects. In the first riddle scene, he challenges Girlie with a riddle, the answer to which—"nothin'" (77)—itself suggests the emptiness of Papacita's facility for verbal cleverness. Mais emphasizes the alienating effect the riddle has on Girlie, describing how she "laughed with him in spite of herself" (77). Papacita's next riddle, told in a club for the benefit of Minette, whom he is trying to seduce away from Brother Man, reinforces the unpleasant exclusivity that motivates Papacita's riddling proclivities. The answer to this riddle, "Jonah in de belly of de whale" (93), is a clear figure of separation from society, and the narrator notes how, in telling the answer, Papacita "laughed more than anyone; he always managed to get the best of his jokes, both ways" (93). Evoking both double dealing and double talk, the characterization of his opportunistic cleverness continues the suggestion that for Papacita, riddles are an aggressive way of asserting verbal and social mastery. The third and final riddle Papacita tells, to his partner in a counterfeit money scheme, likewise displays the antisocial tendencies at work in the practice, while also suggesting, via its answer of "needle an' thread, sewin' cloth" (148), the way Papacita employs riddles to cover over his own social inadequacies. In this instance, after telling the answer, Papacita laughs loudly but then "stopped laughing suddenly [and] seemed to take notice for the first time he alone was enjoying the joke" (148). Although it hints at the emergence of some self-awareness on Papacita's part, the passage is most concerned with reconfirming the self-serving nature of Papacita's enjoyment of riddles. Instead of being used for enlightenment or even simply a socially binding light humor, the opacity of language characteristic of riddles is, in Papacita's hands, seen as a mechanism for asserting his own private, superior understanding.

Mais holds Brother Man up as an obvious contrast to Papacita, yet the novel's eponymous hero maintains a remarkably similar relationship to language as its antihero. Most strikingly, Brother Man's words are curiously dependent on tone and gesture to guarantee their efficacy, a trait that Mais's book emphasizes in its holy Rastafarian protagonist from the outset.[25] The first description of Brother Man, after a fleeting glance at his unremarkable "medium height, medium build" (22) and his long hair and beard, devotes itself not to his eyes, but to his gaze itself: "he had a far-away, searching look, as though the intensity of his being came to focus in his eyes. Many looked away and

were embarrassed before the quiet intensity of that gaze" (22). The indirect-
ness of this examination—relying on vague simile and the general reported
reaction of others—is conspicuous, as the book struggles to articulate the precise nature of how its hero (transitively, rather than intransitively) looks. The
book struggles, too, to convey the precise nature of its hero's words. Just after
Brother Man's first spoken words in the novel—a response to Minette's question about the nature of love—the narrator starkly admits to an inability to do
justice to their affective and semantic significance. Brother Man's speech contains something ineffably related, yet crucial, to its sense: "somehow the words
didn't sound banal, coming from him. He spoke with such simple directness
that it seemed to give a new import to everything he said. It was as though
the common words of everyday usage meant something more, coming from
his lips, than they did in the casual giving and taking of change in conversation, the way it was with other folks" (23–24). The anxious imprecision of this
description, rather surprisingly, calls attention to the novel's own descriptive
incapacity, simultaneously locating an enigmatic fluency, beyond the reach of
words, in its protagonist.

The extra-linguistic qualities of Brother Man's rhetorical persuasion are
consistently raised by the novel as it portrays his attempts to instill righteous-
ness in his neighbors. In an early conversation with Minette, whom Brother
Man has selflessly saved from a life of prostitution, simply the tone of his voice
is instrumental in defusing the fraught question she implicitly raises: "she
felt the gentle rebuke of his words, the subtle rebuke in the very gentleness of
his tone, and was suddenly abashed" (40). A bit later it is Brother Man's earnest gaze that makes Minette feel guilty for flirting with Papacita in the street:
"His gaze gave nothing away; all the same she had a funny sort of feeling way
down. She wondered if he had seen anything through the window" (63). This
power is not simply a product of the couple's increasingly intimate relations,
either (though that, too, takes the form of silent communication, "something
that went without words" [137]), as revealed by Brother Man's ministrations
to other members of the community. Mais suggests that Cordy's fever begins
to dissipate when Brother Man tells her he is praying for her, "and there was
that good wholesome smile on his face, and deep conviction in his voice" (65).
When Cordy brings her sick child, Tad, to Brother Man for help, his physical
movements actually call forth a voice in her head: "She saw him lift [Tad] up
in his hands off the bed, and put aside the clothes she had wrapped him in.
And something moved inside her—yes, moved. And it was as though a voice

was saying to her, 'Woman, be not afraid.'"(65). The identification of "something" that moves inside her is noticeably vague, defying description, while the power of Brother Man's presence interestingly circles back to the figure of a voice speaking, again indicating the anxiety over words and truth that permeates the novel. Elsewhere in the novel, Jesmina is reassured in her fear by the tone of Brother Man's voice: "There was a gentle, soothing quality about his voice that stilled her" (127). Earlier, in fact, frustrated with her sister, Jesmina has summoned his kindly intonations herself, and she is described "as though she could hear Bra' Man's voice, calm and soothing, telling her to be more patient" (95). With this emphasis on gesture and tone, Mais suggests that it is as much in the delivery of his message as in the contents of the message itself that Brother Man's evangelizing is effective.

The implicit parallel between the rhetorical aptitude of Brother Man and that of Papacita reveals the novel's apparent anxiety about the controllability of communication. Mais does make some distinction between these two figures: if Papacita's riddles reinforce an alienated individuality and self-interest, Brother Man's parables are seen to aim at the maintenance of social cohesion. Mais dramatizes the use of parables only once in the novel, describing in detail how Brother Man settles a dispute between a man and his sweetheart, who has given birth to someone else's child while he was away in prison. In making his explicitly Solomon-like decision, Brother Man tells the man to bring three paving stones and stack them one on top of the other. After asking the man— twice, for dramatic emphasis and confirmation—whether he could remove the middle stone without disturbing the others, Brother Man renders his judgment that the man must care for the illegitimate child, if he wishes to stay with his sweetheart. As he explains: "these stones are as yourself and the woman and the child. You on top, the child in the middle, the woman at the bottom" (122–23). This judgment, unlike Papacita's riddles, is grasped immediately by everyone, and the gathered crowd's reaction is revealingly full of good cheer and fellowship: "they laughed richly, and clapped the man who thought he had been wronged on the back, and made loud talk, and laughed, and the man himself started laughing" (123). The repetition of so much laughing, in contrast to the solitary levity of Papacita, conveys Mais's commendation of Brother Man's socially valuable communication. The evaluative distinction between Brother Man's message of selflessness and Papacita's philosophy that "every man had to scuffle for himself" (43) is thus plainly established. However, their creative, implicitly literary method of communication remains similar, and the novel elsewhere suggests that the crowd's almost magical comprehension of Brother Man's allegorical explanation in this scene cannot easily be counted on to repeat itself.

Indeed, linguistic circulation and reception within *Brother Man* are both unpredictable and mysterious, and the narrative trajectory of the novel ultimately suggests a rather bleak forecast for the possibility of communally gratifying, socially productive communication (and thus casts doubt on the viability of its own function as a novel). The progression of the five choruses in the book charts the narrative's teleology of a crestfallen reining-in of hope. The language of the choral sections—seemingly because, rather than in spite, of its communal makeup—emerges as a capricious, disruptive force. The novel's (which is also the chorus's) first sentence evokes the unpleasant din of people's talk: "The tongues in the lane clack-clack almost continuously, going up and down the full scale of human emotions" (7). The onomatopoeic "clack-clack" does not convey approval and is soon related to socially malignant gossip: "slander lurks in ambush to take the weakest and the hindmost, and the tongues clack upon every chance" (8). By the second chorus, the verbal assault has lessened, with the talk taking on the milder form of "casual gossip" (60), while in the succeeding one "people lapse into even more relaxed postures" (106). Their talk seems to parallel their posture: "The intermittent patter of conversation, soliloquy, small-talk, carries on, desultory, rich with raillery, repartee, sometimes—sometimes humourless, turgid, dry" (106). The ambivalent nature of this conversation prevails, but it has receded into a much less insistent, more humane register, and the third chorus ends with the whole lane singing a hymn inspired by Brother Man's rise to holy stature.[26] By the fourth chorus, "there is a feeling of excitement in the air" and more singing of hymns. The people "speak about different things, and after a bit the speech turns upon the ordinary topics of gossip, but the voices are a little less sharp, there is less of that vicious underlining both in tone and content" (138). The language here registers the solid sense of optimism and hope at the beginning of this chapter, and the chorus ends once again with song: "Somebody starts the tune. They lift their voices, all, and sing" (140). In the final chorus, however, after Brother Man's unjust arrest, things take an ominous turn, and the people in the lane "are unquiet, somewhat ill at ease" (172). Their talk reflects their return to uncertainty and suspicion: "They fall into the usual conversational postures, but shift them continually. They speak as though they are afraid their tongues might trip them, and their words discover them in a fault" (172).

In marking the rise and undeserved fall of Brother Man in the lane's esteem, the choruses reveal that the success of Brother Man's rhetoric of hope is exceedingly fragile—quickly and fatally vulnerable to the gossipy whims and self-reinforcing chatter of his neighbors in the lane.

The dangerously contingent efficacy of rhetoric is emphasized in the book's brutal climax as well, when a crowd of people mercilessly beats Brother Man. Following a vicious crime by an anonymous bearded man, the people of Kingston become enflamed by media sensationalism, as the "leading newspapers played up the angle that a community of bearded men in their midst, formed together into a secret cult, was a menace to public safety" (173). This misleading "angle," as Mais disapprovingly makes clear, manipulates people into an anger that "was carefully fanned to a nice conflagration" (174). It is an unreasoning anger in which the novel's innocent hero is caught up. In the description of the mob's violent assault, loudly emotional language easily overcomes Brother Man's quiet attempts to reason with the crowd. As the "clamour and shouting behind grew louder, coarser, shriller," Brother Man attempts to speak, "but his voice was drowned in the shrieks and curses of the mob" (185).[27] These scenes mark the brutally enforced end of Brother Man's time as hero to the people, betraying a sharp fear of the ability of popular discourse to inspire extreme emotion and brutality.

Nevertheless, Mais's second novel still maintains some of the belief in the transformative power of aesthetically rendered words so prevalent in *The Hills Were Joyful Together*. This belief is particularly exemplified in Minette's ecstatic reading of the Bible. This relatively early scene in the novel underscores how her reading about David is positively enchanting: "the unfolding of the story enthralled her" (47), such that she does not notice the passing of time. Minette's enthrallment is related to the intense empathetic feelings she develops from the story: "she became absorbed in the tale, so that she could not have put down the book if she wanted to. For these people, and their lusts and their hates, had become very real to her. They were just as real as the people who lived in the lane" (46). This response—a transcending of the everyday that paradoxically leads back to the everyday—is a plainly redemptive aesthetic moment in the novel and hearkens back to Surjue's transformation in Mais's first novel. Similarly, Minette's magical response to Brother Man's given name, which she discovers written on the flyleaf of his Bible, also suggests Mais's continued investment in the possibilities of linguistic enchantment. Repeating his first name, John, to herself later, "a pleasant warm sensation went clear through her, as though the single syllable set up a mysterious vibration in her being" (147). Elsewhere, however, Minette's responses to language take on more ominous overtones, such as when Brother Man reads the Bible at her bedside: "His voice intoned the lines, deep and sonorous, so that when he stopped reading, she said automatically after him, 'Praise the Lord'" (99). Minette's response expresses both piety and unthinking habit. This latter characteristic is expressly denounced in almost all of Mais's writing, and its appearance (in Brother Man's preeminent "convert," no less) lays bare the crux of the novel's difficulty: how to judge and control the effects inspired by affective language.[28]

Brother Man does not offer a particularly confident answer to this problem. Its title character's (and by implication the novel's) message is ultimately ignored and drowned out by the vast majority of its intended audience, while Brother Man is left with only a few "disciples" (Minette, Jesmina, and Nathaniel), the most important of whom is the woman who shares his bed. Brathwaite suggests that Brother Man's social downfall can be traced to his own failure to subordinate his message to the "collective sound." He explains: "Mais's choruses have this communal function and when Brother Man, subtly tempted by pride of individuation (pp. 174–5) loses beat with this, the chorus becomes «tuneless» (p. 183) and he is struck down by the multitude/ensemble" (*Roots,* 186–87).[29] What Brathwaite sees as pride of individuation, however, seems hard to square with the scene he cites. This scene, in which Brother Man meditates on his abandonment by the people, primarily emphasizes his sorrow that "his service to his people would be at an end" (174). Moreover, the novel's depiction of the multitude—rife with animal imagery, bloodlust, and relish for scatological debasement—is difficult to hold up as a worthy object of adulation. Indeed, the novel goes out of its way to emphasize people's dangerous susceptibility to rhetoric, whether in the form of enflaming journalistic accounts, the mercenary obeahman Bra' Ambo's scare tactics, or the accusatory exhortations to violence by the mob itself; even Brother Man's initial (and ultimately unstable) acclaim is in part based on the spread of rumors about his meeting with the ghost of Old Mag in the street. Contrary to Brathwaite's claim, it is the fact that the people themselves finally refuse to listen to Brother Man's message of peace and love that appears to form the core of the novel's tragic events. In the scene of "proud individuation" to which Brathwaite points, Brother Man delineates the failure of his life's mission: "He had tried to bring a ray of hope into their lives, to make each man aware, somewhere, somehow, of his own innate dignity as a man" (174). Intriguingly, these words echo the prologue of *And Most of All Man,* in which the goal of the work is suggested to be precisely this: teaching humans to understand their own dignity and divinity.[30] This, in turn, offers Brother Man as a stand-in for Mais the author (and Brother Man, of course, does become a writer, composing a personal testament), an author who has been unable to convey his message successfully to more than a very few, especially receptive people.

The novel itself does not seem able, finally, to articulate in words its own concluding, hopeful gesture toward the future. The book ends in a noticeably private, enigmatic moment, as Minette helps the injured Brother Man to the window, where "he saw all things that lay before him in a vision of certitude, and he was alone no longer" (191). He then asks Minette, "You see it, out there, too?" She looks "up above the rooftops where that great light glowed across the sky" and answers, "Yes, John, I have seen it" (191), and proceeds to lead him away from the window. Some readings of this denouement readily come to mind—especially the sense that Minette has now been "converted" into a spiritual prophet herself, in close partnership with Brother Man—but the "certitude" of Brother Man's vision, referred to only in the inexact pronominal "it," is markedly enigmatic. Indeed, possible readings, promoted by the ambiguity surrounding "that great light" at which the characters are actually looking, proliferate, ranging from naturalistic beauty to religious illumination. Brother Man's certitude, as the novel ends, is communicable only to his closest companion, relegating all others, including the novel's audience, to a complementary lack of certitude. In his dissatisfied reading of the ending, Ramchand observes that the "only certitude here, however, is that Bra' Man and Minette love each other" (*West Indian Novel,* 185). However hopeful and suggestive the novel's ending wishes to be, its diminishment to an ambiguous connotative status (in a peculiarly intimate moment) reveals a profound shift from the linguistic exuberance of *The Hills Were Joyful Together.* Much chastened, *Brother Man* casts grave doubt on the efficacy of its own verbal medium, almost literally gesturing to a more plentitudinous meaning beyond the reach of mere language.

An Uncertain Illumination

Black Lightning, Mais's third and final published novel, carries this suspicion of language (and art more generally) yet further, casting doubt on the direct social value of any artistic pursuit and locating true communication in a material, mundane realm that is not contained within the boundaries of human language. The book announces its views most eloquently in its choice of form, eschewing the lyric flights of its predecessors for a stark, laconic style and emphatically relying on simple dialogue and action. Ramchand's review, "Black Lightning," emphasizes the tightly controlled dramatic nature of the novel: "The narrative persuasion of the omniscient author is drastically reduced. Everything depends upon speech and actions.... There is skilful use of off-stage sounds, the wind, the sound of an axe, a woman yoo-hooing in the distance. The characters make entries and exits like the characters in a play." Read alongside of *The Hills Were Joyful Together* and *Brother Man*, Mais's third novel is remarkable for its pared-down language and the straightforward transcription of its narrative events, suggesting a desire to communicate as immediately as possible, in the most simple language and imagery. This tendency is identified by D'Costa in her introduction to the novel, which she sees as having "something of the frozen energy of pictorial art which conveys emotion directly; it strives to appeal to us in ways beyond the reach of words" (7–8). Ramchand, too, remarks the book's paradoxical relation to language, in which "it becomes apparent that abundant dialogue testifies to an articulate inarticulateness. The failure of words is the triumph of intense feeling" ("Black Lightning"). The oddly self-canceling message of *Black Lightning*—implicit in the title itself—emerges as the culmination of Mais's self-reflexive meditation on the strict limits of literary language.

The novel's examination of aesthetic production centers on the protagonist Jake's carving of a Samson sculpture, and the sculpture's creation and subsequent utility thus reflect Mais's notions of literature, as well as artistic practice more broadly. Significantly, Jake's secretive woodworking is catalyzed by what he feels as a lack in the communicative ability of language. In an interesting reversal of Minette's captivating and redemptive relationship to the Bible in *Brother Man*, Jake finds the biblical account of Samson and Delilah too simple to relate to as a realistic human story. Having read the story many times and meditated on its possible meanings, Jake finds himself wondering about Samson and "what must have gone on under the surface between himself and Delilah. Things that the Bible never mentioned at all. Things other than, and more complex, and in a way more disturbing than what was discovered in the bald account" (60). Explicitly addressing the perceived failings of the biblical tale's rendering, Jake's sculpture is his attempt to convey the story's hidden significance, "what must have secretly lain underneath, and had gone before, that the Bible never gave any clue of at all" (60). The painful irony of Jake's effort at clarification is revealed in the dramatic scene when Jake shows the sculpture to Amos, his hunchbacked counterpart and fellow social outsider. Their discussion of the statue, marked by Amos's befuddlement and Jake's repeated failure to apprehend the words of Amos, discloses a deep pessimism regarding art's ability to impart meaning. Jake's attempt to render the biblical Samson more expressively is a resolute failure, as, despite his attempts to assert its meaning as the embodiment of all human suffering, the final meaning of *that* representation is unsatisfactorily absent. Mais figures this interpretive lacuna in Samson's pointing finger, which Jake, in frustration, cannot account for: "But to what end, Amos? Where does the finger point? Down what blind road . . . through what blank wall . . . to what?" (110). The inexpressive locations Jake names emphasize his dawning recognition that the statue's meaning remains infinitely nebulous, and he is forced to acknowledge the sculpture's failure to elicit any ultimate significance: "And it will not come. Something else, but not that" (110). Amos, as well, is unable to account for this absence of meaning, as his stammered response reveals—"I—I can't figure it out either, Jake" (110)—and he reinforces this overwhelming sense of semantic disconnect as the scene comes to a close. Acknowledging Jake's vague feeling that the statue is no longer of Samson, Amos again reaches an interpretive impasse and bluntly rejects Jake's hope that he can name what Jake's statue now represents, saying, "No. I can't, either" (112). This scene's damning depiction of artistic stillbirth is then brought home with mythic force by Mais: just after Amos fearfully flees the attic workshop, Jake is struck by lightning and blinded. Jake thereby takes on the role of the failed, hubristic artist symbolically disciplined by the heavens. It is on this scene that the narrative turns—the chiasmatic structure of Jake's fall and Amos's rise becomes visible from this moment— dramatically marking the novel's distrust in the potential for the coherent, collective comprehension of its emblematic object of art.

As in *Brother Man*, the nervousness about aesthetic production in *Black Lightning* hinges on the way art functions in social space. After his blinding, Jake expresses his fears of art's troublingly willful autonomy, describing how "at last it takes its own end into its own hands, in a manner of speaking, and becomes what *it* wants to be, declaring its own form and meaning" (122). The analogy Jake then proffers between the contingencies of art's meaning and human free will suggests the novel's view of the unruly and unpredictable role that art plays once it has gone into the world. Indeed, throughout the novel, nearly all the valuable scenes involving aesthetic production occur in private, the work's beneficent effects limited to its own practitioners. Amos, an accordion player, is moved to self-realization through his own music several times, but always alone in the forest. The most significant such scene, in which Amos at last recognizes his own value as a friend to Jake and others, occurs in pointed solitude, just after he has met with Bess and Miriam:

> When they were out of sight he took his accordion in his hands and started to play.
> He played softly, to himself, a tune that came out of his head. (151)

The emphasis on the privacy of his artistic communion is unmistakable.[31] When Amos plays for Jake near the end of the novel, Amos attempts to play "something to lift that cloud of despondency that had settled upon Jake" (191). The novel describes how Amos creates the song—"it went with his thoughts as they thronged through his mind" (191)—and details their optimistic insistence that "the storm is past, and all is smiling in the world again" (191). However, the novel again suggests that this is a purely private communication: the chapter concludes with the elliptical petering out of Amos's musically expressed thoughts, never registering any response on Jake's part. Jake's suicide shortly thereafter makes clear that Amos's performance, however privately expressive, failed to connect with its intended audience.

Brathwaite has faulted *Black Lightning* for "moving towards individuation and away from the folk/urban expression of his first two published novels" (*Roots*, 187), yet the novel's critique of art takes aim specifically at the unproductive individuality of high aesthetic production. Jake, the artist figure who proclaims his Samson sculpture "All mine!" (83) in a moment of deranged bliss, is in fact overtly criticized in the novel for his insistence on self-sufficiency and total control of his surroundings. Thus, far from supporting individuality at the expense of community, *Black Lightning* reproves art precisely because of its lack of reliable connection to the people. Discussing the novel's main characters, Jake and Amos, Mais notes the general thrust of the narrative: "It is the story of a strong man's struggle to find self-sufficiency, and how he failed in the least of things and lost all; and of another who grew from weakness to strength, because he found the one thing that the other lacked" (quoted in Carr, "Roger Mais," 25). The strength that Amos discovers is clearly revealed as the ability to help others, or, in Jake's estranged wife

Estella's words, "the stuff that human friendship is made of" (217). Jake, in turn, is haunted by his reliance on others, which Estella also makes clear in her conversation with Amos as the novel ends. Certainly, the most important moments of connection in the novel do not arise from art, but from something more properly thought of as artful everyday communication. The novel abounds, like *Brother Man,* with instances of momentous meaning conveyed not by words alone, but by touch, glance, gesture, and tone. The most illustrative instance of this phenomenon occurs after Jake irritably tells Amos to stop cursing:

> Amos looked at him.
> "I'm sorry, Jake," was all he said.
> But it was like a man speaking a parable, it sounded many notes together in the hearer's mind. (70)

Here, it is Amos's mundane but genuine apology that triggers the effects that *The Hills Were Joyful Together* sought via heightened, oracular prose. Mundane actions and words are also decisive in confirming the long-deferred young love between Glen and Miriam (something Mais considered a crucial antidote to the tragic sadness of Jake's suicide).[32] After uncertainly sniping with each other throughout the novel, these characters at last come together due simply to Glen's sudden, spontaneous concern for Miriam's wound (209); their union is reinforced on the novel's last page by their commonplace talk of the changing seasons and bird migrations and the simple gesture of Glen's drawing Miriam "back into the protective circle of his arm" (222).

Another instance of this more earthbound sense of everyday redemption occurs when George, a character who has undergone a radical (and partially inexplicable) transformation into a compassionate, nature-loving boy, enjoys an exultant communion with Beauty, the horse he has been longing to ride: "it seemed nothing could disrupt that perfect fusion between the boy and the mare" (206). Here, again, Mais appears to locate ethical value in something he conceives of as elemental human experiences, devoid of artifice or even self-conscious presentation. The more pragmatic art of the blacksmith—Jake's profession—is also strongly contrasted with his alienated activities as a sculptor, further underscoring the novel's investment in the value of the everyday. Mais describes the blacksmith shop's activity in a way that emphasizes the magic of its quotidian communicative harmony: "The hammers beat out a rhythmic pattern made up of quick and slow strokes, and the leader by the pattern and measure of the tattoo he beat could communicate to his assistant when he should withhold his own hammer strokes" (178). Moreover, the social value of Jake's work as a blacksmith is described by Jake himself, as he defends his refusal to leave his home village and employ his education and talents elsewhere: "I might have found other things to do that I liked better, that would bring in more money, perhaps; but nothing that would have served the needs of a greater number of people" (101). Ironically, then, *Black Lightning*, itself a work of literary art, ultimately points to art's general lack of social utility—indeed, Jake's sculpture is useful in the end only as firewood. Suspicious of the miscommunication enabled by highly wrought (in more than one sense) artistic practice, the novel asserts common, everyday practice as the only trustworthy basis for intersubjective understanding.

Read together, then, Mais's three published novels delineate a steady shift in attitude toward the appropriate means of art. If the elevated flights of imagistic verse of *The Hills Were Joyful Together* first garnered Mais recognition as a "literary" writer, the progression of his subsequent novels suggests his increasing distrust of the reliability (and by implication the social applicability) of such writing. Contrary to the division between literary and political that characterizes much critical discussion of Mais, his writing, from the outset, displays a pronounced interest in how those two categories intersect and interact.[33] Starting from a Lawrence-inspired philosophy of literature as a sensually transfigurative mechanism for eliciting social change, Mais's novels self-reflexively examine their own medium of (artistic) language, ultimately investing less and less value in the literary and finding moral foundation, somewhat paradoxically, in the everyday and the palpable. It is tempting in this light to figure Mais's authorial trajectory with simplified imagery, from the brash, confident writer who concluded *Form and Substance in Fiction* with a triumphant image of writers and artists ushering in a golden age to Carr's description of Mais in his final days, too frail even for dictation, content to complete "a half dozen small pastels" ("Roger Mais," 15) in quiet solitude.[34] However, Carr's description of these pastels as works that "concentrate the eye upon an intense vividness of colour, texture and particulars" (15) suggests something more than Mais as the chastened writer reduced to a contrite, gestural silence of painting. Indeed, the vitality and sensual particularity Carr observes in these late pastels are at the root of Mais's authorial aesthetic in all of his published novels. If these novels do seem increasingly less confident in the foreseeable effects of language, and more and more insistent on locating a guaranteed meaningfulness in something beyond the reach of their own verbal medium, their various experimental forms all nevertheless relentlessly signal their belief in the redemptive possibilities of human consciousness and communication. While Mais may have become disenchanted by the unpredictability of what he considered to be literature's most crucial characteristic—"imaginative persuasion" (*Form and Substance*, 228)—his novels never ceased striving to awaken his readers into a sense of enchantment with the complex beauty and possibility of the world around them.

Taken in this way, Mais seems an appropriate figure with which to conclude the discussion of West Indian modernism in London at midcentury. Brathwaite notes that Mais's papers reveal an incredibly prolific writer who attempted publication in many places. Letters to and from Mais's agent in the United States (before the publication of his first novel in Great Britain) suggest he was well aware of the necessity of altering his style to fit the tastes of different audiences, including popular or middlebrow ones. Consistent themes and attitudes do appear throughout his writing, but his initial adoption as an experimental "literary" writer points as much to the contingencies of the British publishing market as it does to his own conscious principles of composition. This should not be taken to devalue Mais's achievement as an artist in any way. However, it does point up how the social and historical embeddedness of literature must always be taken into account. Mais was an extremely strong-willed and opinionated artist, long before the composition, let alone the publication, of *The Hills Were Joyful Together*, and the politicized impulses of his aesthetic views can hardly be put into question. Nevertheless, his explicitly Lawrentian aesthetic leanings also fit nicely with the prerogatives of (one part of) the postwar London literary field, such that the systematic openness to experimental writing first catalyzed by Mittelholzer (itself capitalizing on cultural currents stretching back to before World War II) clearly had some role in making Mais's emergence as a published West Indian novelist possible. In such a light, Mais's enchantment—and then disenchantment—with the political utility of literary expression might serve to highlight the shifting contexts within which aesthetic practices always take shape. However one might perceive the ideological investments and lineage of modernist forms, at this crucial moment in West Indian literature a confluence of individual and structural forces made such forms both attractive and powerful not only to Mais but to his most immediate predecessors in print, Lamming, Mittelholzer, and Selvon. Mais's death in 1955 certainly does not mark the end of Windrush literary output—indeed, the boom would certainly reverberate into the next decade, in however attenuated a manner. However, Mais's work's increasing consciousness of the unpredictable and ultimately ungovernable meanings attached to that output helps to highlight the contingent, perhaps necessarily unsettled nature of his generation's engagement with British modernism.[35] Certainly, Mais's brief publishing career in Britain suggests that regardless of how deep-seated the political and aesthetic principles of the Windrush writers were, their literary emergence was also fundamentally facilitated by a particular alignment of social, cultural, and historical forces. If the variable nature of such forces subsequently obliged a shift in tactics, outlook, and allegiance on the part of later authors (not to mention critics) of Caribbean literature, this shift should not overwrite the strategic and intellectual lessons of their predecessors' initial, enabling embrace of modernist practice.

Coda: *Kamau Brathwaite, Wilson Harris, and V. S. Naipaul's Caribbean Voice*

The year 1962 can be seen as something of a watershed for the West Indian presence, both literary and actual, in Britain. Most important, the passage of the Commonwealth Immigrants Act of 1962 decisively restricted the entry of new migrants from the entire ex-empire. Though the flow of immigrants did not dry up immediately—mainly due to the continued ability of spouses and children to join migrants already resident in Britain—the act marks a crucial change in both the perception and the legal status of the West Indian population in Britain. Moreover, the year also marked the dissolution of the West Indies Federation and the subsequent achievement of independence by its two largest (and mutually quarrelsome) members: Jamaica and Trinidad and Tobago. Although these landmark events of official history do not necessarily have immediate ramifications in the cultural world, they do serve as useful indicators of the different directions in which West Indian literature could be said to move after the initial postwar years. Both events suggest an epochal shift in British-Caribbean relations, establishing a much firmer border between the former colonies and their erstwhile colonizer. While far from completely removed from considerations of British policymakers, the islands, serially emerging as independent nation-states, become responsible for their own fates, no longer a legitimate subject of domestic British legislation. This shift also bears significantly on the nature of the Windrush migrants resident in Britain: it effectively allows them to become British by dint of having arrived before the Commonwealth Immigrants Act took effect.[1] Thus, after an initial period of flux, uncertainty, and mixture following World War II, 1962 marks a moment in which the West Indian diasporic community begins officially consolidating into distinct formations, loosely contained under the headings of Caribbean—actually resident in and citizen of an island nation in the region—or Black British—part of a visible minority population situated within Britain itself.

Certain parallels to this drawing apart can be seen in the fortunes of West Indian literature, too, as the period of intense, agonistic interconnection described in the pages of this book draws to a close, and Caribbean literary energies get channeled into distinct, quite different paths. At the center of these changes in the literary scene—perhaps standing athwart them in some sense—is the now towering figure of V. S. Naipaul. From a contemporary perspective, Naipaul, among all the novelists of the Windrush generation, has achieved the most prominence, a status attested to most concretely by the 1990 knighthood bestowed upon him by Queen Elizabeth II and his 2001 Nobel Prize in Literature. During the earlier postwar years, however, Naipaul had a much lower profile as a novelist vis-à-vis his Windrush peers. His initial publication, *The Mystic Masseur,* in 1957, comes well after Lamming, Mais, Mittelholzer, and Selvon had established the early parameters of the postwar West Indian novel, and his immediately subsequent books—*The Suffrage of Elvira* (1958) and *Miguel Street* (1959)—continue in the same comedic, lightly satirical vein as his debut novel, not unnoticed by critics, but likewise not registering with the same serious, high literary force as his predecessors. It is arguably in 1961, with the publication of *A House for Mr. Biswas* (and his being awarded the Somerset Maugham Award), that Naipaul begins to establish himself lastingly in the British world of letters.[2] Although Naipaul should by no means be considered the sole representative of shifts in the Britain-based West Indian literary field, his rise to cultural prominence occurs at a suggestively pivotal moment in both political and cultural terms and, perhaps counterintuitively, helps shed light on the emergent aesthetic formations of both Black British and Anglophone Caribbean literature, as well as, much later, its uneasy consolidation into what is now thought of as postcolonial literature.

In this light, it is surely provocative that the two books Naipaul published subsequent to *A House for Mr. Biswas*—after a well-known artistic and emotional crisis—display rather overt signs of their author's tendentious and controversial disaffiliation with the Caribbean as the grounds of his public and artistic identity.[3] His 1962 nonfiction account of a return trip to the Caribbean, *The Middle Passage,* paints an almost wholly denigrating picture of the region, poignantly portraying Naipaul's own paranoia about becoming trapped back in his home island of Trinidad and presenting its entire narrative in the tradition of English travel writing (most notably and notoriously that established by James Anthony Froude).[4] The book's opening sentence betrays Naipaul's supercilious self-positioning as thoroughly distinct from his fellow Caribbean travelers: "there was such a crowd of immigrant-type West Indians on the boat-train platform at Waterloo that I was glad I was travelling first class to the West Indies" (2). This book, of course, is also where one of Naipaul's most controversial statements appears. Echoing the book's epigraph from Froude that asserts the absence of meaningful human existence in the region, Naipaul proclaims, "history is built around achievement and creation; and nothing was created in the West Indies" (20). In a related gesture of natal disavowal, Naipaul's next novel, *Mr. Stone and the Knights Companion*, published in 1963, represents Naipaul's first attempt to write a novel set entirely in England with English characters. The novel's basic plot structure—of an aging British man discovering some measure of creativity late in life—can be construed in the manner of an allegory of bittersweet creative rebirth pointing to Naipaul's own and certainly suggests the author's reorientation, however hesitant or unfulfilling, toward things English. Naipaul's notorious (and anguished) antipathy toward the Caribbean is by now well known and much discussed, and these two texts seem useful in tracing the beginnings of a pronounced shift in Naipaul's artistic vision and positioning. However, it is from an earlier moment that one can begin to descry the tectonic shifts in West Indian literature in Britain that Naipaul's influence inaugurated—most particularly, when he took over from Henry Swanzy as the editor of *Caribbean Voices* in 1954.

As discussed in the first chapter, this program had an outsized role as the primary arbiter of literary taste for Anglophone Caribbean writing of the era: to return to Gail Low's emphatic assessment, the importance of the show in establishing a unity of taste and practices for writers of the time "cannot be overestimated" ("Publishing Commonwealth," 80–81). The internal BBC politics are intriguing to consider, if largely undocumented, but it seems there was a sense that by 1954 it was "time" for the West Indians to run their own literary show. Swanzy has suggested in an interview that his liberal leanings (at a moment when Britain was having great difficulty maintaining control over its far-flung empire) were a factor in the BBC's gently pointed encouragement that he find other projects to work on, and his letters to friends informing them of his departure from the show betray an understated sense that he was not doing so entirely willingly.[5] Whatever the forces effecting this change in editorship, its results appear in a much clearer light: if Swanzy's tastes tended toward an embrace of the ostensibly liberal aims of prewar literary experimentation, Naipaul's most certainly did not.

Unsurprisingly, perhaps, Naipaul's editorial preferences on *Caribbean Voices* mirror his own writing practices, insisting on a spare, exactingly descriptive prose style, with some allowances for satire (so long as it was not overtly political). His dismissive depiction of the BBC-led literary culture for Commonwealth emigrants in London in the 1950s in his 2001 novel *Half a Life* offers one indication of his disdain for both writers and editors engaged in supposedly highbrow literary pursuits at that time. Naipaul's satirical portrayal of Willie as a writer who thoughtlessly imitates Hemingway and produces largely nonsensical, film-inspired prose stories finds precise parallel in Naipaul's own literary criticism on *Caribbean Voices,* in which he persistently censures writers (especially Garth St. Omer and John Hearne) for trying to sound like Hemingway and suggests that certain writers are too inspired by film and should concentrate more on structure and cohesion. Indeed, Naipaul's on-air commentary aggressively advances an aesthetic project that sounds like an uncanny double of Amis's. Deeply impatient with literary experimentation, Naipaul argues instead for more commonsense language, straightforward stories, and a down-to-earth, lightly humorous writing style. For Naipaul, like his Movement contemporaries, good writing appears on the page "with a vigour and pungency entirely free from affectation" (*CV,* 20 Mar. 1955).

Naipaul's review of Lamming's *The Emigrants,* for example, complains that the novel's "technique is difficult" and its prose "over-dramatic," offering the suggestion that "the book needed some documentary writing" (*CV,* 2 Jan. 1955). Elsewhere, Naipaul decries the "brittle unloveliness of the moderns," which, he says, results in "a coldness, an intellectualizing which does not belong to the poetic temperament" (*CV,* 30 Oct. 1955). On yet another show, he articulates the typical 1950s critique of modernism as too self-concerned and expresses his fear "that this intensity will lead to a niggling hypersensitiveness and eventually to sterility; and, in the end, will isolate the writer from his society more than ever" (*CV,* 8 Apr. 1956). In a 1956 review of the previous nine months of Caribbean literature, Naipaul praises Mittelholzer as "the only one who really can tell a story" and then rebukes the "university writers," including Stuart Hall and Brathwaite, bemoaning that "it is all mind and manner with these young men" and complaining that their work is flat—"not all the pretentiousness of borrowed technique could leaven it"—as well as "unusually open to infection from foreign 'isms' which it would be folly to apply to the West Indies" (*CV*, 16 Sept. 1956). The note of aesthetic isolationism in this last reproof—with its implications of Caribbean cultural nationalism—is perhaps surprising coming from Naipaul, but it is in fact of a piece with the Movement's critiques of experimental writing: both are invested in a somehow natural, unmarked style taken to represent the "normal" state of a national culture, however defined. Moreover, the foreignness that Naipaul abhors does not seem to be British, but European, since, at bottom, he expresses a sense at this time that properly West Indian literature *is* British. In an early discussion of Caribbean literature on the show, Naipaul notes the extinction of the native population of Caribs and Arawaks, pointedly concluding that "there is therefore no binding national tradition; such traditions as exist come from Britain" (*CV*, 12 Dec. 1954). In contrast with Mittelholzer, however, Naipaul displays a quite static understanding of tradition, what Paul Gilroy has strongly critiqued as "the idea of tradition as invariant repetition rather than a stimulus toward innovation and change" (*Black Atlantic*, x). At *Caribbean Voices*, Naipaul seems to have aimed at aligning West Indian writing as closely as possible to an ostensibly stable, unchanging tradition of realism then being noisily revived by Amis's generation in English literature itself.

If Naipaul thus shared the Movement's politics of form, the commonality reverberates in his view of the place of politics in literature as well. From the outset, Naipaul was adamantly in favor of effacing political concerns from the radio show's literary offerings. As he opines early in his tenure: "too often, I feel, a Caribbean Voice has been one of social protest" (*CV*, 26 Dec. 1954). Another transcript finds him commending one poet because "there is only one hint of the nationalism so conspicuous in early Jamaican poetry. Things seem to have changed now. The writer is an individual who no longer needs to be buoyed up by his nationalism" (*CV*, 18 Sept. 1955). On a different show, expressing impatience with stories about the poor, Naipaul pointedly notes that he "would welcome a story about the middle class" (*CV*, 30 Jan. 1955). Race, of course, is also eschewed, perhaps most explicitly when Naipaul complains about "the handy old subject of the burden of being black. Writers are so boring when they are only being black" (*CV*, 16 Sept. 1956). Taken together, these editorial views have some import for Caribbean writers' strategic positioning vis-à-vis the British literary field: that is, Naipaul's taste in style and content exhorts West Indian authors to produce writing that is closer to the so-called universal qualities then assumed to comprise the essence of great English literature, while also erasing the difference, exoticized or otherwise, often stressed about the subjects of the region's writing at the time.[6] Thus, in the context of the British literary marketplace, *Caribbean Voices* under Naipaul in fact encouraged its writers to *efface* the distinctions Swanzy's policies had invited Caribbean writers to maintain, pointing them toward becoming less and less distinguishable—in terms of strongly marked West Indian content, but also formally—from their British counterparts.

A useful marker of this change is the Trinidadian author Michael Anthony, who might be considered the most successful authorial "product" of Naipaul's tenure at *Caribbean Voices*.[7] Anthony's work appeared with remarkable frequency at this time, and Naipaul's encouragement and critique of the work almost precisely shadow the Movement-inflected responses to West Indian novels delineated in the preceding pages of this book. The first work of Anthony's to appear on the show, "The Strange Flower," occurs at the end of 1955, well into Naipaul's tenure, and his stories appear with some frequency thereafter. By March of the following year, a program holds up Anthony as the most successful example of the show's critical guidance. Anthony's work is praised for being "neater and tighter ... with an almost professional directness," and he is favorably contrasted to writers who have succumbed to what is figured as literary and intellectual decadence: in his writing there is "no padding, no showing off, no asides to the reader" (*CV,* 4 Mar. 1956). In May he is again lauded for his directness, and in June for not writing about the color problem. By September, however, Naipaul sees a problem with the work. Commenting on Anthony's story "The Tree," Naipaul expresses worry that Anthony's writing is suffering because he has come to London and fallen into "bad literary company," such that his stories now reveal a "growing affectation, a growing 'prettiness'" (*CV,* 2 Sept. 1956). Two weeks later, in his cumulative review of the past nine months (and apparently oblivious to the ironies of his own position of exile), Naipaul reiterates these anxieties, describing Anthony as "a new writer from Trinidad, now alas! in England, and slowly losing the feel of his island" (*CV,* 16 Sept. 1956).

In the penultimate program of *Caribbean Voices,* Naipaul names Anthony and Leslie Roberts as the "only two new writers of any worth" discovered during his time on the show (*CV,* 31 Aug. 1958). He expresses regret that a last story by Anthony cannot be read on the show, but his description of Anthony's counterpart Roberts (whose story is read on the show) provides a lucid portrait of the aesthetic priorities of Naipaul's editorial reign.[8] Initially, Roberts is praised as "an earthy writer with no literary pretensions," whose stories "are always honest." Naipaul then goes on to praise the verisimilitude of his characters—"you can never doubt that he is writing about real people"—and, more important, the fact that "he also never uses them, as so many West Indian writers do, as material for facile social protest." The subsequent description of Roberts's writing is connotatively rich, suggesting a transcendence of the physical (and, implicitly, the racial) into the rarefied realm of hard-earned literary universality: "There is toil and endeavour in these stories; rather than blood and tears and sweat" (*CV*, 31 Aug. 1958). The broader tension in the script between a salutary groundedness and the contamination of the physical remains unremarked (and arguably structures Naipaul's writing to this day), but the overarching message to write carefully mimetic, commonsense prose is plain enough. In this way, Naipaul's predilections favor a literary style that is aesthetically assimilated into the regnant British mode of writing advocated by Amis and other Movement figures.

This is not to say that West Indian fiction was channeled completely into the mold advocated by Naipaul: there was of course still considerable diversity and quantity of production by West Indian authors in Britain stretching well into the 1960s. Yet Naipaul had unquestionably become a central figure as the decade turned. Naipaul's biographer Patrick French, for example, asserts regarding his subject that "only in 1960 did his star begin to rise" (*World Is*, 180), while in 1963, none other than Kamau Brathwaite (then writing as Edward) claims Naipaul as an avatar of West Indian novelistic revolt in his essay "Roots." Brathwaite makes what would now seem uncharacteristic claims about Naipaul in a characteristically strong manner, naming Naipaul as almost the only exception to the sterility suffered by contemporary Caribbean novelists as a result of exile: "The novels of Vidia Naipaul, then, come at a significant stage in the development of our (British) Caribbean literary tradition. Very little of what has so far been said applies to him and his remarkable series of books . . . [which] have come, almost overnight, to topple the whole hierarchy of our literary values and set up new critical standards of form and order in the West Indian novel" (*Roots*, 39).[9] Importantly, of course, Brathwaite's knowledge of Naipaul's novels in this essay stops with *A House for Mr. Biswas*, but the language of epochal change he employs in describing Naipaul is unmistakable. Oddly, for a figure so readily associated with oppositional formal experiment in his own poetics, Brathwaite's subsequent enumeration

of Naipaul's authorial traits reiterates almost precisely the conventional terms
Naipaul himself employed so frequently in the previous decade. As Brathwaite
maintains, in Naipaul's work "we find a sense of narrative, an ease, a lightness
of touch, an absence of tension, a feeling for proportion, an ear, a power of
characterization" (*Roots,* 39).[10] At the end of the essay Brathwaite explicitly
acknowledges that Naipaul's success as a novelist reveals that "to write really
well about a living society . . . one has simply to be an «old fashioned» writer
like Hardy, Dickens, George Eliot, or Jane Austen. This is what Naipaul is"
(53). The discordance between this critical endorsement of Victorian literary
style and Brathwaite's later aesthetic investments—prominently visible in his
first published collection of poetry, *Rites of Passage,* in 1967—is instructive,
suggesting not only Naipaul's widespread influence by the beginning of the
decade but also the disparate, multifarious tendencies it ultimately created
in the field of West Indian literature. Brathwaite's championing of Naipaul,
surely, did not last long (indeed, he would shortly turn to Mais as a much more
appropriate representative of Caribbean novelistic production in "Jazz and the
West Indian Novel"). However, Brathwaite's own important projects for West
Indian literature, notably the formation of the Caribbean Artists Movement,
display the traces of an aesthetic reaction to Naipaul that helped determine
the diffuse directions in which Anglophone Caribbean writing would flow
through the 1960s and beyond.[11]

The germ of Brathwaite's organizational plan for Caribbean culture
can be discerned in the same 1963 essay in which he praises Naipaul. Noting
the return of many exiled writers to their regional roots, Brathwaite observes
that "all now that is needed to make the story complete is for us to arrange
a Conference of Caribbean Writers and begin the publication of our version
of something on the scale of *Presence Africaine*" (*Roots,* 29), the Paris-based
pan-African journal that began publication in 1947. Ultimately, with the establishment of the Caribbean Artists Movement (CAM) in 1966 and its related
journal, *Savacou,* in 1970, Brathwaite succeeded, however fleetingly or inter-
mittently, in realizing this aspiration. Within a periodization of Anglophone
Caribbean literature, CAM would seem to represent the next major cultural
assemblage to appear after the Windrush generation treated in the preceding pages.[12] In fact, CAM was originally envisioned as an antidote to the perceived decline in West Indian cultural visibility in Britain since the postwar
literary boom. Andrew Salkey, one of the founding members of the group,
remembers this lack of public attention as central to the group's beginning,

as revealed by his recollection of an early conversation with Brathwaite: "'It doesn't seem to me,' he [Brathwaite] said, 'that West Indian writers are being noticed any more. The '50s, yes, they were then noticed. We don't hear from them, they are not in the bookshops, I don't see anybody giving talks in London, and so on. How about it, Andrew?'" (quoted in Walmsley, *Caribbean Artists Movement,* 46). Brathwaite reinforces the sense of frustrated belatedness remembered by Salkey in a footnote to the version of "Jazz and the West Indian Novel" that appears in *Roots.* Noting how, even in the 1980s, Caribbean authors were dependent on metropolitan publishers, he expresses a belief that British publishing firms continue to display a "waning of interest" in "«new», «experimental», «too parochial», «too specialized», «for too narrow a market», «unknown» Caribbean writing." Brathwaite dates this lack of interest specifically to the 1960s, observing that "some say since; Lamming's *The Pleasures of Exile* (1960)," and then protests that almost no "new Caribbean writers have appeared on London publishers' lists since the 60s" (82). The strong association Brathwaite makes here between Caribbean literature and experimentalism is striking, especially when set alongside his earlier praise for Naipaul's Victorian conventionality. CAM itself, as Anne Walmsley records in her authoritative account of the movement, was characterized from its founding moments by similar fissures and divergences, manifested in both its internal and public debates. Although Naipaul simply refused to be involved in CAM, the tensions that animated—and eventually sundered—the organization centered precisely on the axes of style and politics that most exercised him. It is thus in the finally splintered nature of CAM that the antithetical reaction to Naipaul's aesthetic stance becomes most visible, revealing not only the divergent paths taken by Anglophone Caribbean writing in the 1960s but also the different ways in which the Windrush legacy of modernist experiment manifested itself after its 1950s apogee.

The interactions of CAM, its founders, and other West Indian writers certainly seem to map neatly into various emergent divisions discernible in West Indian literature at that time. If Naipaul can be read, as suggested above, as the most prominent example of a conscientiously Anglicizing West Indian author, his protégé Michael Anthony's experience with CAM suggests that he, too, did not fit into the explicitly political, assertively Afro-Caribbean contours assumed by the organization. Describing Anthony's presentation at the first CAM symposium in 1967, Walmsley observes that the author's three published novels "were apparently written in the mainstream European tradition—good stories, with clearly defined and well-developed characters" (*Caribbean Artists Movement*, 65). In his own summation of the presentation, Anthony notes that "my contention was simply that the primary function of the writer was to write, and in our intellectualism we must be careful not to lose sight of the wood for the trees" (quoted in Walmsley, *Caribbean Artists Movement*, 65) and turns to E. M. Forster as his primary authority. In such statements, Anthony clearly resembles his mentor Naipaul, emphasizing simplicity and craft over either intellectual or political concerns, and what Walmsley calls his "expressedly neutral, innocent approach to depicting society" appears to have provoked his fellow panelist Orlando Patterson to a rousing riposte in favor of political commitment (66). Later that year, Anthony caused some unrest at the CAM conference in Kent by avowing, "The novel of protest is not my sort of novel . . . I want to tell a story and tell it well" (Walmsley, *Caribbean Artists Movement*, 104). Although defended by C. L. R. James on the basis of authorial autonomy on this occasion, Anthony seems to have remained on the periphery of the group ever after, never officially presenting at any more of its public events. Anthony's work was still discussed frequently— often admiringly—but his apolitical disposition and "uncommitted" aesthetic sensibility put him well outside the main concerns that CAM developed, and his participation in the movement tapered and then ceased altogether with his move to Brazil in 1968. However causally related, Anthony did not publish another novel until 1973.[13]

At the same time, the founding figures of CAM—Brathwaite, John La Rose, and Salkey—were articulating an emphatically pronounced political viewpoint, under the growing influence of Black Power. In the first public session of CAM, for example, La Rose advocated "the rehabilitation of the African experience" (Walmsley, *Caribbean Artists Movement*, 67) and in a later session reiterated the need to explore more African-centered creative options: "If we do not break our tête-à-tête with Europe, and this self-abasement to a certain kind of form which we have inherited through the language, we cannot explore all these possibilities" (Walmsley, *Caribbean Artists Movement*, 172). Most indicative of this political strain, perhaps, is the August 1969 CAM symposium in which all three founding members presented papers: Brathwaite's "Africa in the Caribbean," Salkey's "The Negritude Movement and Black Awareness," and La Rose's "The Development of Black Experience and the Nature of Black Society in Britain" (Walmsley, *Caribbean Artists Movement*, 241).[14] The titles alone make clear that the major concern of the symposium centers on matters of Africa and the iterations of its diaspora, and indeed, only Brathwaite's title gestures specifically to the Caribbean itself. This discrepancy, in fact, can also be seen as significant, as Brathwaite's appearance at the conference occurred after his having spent a year away from London, in Jamaica. Indeed, Brathwaite's departure to Jamaica to take up a position at the University of the West Indies, Mona, in the fall of 1968 marked the institutional bifurcation of CAM, in which Salkey and La Rose officially took over for Brathwaite in London, while the latter began efforts to establish a new branch in the Caribbean. This bifurcation, in turn, neatly summarizes the two directions in which CAM was splitting—to a politicized concern with race relations in Britain (as well as a broadly international politics of race) and to a focus on establishing a strong cultural and political presence at home in the Caribbean. In many ways, this split can be read as the founding moment of a particularly Black British literary orientation separating itself from the priorities of specifically West Indian writing, especially when one considers La Rose's role (along with his partner, Sarah White) as the founder of New Beacon Books in 1966, which became the first press dedicated to Black British publication in Britain (to be followed, shortly thereafter, by Bogle-L'Oeverture Publications and, much more recently, by Peepal Tree Press). Both of these complementary facets of CAM were highly politicized. However, as Salkey and La Rose became more and more enmeshed in addressing the situation of minorities in Britain, Brathwaite's turn to the Caribbean is more legible as an archetypal postcolonial concern with fashioning a meaningful, independent culture not beholden to the metropole. Although it would be impossible to separate Black British and West Indian literature into two wholly distinct categories even today, their different tendencies with regard to the politicization of culture emerge in this foundational split within CAM.

A final aspect of CAM's fragmented history—its relationship to Wilson Harris—has particular pertinence for an understanding of Caribbean literature's modernist inheritance. Harris is unquestionably the most direct literary descendant of novelists such as Lamming, Mais, Mittelholzer, and Selvon. Harris's dense, mythopoetic novels are overtly experimental in nature, and his essays at the time advocate a pronounced opposition to conventional realist narrative representation. Harris's first novel, *The Palace of the Peacock,* appeared in 1960 and received consideration in a good number of the major journalistic outlets in Britain. After this first book, however, Harris's steady and prolific novelistic output (seven more novels before the decade came to an end) garnered British notice, if at all, only in the *Times Literary Supplement*. Considering that CAM discussions frequently held Harris up as one of the most important examples of contemporary Caribbean artistry, it seems plausible that his lack of visibility in Britain played a key role in catalyzing the movement's foundation. Harris was, according to La Rose's account, felt to "be an important person to be part of" CAM when it was being initiated (Walmsley, *Caribbean Artists Movement*, 43), and at the second CAM conference, both Swanzy and Ivan Van Sertima held up Harris "as the exemplary Caribbean writer" of the time (Walmsley, *Caribbean Artists Movement*, 172). He presented (along with Anthony) at CAM's first symposium, articulating his own vision of a "radical new art of fiction" (Walmsley, *Caribbean Artists Movement*, 64), and he also participated widely in CAM's Kent conference. However, the disagreement voiced there—in which CAM artists were criticized for not allying themselves more directly and publicly with black immigrants in Britain—put Harris in the position of defending the autonomy of the artist. Walmsley bluntly summarizes the effect of this conference's heated exchanges on Harris: "CAM artists were challenged directly to relate to and identify with the immigrant community in Ladbroke Grove and Brixton; as a result key artists withdrew from CAM, notably Wilson Harris" (305). Presaging the later geographical separation within CAM, Harris's devotion to a high-art aesthetic of challenging, opaque, and philosophical prose here splits ways with the group's evolution into an organization with more immediate political ends.

While these internecine divisions may seem far removed from Naipaul's direct influence, one can see emblematized in CAM's fragmentation the eruption of disagreements in precisely the areas in which his aesthetic proclamations fastidiously sought to foreclose discussion. Politics—persistently dismissed by Naipaul as a pertinent concern for literature—plays the most visible role in CAM's disagreements, but discussions of aesthetic style also reverberate loudly. Certainly, as the politicized Black British side of CAM emerged into dominance, the organization's earlier openness to aesthetic variegation contracted accordingly, and it seems far from accidental that the era's two most prominent practitioners of Caribbean experimental writing split off, albeit in vastly different directions, from the group in Britain. Brathwaite's poetics, upon his return to the Caribbean, take on an oppositional mode characteristic of modernism, but they are almost always rhetorically positioned as embodying a Caribbean (largely Afro-Caribbean) form. Brathwaite's famed revolt against the constraints of iambic pentameter is illustrative. As he argues in "History of the Voice," this meter has dominated English verse and imposed a way of thinking on poetry in English: "the pentameter remained, and it carries with it a certain kind of experience, which is not the experience of the hurricane. The hurricane does not roar in pentameter" (*Roots*, 265). Although this formal critique of convention could come straight out of a modernist manifesto, it is here clothed in explicitly folk form. In "Jazz and the West Indian Novel," Brathwaite addresses these consonances more explicitly, as he explains: "I'm trying to outline an alternative to the English Romantic/Victorian cultural tradition which still operates among and on us, despite the «colonial» breakthrough already achieved by Eliot, Pound and Joyce; and despite the presence among us of a folk tradition which in itself, it seems to me, is the basis of an alternative" (*Roots*, 72–73). While he does here acknowledge some similarity between his project and Euro-American modernism, Brathwaite nevertheless insists on the ultimate difference of his proposed cultural solution, and the essay pointedly presents itself to its Caribbean audience as "the delineation of a possible alternative to the European cultural tradition which has been imposed upon us and which we have more or less accepted or absorbed, for obvious reasons, as the only way of going about our business" (*Roots*, 72). Taking jazz as its model for anticolonial cultural resistance, the essay argues for a Caribbean aesthetic that finds its material basis in a specific history of African diasporic practice. In this influential essay (and with increasing explicitness over the course of his career) Brathwaite's modernism is thus rhetorically denuded of its European inheritance, rearticulated in a version of countercultural autonomy that resonates with the decolonizing emphasis of many of the more recent incarnations of postcolonial literary criticism.

On the other hand, Harris, who has lived in Britain for more or less his entire career, is much less hesitant to represent his aesthetic philosophy as arising out of both European and Caribbean sources. A contrast with Brathwaite can be made even at the titular level: if Brathwaite's well-known essay collection, *Roots,* emphasizes a subterranean African presence, Harris's *Tradition, the Writer and Society* pays explicit homage to Eliot's "Tradition and the Individual Talent." In the collection's central essay, "Tradition and the West Indian Novel," Harris, in archetypal modernist fashion, makes strenuous claims against the appropriateness of "the framework of the nineteenth-century novel" (29) for West Indian literature. Harris faults Naipaul specifically for submitting to this framework, maintaining that it is responsible for the sad fact that the latter's fiction "never erupts into a revolutionary or alien question of spirit, but serves ultimately to consolidate one's preconception of humanity" (40). At the close of the essay, Harris observes the formal conformism of most West Indian novelists, asserting: "they may conceive of themselves in the most radical political light but their approach to art and literature is one which consolidates the most conventional and documentary techniques in the novel" (45). Against what he sees as the narrow constraints of such artistic practices, Harris finds surprising cynosures in "many of the great Victorians—Ruskin, Gerard Manley Hopkins, Dickens in *Bleak House*" (45), as well as grounding figures of European modernism, "Pound and Eliot, Joyce and Wyndham Lewis," all of whom, to Harris's mind, "remain 'explosive' while many a fashionable rebel grows to be superficial and opportunistic" (46). The staggering range of European cultural touchstones employed by Harris in the book—encompassing, among others, Beckett, Dante, Dostoyevsky, Giotto, Kafka, Henry Moore, and Petrarch—illustrates the cultural inclusiveness at the base of Harris's understanding of something he nevertheless names West Indian tradition. Harris's fiction, too, in keeping with the apparent circumstances of his break with CAM, rejects the "national and political and social simplifications of experience in the world" (30) that he associates with the mainstream novel tradition. His writing generally carries its politics in a much less overt fashion, relying on subtle mediations between art and consciousness as the only possible location of its political purchase. Consequently, Harris's work has often seemed amenable to critics working in the strain of postcolonial literary studies emerging out of the Commonwealth literature paradigm, with its deemphasizing of politics in favor of a more unifying, allegedly universal approach to literature.[15]

Thus, two broad, antithetical options emerge in the lineage of what could be thought of as Caribbean modernism after Windrush: either the strongly marked cultural separatism of Braithwaite's aesthetics, denying the taint of the European in an effort to preserve its political integrity, or the more ecumenical experimental posture of Harris, vulnerable to critiques of pandering to metropolitan expectations and potentially guilty of evaporating its politics into a transcendent mist of high artistic style. As this book has tried to illustrate, such a view of Anglophone Caribbean literature's possible engagements with modernism is far too schematic and binaristic, offering an analytically sterile false choice between metropolitan and Caribbean. It is unable to capture the Windrush writers' sophisticated involvement with the lingering remainders of the

British modernist tradition, an involvement that embraced the unruly energy and utopian critique characteristic of its European forebears while remaining deeply anticolonial in its political message. A return to the scene of early Windrush production also gives the lie to any romantic tales of lonely postcolonial literary heroism at the crucial moment of decolonization, showing instead that from its very beginnings, Anglophone Caribbean literature was in fact constituted by its paradoxical positioning both in and against metropolitan European high culture. Far from shying away from this engagement, writers like Lamming, Mais, Mittelholzer, and Selvon—and, in a different way, Naipaul—all eagerly embraced the challenge of constructing a cultural movement with the erstwhile tools of imperial oppression. The fact that this generation of writers established an effective position in the field of postwar British writing as the inheritors of the modernist tradition should not be taken to mean that the roots of Anglophone Caribbean literature are utterly, inalterably British, any more than one could make the case that these writers wrested modernism wholly away from its European bases and transformed it into a straightforwardly postcolonial practice. The heuristic utility and historical importance of these distinct literary categories cannot be gainsaid. However, this need not foreclose an understanding of the more broadly global, relational dynamics whereby the very categories themselves have come into being. To state that at its foundational moments, West Indian literature was already densely and unavoidably transnational may risk stating the obvious, but such obviousness can easily be overlooked in favor of more self-ratifying, self-protective claims. Thus, however obvious, such a statement might also be taken as a reminder—echoed in the very practices of the Windrush writers examined here—of the intellectual need to unsettle one's own comfortable critical position and engage anew with the familiar other against which that position is typically constructed.

Notes

Introduction

1. The term *Windrush* derives from the name of the ship, the SS *Empire Windrush,* that brought Caribbean immigrants to England in 1948.

2. *West Indian,* though based on Christopher Columbus's erroneous geography, is the term most often used in the postwar years to refer to people from the English-speaking Caribbean (and it still, in the University of the West Indies and the supranational cricket team, has contemporary relevance). The preferred term is now *Anglophone Caribbean,* used in order both to distance the islands from Columbus-era European presumption and to distinguish among the language groups in the region. This book will employ both *West Indian* and *Anglophone Caribbean* in a more or less interchangeable way, largely for reasons of style and to avoid repetition, rather than with regard to any distinct semantic or political intent. *Caribbean* will also be employed in circumstances where the Anglophone context is either already obvious or unimportant.

3. Eysteinsson acknowledges that this malleability and contention are characteristic of all literary concepts but suggests that, since the modern is still so closely allied to our sense of the present, discussions of modernism appear to take on a particular sense of urgency or importance.

4. The institutional authority with which Levin (and later Beebe) speaks attests to the clear shift in the balance of power (political, economic, and not coincidentally academic) from Britain to the United States after World War II.

5. In his chapter on literature and painting, Spender in fact cites Levin's essay, endorsing and employing his fellow critic's characterizations of Eliot and Pablo Picasso.

6. Notwithstanding Laura Riding and Robert Graves's 1928 *A Survey of Modernist Poetry,* the term *modernism* does not seem to have been employed with any consistency until well into the second half of the twentieth century. The *Oxford*

English Dictionary's tracing of the term with reference to literature shows that it was only rarely employed without quotation marks until the late 1960s.

7. Critics such as Alison Donnell, Evelyn O'Callaghan, Leah Rosenberg, and Faith Smith, among others, have persuasively argued against uncritical acceptance of a romanticized Windrush myth of origins, suggesting that this has worked against a more inclusive understanding of Anglophone Caribbean literature and its roots.

8. Both Lamming (1957) and Naipaul (1961) won the W. Somerset Maugham Award during this period, while Mittelholzer (1952), Lamming (1955), and Selvon (1955, 1968) received Guggenheim Fellowships. The figure for novels published in the United Kingdom during this period is taken from Ramchand's "Year by Year Bibliography" in *The West Indian Novel and Its Background.*

9. See Miller's *Late Modernism* and Esty's *A Shrinking Island.*

10. Mao and Walkowitz provide an excellent and wide-ranging bibliography of scholars engaged in this kind of work ("New Modernist Studies"). Numerous later works in the same vein but published after their article appeared could be cited, but those that include Caribbean-specific subject matter include Matthew Hart's *Nations of Nothing But Poetry* and Anita Patterson's *Race, American Literature, and Transnational Modernisms.*

11. Critics of postmodernist and postcolonial literatures, emerging into prominence at around the same time, also invested time distinguishing their critical practices from each other. See Kwame Anthony Appiah's "Is the Post- in Postmodernism the Post- in Postcolonial?" and Linda Hutcheon's "'Circling the Downspout of Empire': Post-Colonialism and Postmodernism" for influential examples of this debate.

12. Other prominent examples of this early antipathy can be found in Kumkum Sangari's "The Politics of the Possible" and in the entry for modernism in Bill Ashcroft, Gareth Griffiths, and Helen Tiffin's *Post-Colonial Studies: The Key Concepts.*

13. See also Howard J. Booth and Nigel Rigby's *Modernism and Empire* and Richard Begam and Michael Valdez Moses's *Colonialism: British and Irish Literature, 1899–1939;* both collections are explicitly aimed at counteracting the straightforward association of modernism with imperialism.

14. Neil Lazarus is another critic who has fruitfully examined the connections between modernist and postcolonial literature. See, e.g., "The Politics of Postcolonial Modernism."

15. See Bourdieu's *The Rules of Art: Genesis and Structure of the Literary Field* for Bourdieu's most thorough accounting of this phenomenon in literature. David Swartz's *Culture and Power: The Sociology of Pierre Bourdieu* provides an astute, readable overview of Bourdieu's cultural theory, to which my own thinking is indebted.

16. See Joe Cleary's "The World Literary System: Atlas and Epitaph" and Christopher Prendergast's "The World Republic of Letters" for early, comprehensive, and insightful critical assessments of Casanova's book.

17. This point bears comparison with Edward Said's notion of the "contrapuntal." Although from a quite different critical lineage, Said's concept is equally concerned

with conveying "a more urgent sense of the interdependence between things" (*Culture and Imperialism,* 61).

18. Although not specifically discussed in this book, reviews from Caribbean sources tell an interesting parallel story: while culturally focused journals like *BIM* and *Kyk-over-al* were frequently amenable to Windrush experimentation, many of the more mainstream establishment organs, especially Jamaica's *Daily Gleaner,* conveyed suspicion of the works' modernist overtones.

19. The elided words from this passage—"and modernity"—illuminate a critical disagreement. To be sure, *Migrant Modernism* embraces, and indeed takes its inspiration from, the basic premise of Gikandi's book. However, the book's occasional conflation of modernism with modernity overlooks the former's often agonistic relationship with the latter, implicitly eliminating the possibility that modernist practice might function as a productive critique of modernity. Susan Stanford Friedman has been an influential voice in arguing for modernism as defined primarily by its complex and ambiguous relation to modernity; see, e.g., her "Planetarity: Musing Modernist Studies."

20. Michael G. Malouf's *Transatlantic Solidarities: Irish Nationalism and Caribbean Poetics,* while not interested in modernism per se, has a similar interest in making connections across disciplinary and cultural domains assumed to be separate.

21. Emery's delineation of how modernist aesthetics helps articulate a resistant subjectivity is illuminating (*Modernism, the Visual*). If the book's broad historical sweep—encompassing the early twentieth century to the present day—may give the appearance of monumentalizing both the oppositionality of Caribbean modernist aesthetics and the colonial oppression against which Emery sees it reacting, it nevertheless identifies a crucial ground of struggle—the visual—staked out in Anglophone Caribbean artistic practice.

22. Dash's book *The Other America: Caribbean Literature in a New World Context* undertakes an examination of modernism in a trans-Caribbean context, including Anglophone, Francophone, and Hispanophone literature within its purview. It makes a convincing demonstration of modernism as an important epistemological disposition across Caribbean literature, though such unifying breadth tends to underplay the widely divergent political and cultural histories in which modernism arose within the separate linguistic regions.

23. *Caribbean Voices* was certainly the most important institution enabling the establishment of the Windrush writers in London. It will be discussed in more detail in chapter 1.

24. The importance of fluid, mobile critique to Caribbean literature has been emphasized through critical terms other than *modernism.* For example, Glyne Griffith's *Deconstruction, Imperialism and the West Indian Novel* employs the notion of deconstruction (itself heavily indebted to modernism for many commentators) as a useful way of characterizing the nature of West Indian literature, while Antonio Benítez-Rojo uses postmodernism (also heavily indebted to modernism and perhaps not quite historically accurate in the case of Windrush) as his critical lens.

25. That these writers all came to prominence as novelists is not accidental. Although only Mittelholzer originally considered himself to be primarily a novelist, the exigencies of publishing in Britain at the time largely worked to reward Commonwealth novelists, rather than poets or even dramatists, the nature of whose work, of course, could be more easily sustained independent of the institutional literary resources concentrated in London. Interestingly, Henry Swanzy's letters reveal that in the late 1950s, even so manifest a poetic talent as Derek Walcott was composing a novel manuscript.

26. Some commentators include V. S. Reid's *New Day*, published in 1949, with these early Windrush novels; however, Reid's book was first published in New York, and though available a year later in Britain, it did not receive the same notice or have the magnitude of impact in the United Kingdom as the novels discussed here. Indeed, so magnetic was the pull of London literary possibilities that Reid published his second novel, *The Leopard*, in 1958 with Heinemann in Britain, as well as Viking in the United States.

27. See Edmondson, *Making Men: Gender, Literary Authority, and Women's Writing in Caribbean Narrative*. Michelle Ann Stephens's *Black Empire: The Masculine Global Imaginary of Caribbean Intellectuals in the United States, 1914–1962* is another important examination of the gendered nature of Caribbean political thought during the era of decolonization.

28. Donnell's "Heard but Not Seen: Women's Short Stories and the BBC's *Caribbean Voices* Programme" explores the gendered dynamics of the era's literary production through the lens of genre.

29. Perhaps relatedly, their writing also fits, broadly speaking, into a mimetic realist paradigm. Jean Rhys is an obvious exception to this pattern, but her writing occurs either well before the Windrush writers' emergence or well after. Moreover, Rhys was generally considered a British author until the late 1960s. Emery, in particular, perceptively established Rhys as a modernist Caribbean author in *Jean Rhys at "World's End": Novels of Colonial and Sexual Exile*.

30. This book's principle of selection is based on the claim that it is the first authors to publish novels in the British marketplace who had the most prestige and profile during the 1950s. Such selection thus leaves to the side quite a few other (male) Windrush novelists who, while important, were neither as widely recognized nor as clearly experimental, including figures such as Jan Carew, John Hearne, Reid, and Andrew Salkey.

31. In significant ways, this formative stage of West Indian literature begins its life, from its very inception, as "global literature" in the sense employed by David Damrosch; i.e., its initial release already sees it having moved out of its "origin country" to be received and interpreted in a different cultural milieu. Similarly, Gail Low has observed how West Indian "literary history of the fifties and sixties is a history of transnational connections in a way that reminds us that our current generation's claims to cultural cosmopolitanism are not originary" ("Publishing Commonwealth," 91).

32. In quite different ways, both Nicholas Brown's *Utopian Generations: The Political Horizon of Twentieth-Century Literature* and Marianne DeKoven's *Rich and*

Strange: Gender, History, Modernism note utopian political energies as a fundamental characteristic of modernist literature and the geographical locations to which it arguably dispersed. John Marx's *The Modernist Novel and the Decline of Empire* advances a similarly expansive case with a somewhat different tonality, suggesting that modernism was a key imaginative component in the rise of a new, dispersed global network of administration with (various forms of) the English language as its common idiom.

1.   At the Scene of the Time

1. Lamming's knowledge of Amis certainly belies his later claims in an interview with David Scott in *Small Axe* that in the 1950s he was not paying attention to English writers and critics, though this does not undermine his claim that French writers (loathed by the Movement writers) were most influential on him at that time.

2. It is worth mentioning Sukhdev Sandhu's *London Calling: How Black and Asian Writers Imagined a City* as a work that suggests something of a reciprocal relationship between immigrant writers and the metropolitan space of London, albeit largely in the imaginative realm and with considerable emphasis, still, on the writers' own creative agency.

3. Low's monograph *Publishing the Postcolonial* engages directly with the interactions between several Windrush writers and the British publishing world. Low conveys broad agreement with Kalliney's approach but deals primarily with 1960s-era publications. On the other hand, her emphasis on how the West Indian writers, unlike their fellow Commonwealth writers, published outside the educational arena lends support to claims here that Windrush writers were welcomed as "high" cultural producers.

4. It should be noted that the major figures of the Movement generally denied that they were part of any group. Although acquainted with each other, these writers maintained only a loose affiliation based on age and disposition rather than a consciously articulated aesthetic project. Later in the 1950s, inspired by the popularity of playwright John Osborne's *Look Back in Anger,* the label of choice used to describe this generation of writers became "Angry Young Men." While each of the terms has both salience and shortcomings, the original name "Movement" will be employed here throughout, in deference to the term's less restrictive range and the (rightly challenged now, but at the time quite accepted) connotations of a fiercely avant-garde sensibility.

5. Francis Wyndham's article "New West Indian Writers" explicitly argues that writing by West Indian writers is the place to look in postwar British letters for a continuation of the prewar modernist tradition: "in England during the 1950s a handful of West Indian writers are producing fresh and interesting books, unusual both in content and in style" (188). The review by Amis that Lamming excoriates, "Fresh Winds from the West," suggests a similar (if less celebratory) acceptance of this alignment.

6. See Bourdieu's *Distinction: A Social Critique of the Judgement of Taste* for a comprehensive account of this term, which is somewhat akin to Raymond Williams's "structure of feeling."

7. Paul Gilroy's *The Black Atlantic,* although it pays little attention to the Ca-

ribbean proper, is another important voice in this regard, asserting that the diasporic culture named by the book's title is a constitutive feature of modernity. As noted in the introduction to this book, Gikandi's starting point in *Writing in Limbo* is also closely related to an understanding of the Caribbean as necessarily enmeshed in modernity.

8. Both Raymond Williams's *The Politics of Modernism* and Elleke Boehmer's *Colonial and Postcolonial Literature* note the striking conjunction between colonial immigration to the imperial metropolis and the development of modernist practice. The generative forces of cultural mixture and estrangement they attribute to metropolitan space seem in many ways equally appropriate as a description of the Caribbean since 1492.

9. Collymore, of course, was the editor of *BIM* and was influential in incubating the careers not only of Lamming, Brathwaite, and Austin Clarke but, through *BIM*, almost all of the Windrush generation. For accounts of Collymore's crucial role in the period's literature, see Philip Nanton's *Remembering the Sea: An Introduction to Frank A. Collymore* and Edward Baugh's *Frank Collymore: A Biography*.

10. Lamming has sometimes included Joyce as an important literary forebear as well ("Interview with Mr. George Lamming," 100), while in terms of poetry, he names Thomas Hardy as a crucial figure due to his emphasis on sound and rhythm. In such discussions, Lamming also consistently returns to H. G. Wells's book *The Outline of History* as a catalyzing influence for exposing him to a much broader idea of history, beyond the narrowly British-centered version in which he was schooled.

11. The two letters to Collymore referred to here are dated Tuesday, Aug. 1949, and 5 Aug. 1949, respectively. They are in the Frank Collymore Collection at the Barbados Department of Archives (hereafter the Collymore Collection).

12. Selvon's article can be found in *Foreday Morning: Selected Prose 1946–1986*.

13. See Guari Viswanathan's *Masks of Conquest: Literary Study and British Rule in India* for an important critical account of the function of literature in colonial British education.

14. Both Gikandi and Edmonson, in quite different ways, have suggested the continuing influence of Victorian mores on the formation of Caribbean political and cultural subjectivity.

15. London, as envisioned here, is understood in ways similar to Brent Hayes Edwards's characterization of Paris in *The Practice of Diaspora*, as a site that both facilitates and is determined by transnational interchange and exchange. As Edwards observes, "to ask about the function of Paris is to ask a broader set of interrelated questions about the role of outernational sites" (4). Such a view, of course, has parallel implications when asking about the Caribbean.

16. Matthew Mead has convincingly demystified the (often verifiably false) elements that have gone into forming the conventional Windrush narrative, though he too insists on its continued importance to the British cultural imaginary.

17. The Caribbean region's average yearly emigration to Britain was indeed remarkable during this period, rising from less than 1,000 in the years before 1951 to 32,850 during the years from 1955 until the severely restrictive Commonwealth Immi-

gration Act of 1962. Peter Fryer's *Staying Power* notes that there were around 55,000 Indians and Pakistanis in Britain by 1958, a considerable increase in their population, but nevertheless vastly smaller in number than the Caribbean community.

18. Useful historical accounts of Britain's geopolitical struggles in this period can be found in David Childs's *Britain since 1945: A Political History,* John Darwin's *Britain and Decolonisation,* and vol. 1 of Keith Middlemas's *Power, Competition and the State.*

19. Indeed, this class confusion provides much of the subject matter for many of the most prominent novels of the time, not least those of Amis, John Braine, Osborne, Alan Sillitoe, and Wain. Upper-class panegyrics on the ostensible eclipse of aristocratic England—such as Evelyn Waugh's *Brideshead Revisited* and Angela Thirkell's *Peace Breaks Out*—also literarily reflect (albeit from a much different social position) the sense of shifting class dynamics.

20. Accounting in an interesting way for these odd political overlaps, Kalliney's *Cities of Affluence and Anger* argues that postwar Britain ultimately viewed the cultural distinctiveness of the class system itself as an important part of British identity.

21. Both Kathleen Paul and Paul Gilroy have noted the compelling connections between the rise of a postwar British national identity and discourses of racial exclusivity, further suggesting the fraught sociocultural landscape in which the Windrush writers initially found themselves.

22. More recently, critics such as Bradbury, Gasiorek, Dominic Head, and MacKay and Stonebridge have convincingly problematized the simplified narrative of a resurgent postwar realism at the utter expense of modernism. Nevertheless, they still acknowledge the period's primary tendency away from modernist aesthetics.

23. See also Blake Morrison, Alan Sinfield, Randall Stevenson, and William Van O'Connor, who all generally assess the major literary trend of the era as being explicitly opposed to the formal experimentation of writers like Joyce, Woolf, and Lawrence.

24. Arnold Bennett, famously, was the focus of Woolf's attack on realist fiction in "Mr. Bennett and Mrs Brown," and it is no accident that the subject of Wilson's article, a revival of Bennett's popularity, was helped in no small part by the advocacy of Wain, who also published an appreciation of Bennett in his *Preliminary Essays.*

25. Bloomsbury, the name commonly attached to the circle of friends associated with Woolf, was frequently used as a shorthand term for modernism at the time. In terms of literary criticism, Wyndham's view is not unrepresentative. Indeed, as early as 1952 the *Times Literary Supplement* (*TLS*) notes that contemporary writers "lack the zest for experiment that marked young men and women in the twenties" (Symons, "Uncommitted Talents," iii). Anthony Quinton observes in his 1958 consideration of the state of the novel in *London Magazine,* as well, that "the techniques of current fiction are resolutely traditional" and that "there is no notable writer openly dedicated to the idea of literary experiment" (Quinton et al., "New Novelists," 15).

26. Both Head and Gasiorek compellingly trouble the distinction between "realist" and "experimental," thereby undermining the very terms by which the common appraisal of the decade's literature is made. While from a purely literary perspective,

this argument is both important and convincing, it does not extend its efficacy into the historical or sociological realm: the authors and critics of the time emphatically positioned themselves on one side or the other of the realist-experimental debate, giving the terms legitimate purchase in an understanding of the literary production of the time.

27. Kalliney, though not specifically citing Ritchie, descries the same generational dynamics in the period, as discussed in more detail below.

28. In the literary struggles for critical supremacy in the 1950s, Lehmann quite clearly represented the older establishment to writers like Wain and Amis. An explicit rivalry emerged in 1953, when Wain's BBC radio program *First Readings* took over for Lehmann's *New Soundings*, positioning its editorial philosophy as diametrically opposed to that of its predecessor. Not coincidentally, Lehmann was also one of the earliest British champions of West Indian writing.

29. The program, begun by the Jamaican Una Marson, was broadcast to the Caribbean from 12 Mar. 1945 to 7 Sept. 1958. Swanzy took over as producer in 1946. V. S. Naipaul took over from Swanzy in the later years of the program, beginning in 1954. From 1956, various others also took on editing duties, often Mittelholzer. With the exception of Naipaul, who arrived on scholarship to Oxford, all of the major authors treated in this book had published pieces on the program before coming to England. In the case of Lamming, Mittelholzer, and Selvon, the primary reason for migrating evolved out of their success on the show.

30. All citations from *Caribbean Voices* are taken from the written transcripts at the BBC Written Archives Center (WAC), under the reference number R34/473/1. Throughout, they will be cited by *CV,* followed by the date of the program.

31. It is noteworthy that this month of experimentalism on *Caribbean Voices* occurs almost immediately after Lamming and Selvon begin to appear regularly as readers on the program.

32. A more cynical view of the show would note the paternalist implications of Swanzy's influence emanating from metropolitan London out to the benighted territories; in one critic's view, his influence was disturbingly strong at the time: "When Swanzy sneezed, the whole Caribbean caught a cold" ("What Does Mr. Swanzy Want?"). Swanzy was quite aware of this troublesome aspect of his position, frequently noting his outsider status, verbalizing his discomfort about sitting in judgment despite his lack of expertise, and reading aloud comments from listeners specifically criticizing the British assumptions inherent in the program.

33. It should be stressed that the type of ecumenical, transcultural tradition generally advocated by *Caribbean Voices* under Swanzy did not preclude a strong emphasis on formulating an alternative and distinct "national-regional" identity in opposition to dominant notions of Englishness: the goal of the program was overtly geared toward Caribbean self-realization. Indeed, Swanzy was notorious for insisting on "local color" in the submissions as part of a consistent effort to avoid the formation of a West Indian literature submissively subordinate to British or European canons of taste and suitability.

34. While it is tempting to see this eager metropolitan embrace of West Indian writers as yet another devious method of cooptation whereby the colonizing culture

ensures its dominance, Kalliney argues that such a view is too simple, noting that "we cannot assume that success in London's literary world implies political complicity any more than we can assert that hostility to modernist aesthetics guarantees a form of militancy" ("Metropolitan Modernism," 97).

35. Many other critics, including Lodge, Morrison, and Taylor, share such a view of Amis's antimodernist bent, which is particularly evident in his prolific journalism of the time.

36. Perhaps unsurprisingly, the Movement's emphasis on Englishness employs an almost exclusively masculine, heterosexual frame of reference. Foreignness, the wrong kind of femininity, and homosexuality are all lumped together as undesirable or improperly English.

37. Bradbury's "No, Not Bloomsbury" identifies the novel's vernacular voicing of protest against pretension, complexity, and the distractions of the far away as its most salient contribution to the ethos of postwar literary production.

38. As Lodge notes in his article "The Modern, the Contemporary, and the Importance of Being Amis," Amis traveled to Portugal and wrote the novel after winning the Somerset Maugham Award, an award designed to encourage writers to travel as a progressive gesture toward international understanding and cultural connection. The novel thus can be read as a private joke mocking the ideas behind the award.

39. Lodge finds a similar championing of everyday expression in *Lucky Jim*, connecting it with the "ordinary language" philosophy influential during Amis's time at Oxford as a student.

40. Lord Elton's anti-immigrant tract, *The Unarmed Invasion*, is one of the more egregious titular expressions of this attitude, while even Sheila Patterson's largely sympathetic study of West Indian migration, *Dark Strangers*, characterizes the status of its subjects as one of racialized unbelonging.

41. Embarrassingly falling prey to popular misconceptions, Spender mistakes Lamming's nationality as Jamaican.

42. Spender thus also perpetuates a trope, identified by Low as widespread, of the fresh, new, vital (primitive) literature able to infuse some energy and life into the tired, old English literary scene.

43. Although it was published anonymously, Arthur Calder Marshall is the author of this piece, "Caribbean Voices," and it appears under his name in the bibliography.

44. A prime indicator of these attitudes taken up by Morrison and other critics is the almost magical absorption into the upper class of the heroes of *Lucky Jim* and Wain's *Hurry on Down* despite most of the novels' energy being devoted to encouraging the reader to frown upon this very class of people.

45. Contemporary critics noted this tendency too; Angus Wilson describes the "neo-philistine, neo-realistic" attitude of these writers as characterized mainly by "self-interest ennobled by the violence of its expression or modified by sentimental clowning" ("Mood of the Month—III," 41), while Frank Hilton, a bit more glibly, describes this new class as "an army of rag-tag and bobtail new men who are fed up with you, fed

up with war, fed up with politics, fed up with rationing, and feel it is time that the good things in life came their way" ("Britain's New Class," 60). V. S. Pritchett likewise dismisses the political earnestness of the Movement, flatly stating that "it rejects committal. Its rancors are private" ("These Writers," 1).

46. In his Feb. 1957 foreword to *London Magazine,* a special issue on South African writing, Lehmann expresses similar optimistic support for Commonwealth writing, singling out the British West Indies as an especially fruitful literary region; in his Nov. 1958 foreword, Lehmann reinforces this view, distinguishing between "the novel in England" and "the novel written in English," with only the latter providing hope for lasting literary greatness (9).

47. The Suez crisis seems an uncannily appropriate emblem of political concern for the period, imbued as it is with its (unsuccessfully consummated) notions of reasserting British imperial power in the Middle East.

48. See Rushdie's "Outside the Whale."

49. Lessing's observations here find support in Rich's and Patterson's accounts of the period, which note a startling lack of knowledge on the part of UK citizens regarding their country's imperial holdings.

50. This is not to imply that the subject was not taken up in literature, as writers like Colin MacInnes and Alan Sillitoe deal relatively sympathetically, if problematically, with black immigrant characters in their novels. However, the Movement writers, along with their masculinist tendencies, generally included race only via a kind of casual racism in their works, such as Osborne's evocation of "some dirty old Arab, sticking his fingers into some mess of lamb fat and gristle" (*Look Back in Anger,* 19), Wain's description of his hungover character's mouth "like an Arab's armpit" (*Hurry on Down,* 233), or Amis's consistent mockery of foreigners in novels like *I Like It Here.*

51. Race was, not surprisingly, a particular topic on which the West Indian authors wished to be heard. Coupled with the steady stream of overt racism Caribbean migrants faced at this time was the complacent British self-conception of being unprejudiced and wholly fair-minded. As Walvin wryly observes, in midcentury Britain, "it was widely assumed by many prominent spokesmen and politicians in the host society [the United Kingdom] that whereas discrimination existed in other parts of the world (in the U.S.A., and South Africa, for instance), Britain was unusually free of this scourge" (*Passage to Britain,* 124).

52. Naipaul provides an important exception here, as he fits in quite readily with the Movement emphasis on apolitical, sparely literalist, "humane," and satirically comic prose. He rose to prominence just after the writers on which this book focuses, and his subsequently decisive influence on the end (and subsequent reception) of Windrush writing will be discussed in the book's concluding pages.

2.   "Child of Ferment"

1. At the time of writing, Peepal Tree Press had just reissued several of Mittelholzer's novels, with plans for more, as well as for a biography and a collection of critical essays.

2. Geoffrey Wagner's "Edgar Mittelholzer: Symptoms and Shadows" makes the case for Mittelholzer's fascism most directly, but Victor Chang's biographical treatment, A. J. Seymour's survey of Mittelholzer's novels, and Russell McDougall's analysis of *My Bones and My Flute* all suggest similar judgments.

3. The literature on the relationship between British modernism and its intersections with either a reactionary worldview or fascist politics is voluminous. A sampling of key texts might include Robert Casillo's *The Genealogy of Demons: Anti-Semitism, Fascism, and the Myths of Ezra Pound;* Elizabeth Cullingford's *Yeats, Ireland and Fascism;* Charles Ferrall's *Modernist Writing and Reactionary Politics;* John R. Harrison's *The Reactionaries;* Fredric Jameson's *Fables of Aggression: Wyndham Lewis, the Modernist as Fascist;* Peter Nicholls's *Ezra Pound: Politics, Economics, and Writing;* Michael North's *The Political Aesthetic of Yeats, Eliot, and Pound;* and Vincent Sherry's *Ezra Pound, Wyndham Lewis, and Radical Modernism.*

4. Mittelholzer was famously productive, composing, on average, well more than one novel a year for most of his writing life, despite the protestations of his publishers.

5. Mittelholzer's somewhat ghoulishly spectacular suicide—via self-immolation—has likewise contributed unfavorably to his critical reputation, allowing his work to be framed as the product of an irrational, unbalanced mind.

6. The valorized figures throughout Mittelholzer's work share this drive to singularity, including Harpo's fierce individualism in *The Aloneness of Mrs. Chatham* and Paul's stubborn iconoclasm in *Uncle Paul,* among numerous others. The relation of Mittelholzer's characters to the world—characterized by constant, strenuous struggle to locate a space of autonomy uncorrupted by the dictates of social expectation—can be likened in some sense to Mittelholzer's restive forays into multiple literary styles.

7. Mittelholzer's first novel, *Corentyne Thunder,* was published in London by Eyre & Spottiswoode in 1941 but, in some part due to the urgent distractions of World War II, never received much critical attention or notice.

8. Mittelholzer's letter to Frank Collymore of 19 June 1949 (Collymore Collection) reveals his proud sense that the novel had successfully appealed to the experimental, high-art tastes of the Woolfs' publishing house: "The treatment is very unusual (difficult to explain here), and I daresay it is what must have appealed to the Hogarth Press more than anything else, for, as you probably know, they publish very few novels, and those few are generally of an original or novel treatment or technique."

9. The orthographic levity of "The Sibilant and the Lost" prefigures the playful aspects of the experimental Oulipo tradition, particularly as practiced by Georges Perec. The story was reviewed on air by Arthur Calder Marshall, who dismisses it as a stunt and explains that Mittelholzer is having fun with the fact that the BBC typically frowns on too many *s* sounds because of the difficulty in pronouncing them audibly into a microphone.

10. Jacqueline Mittelholzer notes as well that "*A Morning at the Office* has been likened to Woolf's *The Waves,*" though, keeping true to her husband's instincts, she does not agree with the parallel ("Idyll and the Warrior," 64).

11. Marshall's later, 1955 commentary on Mittelholzer in *TLS* also focuses on his

technique, though, as discussed in the first chapter, he advances a rather more patronizing interpretation of it.

12. This review has no author named. It can be found in the bibliography, listed as "Review of *Latticed Echoes*."

13. Ironically, the introduction in the first case is also for a Selvon short story, which Mittelholzer takes as evidence that his fellow author has no technical mastery.

14. West Indian literary reviews, on the whole, were somewhat more sympathetic to Mittelholzer's experimentation, even concerning the more labored leitmotiv technique. See, e.g., the reviews of *Latticed Echoes* by A. J. Seymour (in *Kyk-over-al*) and by Harold Marshall (in *BIM*). Joyce and Woolf were also frequently mentioned as stylistic precursors in the West Indian reviews of Mittelholzer throughout his career.

15. Mittelholzer often seems to advance the Movement view of modernist technique as dubious intellectual chicanery, despite engaging overtly in the same strategies himself. Ironically, the critiques contained in his satirical take on the literature of futurity (which is represented as being interested solely in sound rather than semantic sense) in *A Twinkling in the Twilight* and his dismissive presentation of Susan's novel-writing strategy of piling "sentence upon sentence so as to achieve the highest degree of unreadability" (194) in *The Aloneness of Mrs. Chatham* sound startlingly similar to critiques reviewers leveled at *Latticed Echoes* and *Thunder Returning*.

16. The second set of ellipsis points in the quotation is per the original.

17. Equally typical of Mittelholzer, the implied subject of reform would have to be, more than any other character, Horace, the lowest-ranking member on the office's social scale. While the moral guidelines would apply to all, in the novel, Horace is the only real casualty of the tendency toward paranoid interpretation condemned in the novel.

18. Michael Gilkes interprets the Jen as representing "the repressed, creative self" ("Spirit in the Bottle," 243). Though complementary to the above reading, Gilkes's view narrows the story's social application down to the aesthetic sphere only. Howard's reading of the Jen as a frustrated longing can also be seen as complementary, though his interpretation emphasizes the sexual urge and suggests a deterministic view of the Jen as unavoidable.

19. Many of Mittelholzer's characters express similar, explicitly valorized views in favor of tolerance, such as in *Uncle Paul, Eltonsbrody, The Wounded and the Worried,* and *Shadows Move Among Them,* among other novels. However, the stricture is oddly unidirectional, somehow allowing for social eccentricity and subversion in Mittelholzer-approved ways while not applying to certain crimes, sexual behaviors, political views, and even cultural dispositions of which Mittelholzer viscerally disapproved.

20. As in many other things, Mittelholzer had a strangely ambivalent attitude toward homosexuality. While he seems to have been wary or even dismissive of feminine traits in men—particularly evident in his autobiography, *A Swarthy Boy* (28, 64, 84, 113, 128)—he gives gay characters (always overly effeminate men) quite positive roles in many of his novels, such as Graham and Uncle Raphael in the Kaywana trilogy and Archie in *The Aloneness of Mrs. Chatham.* In "Malicious Morality," a column for the *Barbados Ad-*

vocate, Mittelholzer suggests tolerance of gay behavior to be a virtue of ancient societies. In another such column, "Sexual Inverts," though he opines that tolerating too many open homosexuals would be "a menace to society," he nevertheless approvingly notes that "homosexuals have figured, and still figure, among the cream of the world's culture." Moreover, Mittelholzer takes the trouble to write a letter to the editor of the *TLS,* asserting that its review of *The Piling of the Clouds* is mistaken in detecting any animus toward "homosexuals" in the novel. He takes pains to note that, though the book does condemn many types of people ("unilateralists, pacifists, neutralists, and various kinds of pseudo-liberals," as well as violent criminals), homosexuals are emphatically not included.

21. The ellipsis points in the quotation are per the original.

22. This formulation arises in his response to the question "Is there a West Indian way of life?" which appeared in *Kyk-over-al* in 1955, discussed below. The employment of "primitive" as a characterization of African-derived folk tales is also revealing: Mittelholzer famously disputed the use of such terms (especially "native") to describe people from the Caribbean but did not hesitate to use them to describe inhabitants of *other* areas of the world, notably Africa.

23. Perhaps the most concrete manifestation of this urge is the Kaywana trilogy, which, with its historical sweep and geographical focus, seems intended to serve as an imaginative national epic for Guyana.

24. Many of these formulations occur in his columns discussing religious thought—Mittelholzer seems to have been taken aback by the overt, deeply conservative religiosity he witnessed in Barbados—but the general outlines of his iconoclasm enter fluidly into other spheres, especially the cultural and social ones: consensus in these areas was also considered stultifying and potentially dangerous. One of Mittelholzer's favorite targets in the social sphere was the unthinking duplication of European sartorial styles in a West Indian climate completely unsuitable for them.

25. Other of Menand's descriptions of Eliot also seem appropriate to Mittelholzer, such as the notion that "Eliot was an avant-gardist, but he was also a critic of avant-garde aspirations" and the sense that Eliot and others "engaged in a good deal of shouting against the nineteenth century and . . . at the same time did their best in various ways to live up to the nineteenth century's cultural standards" (*Discovering Modernism,* 4).

26. In the Caribbean context, of course, the Eliotic concept of tradition has proven widely influential. Wilson Harris's essays in *Tradition, the Writer and Society* draw explicitly on Eliot's work, and both Walcott and Brathwaite also look to Eliot as a critical lodestar. For an in-depth examination of the Eliotic influences on these latter two, see Charles Pollard's *New World Modernisms.*

27. In *The Piling of the Clouds* Peter articulates a version of this gradualist view, telling Charles, "You can't reform people overnight. The outlooks of people can only be changed by a cataclysm or by evolution" (82).

28. It seems fair to say that Mittelholzer willfully ignored the symbolic political implications of a more Afrocentric cultural outlook in his advocacy of a predominantly

European cultural tradition. It is also the case, however, that his arguments pay more attention to the historical weight and prevalence of European norms, rather than their "naturalness" or innate, universal applicability. Nevertheless, the racial underside of Mittelholzer's assertion of a West Indian identity frequently emerges as a distinction between the "civilized" nature of West Indian society and the "primitive," African way of life that still persisted (to Mittelholzer's mind) in twentieth-century Africa.

29. Such a view has compelling similarities with Lamming's notion of a "backward glance," although for Lamming the greater emphasis is on innovation and newness rather than the encumbrance of history.

30. Mittelholzer cites no particular review, and its bibliographical details remain unrecovered at this time.

31. Interestingly, in 1954, Mittelholzer wrote a review of Woolf's posthumous *A Writer's Diary,* in which he lauds her, and the Bloomsbury circle in general, as representative of a more wholesome time in which "civilized people could genuinely be interested in the finer things of living for the sake of these finer things—and not for the sake of commercial involvements" ("Dying Integrity"). Thus, despite his discomfort with technical comparisons with Woolf, Mittelholzer comes down clearly on the side (in this case, anyway) of the aesthetic bête noir of the Movement and its acolytes.

32. Mittelholzer had something of an obsession about his family's Swiss-German heritage and the forceful prestige of German culture, so it is no accident that Richard, the hero, also identifies himself as having German ancestry. In many ways, Germany stood as a convenient affiliation for Mittelholzer, appropriately distant from both Guyanese and British connection and likewise far enough removed to avoid dominance in his own upbringing. Emily's analysis of her father's obsession with Germanness in this episode (127–28) explicitly echoes such a reading of compensatory reaction-formation, though, as is typical in Mittelholzer, this analysis is ultimately discounted as too inattentive to genetic inheritance to be viable.

33. It is certainly imaginable that the third novel could have ended similarly to *A Tale of Three Places,* in which the protagonist calmly and decisively chooses to leave his passionate, soul-mate paramour and return to the regularizing routine of familial responsibility.

34. This ridiculing of the pompous self-certainty of characters espousing what are commonly thought of as Mittelholzer's own views—Paul even admits to his priggish tendency to spew "junk" out at his interlocutors in *Uncle Paul*—adds a surprisingly consistent, if understated self-conscious critique of such views. This critique perhaps finds its apogee in Mittelholzer's last two novels, *The Aloneness of Mrs. Chatham* and *The Jilkington Drama,* in which multiple characters have both conflicting and overlapping traits typically valorized by Mittelholzer, such that a simple, straightforward understanding of what is most valued in the novels is not realistically obtainable. More sweepingly, Gilkes, one of Mittelholzer's most perceptive and persuasive readers, has asserted, "it is never safe in reading his work to accept a superficial estimate (even if it appears to be Mittelholzer's own) of events or characters" ("Edgar Mittelholzer," 134).

35. The "Guide to Leitmotivs" provided at the end of *Thunder Returning* lists

Richard's compound leitmotiv as: "Perpetually . . . distant artillery . . . bass buzzing . . . giant bees trapped . . . basement . . . core . . . detached . . . fight . . . march . . . Create . . . image . . . feather-bed tilting . . . dark . . . waves . . . daze . . . actuality . . . fancy . . . dipping . . . rocking . . . illusion . . . insecurity . . . circumference" (237, original ellipses).

36. The bull frogs and their distinctive "quark" sound are explicitly named as part of the British Guiana leitmotiv in the appendix of *Thunder Returning* (237). Perhaps revealingly, Mittelholzer does not formally name any images specific to Richard and Lindy's lovemaking in the appendix.

37. The passage clearly suggests the procreative potential as well, since Lindy observes that the day is an ideal one for her in terms of fertility, and of course, it later emerges that she and Richard did conceive a child that day.

38. Birbalsingh, in assessing the importantly experimental nature of Mittelholzer's literary accomplishments, predicts success in almost precisely these terms, opining that "Mittelholzer will gradually come to be regarded as the true innovator of a literature that is finally free from parochialism" ("Edgar Mittelholzer," 103).

3.   Engaging the Reader

1. Lamming originally intended to be a poet, and though he ultimately became known as a novelist, his prose still bears palpable traces of this early lyrical ambition. The critic Ian Munro sees less value in Lamming's early poetry than Swanzy does, dismissing it as "experimental and often overly imitative" ("Early Work of George Lamming," 327).

2. While one might take issue with the cultural and historical homogeneity implied by his book's general assumption that "all modern readers subscribed to the same hierarchy of value" (*Difficulties of Modernism,* 63), Diepeveen convincingly documents a consistent tension between advocates of stylistic complexity or simplicity in twentieth-century literature.

3. On the other hand, his status as "new" (i.e., ethnically other) could be argued as an advantage in the British publishing competition: Lamming was frequently reviewed together with African American authors such as James Baldwin and Africans such as Amos Tutuola, and the market for books written by people of African descent—targeted mainly toward the guilty liberal British conscience—was certainly expanding.

4. Esty's *A Shrinking Island* adeptly illustrates British authors' struggle to adapt modernism to nativism in a strain of late modernism. Esty includes readings of Selvon and Lamming as participants in the anthropological turn he identifies taking shape in the middle of the century. While his readings of these two West Indian authors convincingly illustrate how their novels work to displace Englishness as a universal category, they do not strongly register the cultural politics of Lamming's and Selvon's formal choices (and in some ways suggest that the authors' primary interest lies in portraying British people and customs).

5. Lamming recounts this episode in *The Pleasures of Exile* as well (56–57).

6. In a BBC radio interview about a British antiracism bill, Lamming suggests

an empirical model for this double sense of "engagement," asserting that he sometimes encourages racist expression to facilitate an argument, after which, at least, some lines of communication can be said to have been formed ("This Time of Day"). In later writings, Lamming has also emphasized the need to recognize the importance of conflict as a creative process that is "accepted as a norm and not a distortion" (*Sovereignty of the Imagination*, 58).

7. Interestingly, in contemplating the British government's initial 1944 discussion of the establishment of tertiary education in their Caribbean colonies, Lamming uses markedly similar terminology to Woolf's: "It is at this critical juncture when new definitions will have to be found to clarify the meaning of the word 'civilization' that the meetings to consider the creation of the University of the West Indies took place" (*Sovereignty of the Imagination*, 23).

8. Marshall makes exactly the same comparison in his *Caribbean Voices* review of the novel (*CV*, 22 Mar. 1953).

9. Pritchett's choice of possessive pronoun reveals much: although Britain encouraged its colonized population to consider themselves British, the reality in the home country was quite removed from this ideal of national solidarity. In literary reviews of the time, there is a symptomatic oscillation between differentiating and claiming the writing of the Commonwealth.

10. The reviewer is not named, so the review appears in the bibliography under its title, "New Fiction."

11. Edward Said's *Orientalism* is a fundamental and originary postcolonial text in pointing out precisely how organized (and thus easily internalized) the effect of colonial discourse can be.

12. In such a context, it is also useful to note Diepeveen's assessment that antidifficulty arguments almost always employ a language of normativity in which "difficulty is typically presented as an abnormal state of affairs" (*Difficulties of Modernism*, 74)—an appealing trait if one is seeking distinction of some kind.

13. See pages 33–34.

14. Of course, for many commentators, including Lamming himself, this blending of the narration between first and third person, between a singular subject and a more plural village-oriented one, articulates via formal qualities precisely the hesitation and struggle between individual and community on which the book's content focuses.

15. This discourse of development, here couched within the terms of the literary, has obvious overlaps with the era's familiar political claims that British colonies were not yet ready or mature enough for independence.

16. This *London Times* review is also unattributed. It is alphabetized in the bibliography under its title.

17. Nadi Edwards has likewise asserted that Lamming's advocacy of a newfound linguistic agency should be seen as a central aim of "the complex experimental narratives that constitute his fiction," though Edwards ultimately reads this agency as resolutely vernacular and anti-Western ("George Lamming's Literary Nationalism," 61).

18. Indeed, although it is largely a matter of emphasis, it could be argued that the concentrated focus on English identity that Esty identifies both presupposes and consolidates an even firmer conception of what is considered "not-English." Both Ian Baucom and Gikandi, as Esty notes, provide compelling witness to the necessary re-imaginings of Englishness accompanying the migration of former colonial subjects to metropolitan England.

19. The first item in the series, oddly, is *The Waste Land,* which the author apparently likewise sees as an object of mainly anthropological interest and, like the others, a dire expression of the breakdown of the rules of language. The sense in the review is of West Indian writing as degenerate, just like the writings of the modernists, and indeed, both Mittelholzer and Lamming are specifically rebuked by the author for the pretension of their experimental aims.

20. C. L. R. James wrote a letter to the editor that appears in the 28 Sept. 1962 *TLS,* asserting that West Indian novels provide far more than simply insights into Caribbean life and placing the article's (then anonymous) author in the nefarious tradition of James Anthony Froude.

21. John Plotz has argued in a similar vein about Lamming's authorial attempt to "re-possess" what the Empire perceives as objects, though his emphasis on the far-reaching potency of creative imagination may seem undue given Lamming's clear-eyed view of the material restraints imposed by imperial history.

22. Mimi Sheller's *Consuming the Caribbean,* in its *longue durée* analysis of the products and images traveling between England and the Caribbean since Columbus, makes provocative use of the metaphor of consumption and its very literal, material effects on the bodies, psyches, and landscapes of the Caribbean people.

23. Emery provides an illuminating reading of this scene, noting that Lamming employs "modernist devices" to portray how the incident, for Dickson, "has altered his deepest sense of himself as a person in time and space" (*Modernism, the Visual,* 162). In her reading, Emery emphasizes how emigrant men are feminized by the colonial gaze in the novel, usefully connecting this phenomenon with earlier historical instances of imperial interest in observing exhibits of exotic, eroticized women.

24. Many critics, including Nair, M. Morris, and Paquet, have viewed the "Author's Note" in a negative light, considering it unwieldy, unnecessary, or even, in Nair's case, in direct opposition to the overarching message of the novel. The reading here suggests that the passage's emphasis on self-critical humility in the face of difference is in direct agreement with the novel's ethos.

25. Imre Szeman is among the most recent critics to assert that, for Lamming, the novel genre was attractive because of its capacity for use as a pedagogic technology (*Zones of Instability,* 76). Forbes, Gikandi, Joyce Jonas, and Avis G. McDonald have also all drawn attention to the investment Lamming's work makes in underscoring the relationship of reader to text.

26. As Curdella Forbes has noted in " . . . And the Dumb Speak," Lamming's fiction often operates *as* theory, enacting theoretical principles rather than simply de-

scribing or presenting them. Forbes connects the opacity of Lamming's texts to the indecipherability of the human (specifically Caribbean) body in *The Emigrants,* arguing that this hermeneutical resistance creates space for a liberating self-fashioning.

27. This manuscript can be found in the Sam Selvon Collection, University of the West Indies (UWI), St. Augustine, item 88, p. 8 (hereafter the Selvon Collection).

28. The parallel is interesting in that the Movement writers also considered themselves heirs to the same eighteenth-century novelists, the difference surely being that Lamming is comparing sociocultural function, while Amis and company were trying to simulate actual writing style. Lamming's point is also about new cultural beginnings, while the overriding tendency of the Movement was to *return* to "real Englishness."

29. This is not to say that Lamming did not have readers in the Caribbean. He clearly received, on the whole, a serious and often enthusiastic reception among the reviewers of regional journals and newspapers. Moreover, browsing the archive of Barbados's *Sunday Advocate* reveals that both major booksellers of the island—Advocate Stationery and the book department of C. F. Harrison & Co.—advertised Lamming's novels for sale. Indeed, Advocate Stationery not only initially devoted a rare, single advertisement wholly to *In the Castle of My Skin* but also put out a second one a month later to announce the receipt of a second shipment of the novel, indicating a certain level of (largely middle-class) popularity for the book.

30. Lamming's 1956 speech "The Negro Writer and His World," discussed below, is an eloquent testament to his carefully calibrated universalism. Without sacrificing an anticolonial, antiracist politics, Lamming nevertheless strongly insists that black writers cannot lose sight of how their plight can be rendered, and hence comprehended, as a universal condition.

31. In his introduction to the University of Michigan Press's paperback edition of *In the Castle of My Skin,* Lamming explicitly parallels what he characterizes as the authoritarian leanings of contemporary pan-Africanists in Barbados with the old colonial ideology, emphasizing, in keeping with Fanon, that the imperialist mindset is not merely the monopoly of the original colonizing power. Shephard and Singh, from *Of Age and Innocence,* are particular examples of such behavior in Lamming's fiction.

32. Lamming generally includes all who read the English language within the rubric of "English reading," asserting that English is also and emphatically a West Indian language. Caryl Phillips notes the utopian nature of Lamming's ideas of altering the nature of reading, cautioning that it would be unwise to "underestimate the impervious nature of British society" (*New World Order,* 236). Nevertheless, Phillips lists himself as someone profoundly affected by reading both Lamming's and Selvon's writing.

33. McDonald analyzes a complementary passage on reading in *Natives of My Person,* in which the Commandant, reading over his old diary entries, appears to recognize the self-serving contradictions in his writing.

34. A comment about Mark's private artistry accidentally falling into its readership's hands rather than being consciously communicated could also be read into this scene. Lamming sees Mark's inability to communicate meaningfully, even with those who are closest to him, as his greatest flaw ("Sovereignty of the Imagination," 145). For

Lamming this is an explicit failure for a writer, who is obliged by his function as writer to be a public figure, of however limited a kind.

35. James Proctor's *Dwelling Places,* in its analysis of spatial representations in Black British literature, has an extended discussion of the barbershops and hair salons in Lamming's novels as places of succor and community. Paquet, on the other hand, reads these spaces as negative embodiments of British social prejudice.

36. It is perhaps not coincidental that Attridge here acknowledges a debt to Sartre's *What Is Literature?,* as this book is one that Lamming has identified as formative in his understanding of the role of a writer. Both Janet Butler ("Existentialism of George Lamming") and Emery (*Modernism, the Visual*) have discussed the Sartrean influence on Lamming's thought.

37. Lamming takes this phrase from a speech by the Guyanese poet Martin Carter. Emery's examination of the important ways in which Fola both sees and acknowledges being seen in *Season of Adventure* outlines a similar sense—in the register of the visual—of Lamming's affirmation of creative, self-reflexive reciprocity (*Modernism, the Visual,* 165).

38. In the anxiety it evinces with regard to the communal cohesion of even the smallest scale of local inhabitation, *In the Castle of My Skin* bears some striking resemblances to Woolf's *Between the Acts,* which catalogs the conflicting consciousnesses of English villagers on the cusp of World War II.

39. Critics who, to varying degrees, view Trumper as the novel's predominant affirmative character include Butler, Eugenia Collier, Munro, Mbatau Kaburu Wa Ngai, Paquet, and Ngugi wa Thiong'o. Lamming's 1983 introduction to the novel makes an indirect critique of Trumper's advocacy of purely racial solidarity, dismissing the reactive response of a "rhapsodic and uncritical embrace of Africa as a mother once stolen and now miraculously restored" (xlv). Lamming cites the voice of the ancestral spirit who speaks, significantly, through Pa, warning against such Garveyite romanticism, as a powerful rebuttal of precisely this viewpoint in his novel.

40. Trumper, in his lack of interest in what G. is trying to say, parallels the narrator's unnamed friend in *The Emigrants,* discussed above. Lamming's latest views are in concord with such a suspicion of Trumper's disavowal of further questioning, as he equates simply being as a process of continual enquiry (*Sovereignty of the Imagination,* 35). As Patrick Taylor likewise observes, Trumper, in not remaining open to new knowledge, "is in danger of becoming a 'corpse'" (*Narrative of Liberation,* 222).

41. The gendered language in Lamming's address reveals the assumptions and expectations with regard to "the Negro Writer" at the time of the conference, as well as the general status of what was then called Negro writing as an almost exclusively male artistic preserve.

42. Jonas similarly notes that Lamming's (and Wilson Harris's) work demands "the reader's active participation in a deconstructive rewriting of texts" (*Anancy in the Great House,* 2).

43. Richard Clarke has noted the emphasis Lamming puts on Marxist notions of agency, with their insistence on recognizing both the restraints of one's social and his-

torical situatedness and the creative power of human endeavor. Although possibly too sanguine about the efficacy of Lamming's texts in the social realm, Patrick Taylor takes a similar view of Lamming's aims, using his novels as examples of liberating narratives that "transform the socio-political totality so that lived history becomes open possibility" (*Narrative of Liberation,* 189).

44. The utopian nature of this project is palpable, and Lamming's long literary silence suggests something of his ultimate evaluation of its viability. Rafael Dalleo has suggested an explanation for Lamming's turn away from novel writing, arguing that the anticolonial content of his novels had increasingly little purchase in a world becoming dominated by the imperatives of the United States. The contours of this argument are compelling, though the contents of Lamming's novels, beginning as early as *Of Age and Innocence,* extend well beyond the merely anticolonial into a critique of independence and postindependence Caribbean possibilities. It would seem, as well, that Lamming is most concerned with the *form* of media in which he works, variably expressing interest in drama, radio, television, film, and political speeches later in life.

4.   A Commoner Cosmopolitanism

1. Selvon himself encouraged such an image in some cases, indeed once referring to himself in an interview with Reed Dasenbrock and Feroza Jussawalla as "what one would perhaps call a primitive writer" (118). At other times, of course, he capably discusses technique and form in interviews while maintaining an insistence on the relatively autodidactic origin of his achievements.

2. The resilience of such views can be seen in Margaret Paul Joseph's assessment of Selvon, which provides an overarching characterization of Selvon's work that echoes Birbalsingh quite closely. Joseph lays emphasis at the outset of her discussion of Selvon on his "gentle comedy, his compassionate realism, and his subtle pathos" (*Caliban in Exile,* 84).

3. Barratt's article initially appeared in 1981 in *English Studies in Canada* and will be quoted throughout in its original form.

4. Gordon Rohlehr's article "Literature and the Folk," although not concerned with issues of European influence, is an important meditation on how the term *folk* cannot properly capture the complexity of geography, class, and race in the Caribbean. Rohlehr uses the multiplicity of "folk" subjects found in Selvon's writing as a prominent example of this complexity.

5. It was only in the 1990s that Joyce's anticolonial politics become generally recognized by literary scholars. Cheng's "Of Canons, Colonies, and Critics: The Ethics and Politics of Postcolonial Joyce Studies" provides a useful overview of the rise of this critical urge to question the canonical assumptions of Joyce as primarily an apolitical stylist.

6. In interviews, Selvon often emphasizes the egalitarian, universalist aims of *A Brighter Sun,* such as when he tells Ramchand "it still amazes me that when some people talk about that novel they mention the Tiger-Joe relationship as a racial statement.

To me I was just portraying the relationship that existed between two human beings and that was all" ("Sam Selvon Talking," 97).

7. Conversely, one of Selvon's most common complaints about the British was in fact their woeful ignorance of the very existence of Trinidad. He presented much of his writing as a means of closing this gap in knowledge.

8. This item, dated 31 Mar. 1952, appears in Selvon's personal papers in the Selvon Collection, item 267.

9. Selvon's papers held in the Selvon Collection indicate that the American response to *A Brighter Sun* followed in much the same vein as the British one, focusing especially on the perceived simplicity of the author and his work. Especially in the case of his early novels, Selvon seems to have kept himself well informed about what reviewers said about his books on both sides of the Atlantic via a news-clipping service. Intriguingly, given Selvon's famed optimism, the complimentary words or phrases in the clippings are all underlined (though whether this was done by Selvon or by the clipping service is unclear).

10. The *TLS* database does not identify the author of this piece. It is listed in the bibliography by its title.

11. A handful of American reviews did register the book's broader message of a shared humanity, including reviews in the *Tuscon Citizen* (Selvon Collection, item 270), the *Hartford Courant* (item 368), and the *Louisville Courier-Journal* (item 396).

12. In conversation with Peter Nazareth, Selvon suggests that this message of human universality characterized all of his writings: "I think that in my work this is one of the things that I tried to explain—that human beings from any part of the world think and experience the whole range of human emotion and experience" (81).

13. Roydon Salick's *The Novels of Samuel Selvon* notes that the original conception Selvon had for the title of his first novel was an even more "peasant-oriented" one—*Soul and Soil* (16).

14. The focus of this novel has led commentators such as Susheila Nasta to characterize it, along with *I Hear Thunder*, as a middle-class novel. The other categories Nasta employs are peasant novels (including the Tiger novels, *The Plains of Caroni*, and *Those Who Eat the Cascadura*) and immigrant novels (encompassing the Moses trilogy and *The Housing Lark*). Salick employs these categories in structuring his monograph on Selvon's novels.

15. Ramchand goes a step further, asserting that Tiger, Foster, and Moses, the central figure of *The Lonely Londoners*, represent the "quintessential Selvon hero" in their collective tendency toward reflective engagement with philosophical issues of "Time, Death, Friendship, and the Meaning of Life" ("Celebrating Sam Selvon," 49).

16. Somewhat ironically, given the metropolitan conflation of Tiger and Selvon, it is Foster's background that more closely resembles Selvon's own. Indeed, though this is often overlooked, Selvon claimed that his "middle-class" novels (*An Island is a World* and *I Hear Thunder*) best reflected his own personal experiences and thoughts ("Old-talk," 120), while insisting that *A Brighter Sun* was very far removed from his actual life in Trinidad. As he tells Daryl Cumber Dance, "when *A Brighter Sun* was published,

everyone thought that, well, there must be a great deal of biographical material in this book, and strictly speaking, there is absolutely none at all" ("Conversation with Samuel Selvon," 249).

17. Selvon's intricate negotiation of the particular and the collective resonates with Natalie Melas's compelling concept of "dissimilation," articulated in *All the Difference in the World: Postcoloniality and the Ends of Comparison* and associated by her with both modernist and postcolonial Caribbean literary forms.

18. This letter does actually begin with a note of its location—London—all the way on the right margin of the page, so there is some chance that this might alert a careful reader that the letter is from Foster, whom the reader already knows to be in London. However, the fact that the place name is on the right margin makes it easy to miss, and there is certainly no reason that Rena herself could not be in London. Most compellingly, of course, the previous sentence contains a strong implication that any letter that follows would be the one under discussion.

19. The insistent, unceasing blurring of the lines between "characters" found in *Finnegans Wake* is likewise a technique that seeks to enunciate the same sense of simultaneous unity and difference.

20. In interviews, this view closely tracks Selvon's preference for open-minded cultural assimilation. He tells Nazareth that he thinks West Indians have a particular capacity for such assimilation ("Interview with Sam Selvon," 432), and the ideal definition of "Caribbean man" he provides to Dance has a similar emphasis: "you're not Indian, you're not Black, you're not even white; you assimilate all these cultures and you turn out to be a different man who is the Caribbean man" ("Conversation with Samuel Selvon," 253). In both instances, there is a simultaneous emphasis on cross-cultural openness anchored in local (Caribbean) roots.

21. Similarly, although critics like Birbalsingh and Ramchand have assailed his nationalist credentials, Selvon in fact embraced his own national identification throughout his career, describing himself in conversation with Nazareth as a "real born Trinidadian, you can't get away from it" ("Interview with Sam Selvon," 83).

22. In *A Portrait of the Artist as a Young Man*, Joyce suggests a similar connection between personal and cosmic in what Stephen has written on the flyleaf of his geography book, which names "himself, his name and where he was" in ascending order from his school, town, county, country, and continent on to "The World" and "The Universe" (15).

23. Rebecca Walkowitz employs a similar sense of cosmopolitanism, suggesting that modernist narrative styles are especially well suited to communicating such a disruptive epistemological intervention (see *Cosmopolitan Style*).

24. Interestingly, Salick, a Caribbean critic, also censures the overly European nature of the novel, opining that Selvon's attempt to craft a localized version of "more famous European existentialist heroes presents serious problems of credibility" (*Novels of Samuel Selvon*, 83). Both critics thus suggest that existentialism has no authentic place in Caribbean fiction.

25. This review is discussed in more detail in chapter 1 (33–34).

26. This article is titled "Two Novels by Selvon" and is item 261 in the Selvon Collection.

27. Selvon critics have yet to settle on a name for the language used in his "dialect novels," characterizing it variously as Trinidadian, modified West Indian Standard, creole, and many other loosely defined terms. The most commonly approved term today is probably creole. Matthew Hart's *Nations of Nothing But Poetry* places Selvon's language into the evocative category of the "synthetic vernacular," which Hart considers emblematic of modernist poetics.

28. Although Selvon is often credited with writing the first (modern) West Indian novel entirely in dialect form, Ramchand and other critics have pointed out that Vic Reid's *New Day,* narrated in a Jamaican dialect, preceded Selvon's novel by seven years. However, Ramchand insists on a crucial distinction between the two novels: while Reid's book is told in the first person, with the narrator implied to be a relatively uneducated, oral teller, Selvon's novel is the first to use dialect for a *third-person* narrative voice that is not refracted through any characters but takes on all the authority and objectivity implied by third-person narration (*West Indian Novel,* 101–2).

29. The segment on *The Lonely Londoners* in David Dabydeen and Nana Wilson-Tagoe's *A Reader's Guide to West Indian and Black British Literature* is an early, important (though perhaps overemphatic) delineation of the novel's distress over British racism.

30. Page A of a screenplay Selvon wrote for *The Lonely Londoners* (Selvon Collection, item 151) provides a particularly clear insight into Selvon's thinking regarding the novel, describing the purpose of the film in unequivocal terms as that of evenhanded education and transethnic identification: "its purpose is to show that [immigrant West Indians] behave as anybody else in certain given situations, and the audience should identify themselves and not be dished out with the popular concepts of the tribulations and hardships of black people. On the other hand, neither should it be a propaganda piece exhibiting the nobilities and durabilities of the negro."

31. Interestingly, Galahad, perhaps the most important character aside from Moses, is remembered appearing with Harris in the park, "both of them dress like Englishmen, with bowler hat and umbrella, and the *Times* sticking out of the jacket pocket so the name would show" (140). Moreover, Selvon attaches this characterization to the character George in "Come Back to Grenada" (*Foreday Morning,* 177), an early iteration of *The Lonely Londoners,* in which George embodies the experiences of both Moses and Galahad, further suggesting the breadth of acceptable "West Indianness" in Selvon's London novel.

32. In being the social unifier, Harris bears comparison to Clarissa Dalloway in Woolf's *Mrs. Dalloway.*

33. Jennifer Rahim pays particular attention to this scene in "(Not) Knowing the Difference: Calypso Overseas and the Sound of Belonging in Selected Narratives of Migration." She, too, notes that Moses registers some disapproval of the "excessiveness and potentially counterproductive behavioral modes of the 'boys'" (par. 9) and argues that it would be reductive to read Harris as a wholly negative sign of "one-sided accom-

modation" (par. 10). However, Rahim ultimately reads Harris's Englishness as a subversive "excessive identity performance" (par. 12), akin to his fellow West Indians' more direct refusals of British social norms, rather than as a potentially authentic gesture of cultural rapprochement.

34. An early essay by Selvon, "Thoughts . . . Here and There" (Selvon Collection, item 548), also explicitly remarks the need for West Indians to shed acquaintances and ways of thinking maintained merely out of comfortable habit, particularly decrying the stolid determinism evoked by the phrase "what is to is must is," a phrase that has been singled out and cited by some critics as an approving expression of West Indian resilience, rather than the narrow defeatism that Selvon suggests in this essay.

35. As Nick Bentley observes regarding Selvon's third novel: "for an addressee belonging to dominant white culture the text re-activates the very stereotypes it claims to challenge" ("Black London," 43). Bentley also asserts the more positive, yet still firmly separatizing, implications for a black audience, to whom the text can "represent an empowering framework of cultural differentiation and celebration" (43).

36. This quotation is taken from a clipping of an advertisement for a series of six stories by Selvon to appear, in a series called "London Calypso," on the front page of the paper's edition of 30 Mar. 1957 (Selvon Collection, item 281).

37. Some reviewers, it is true, note the dialect narration as obtrusive or artificial. For example, Quigly describes it as "a literary trick rather than the author's authentic voice," while the *London Times* notes the novel's "effective if self-conscious use of dialect." Thus, it seems clear, if it was perceived as consciously crafted, the dialect was suspicious for not being "natural."

38. The review, which appeared on 12 Jan. 1957, is item 321 in the Selvon Collection.

39. To be fair, while Betjeman seems to discount Selvon's conscious artistry and ability, his review does register that the novel should not be read as a purely comic production. On the other hand, Betjeman makes the frustratingly familiar error of grouping all West Indian immigrants under the category of "Jamaican." His review, which appeared on 21 Dec. 1956, is item 365 in the Selvon Collection.

40. The American reviews similarly reinforce this familiar separation. See, e.g., John Hicks in the *St. Louis Post-Dispatch* (Selvon Collection, item 402) and Evelyn Levy in the *Baltimore Sunday Sun* (item 420).

41. Much of the material in Selvon's papers at the Harry Ransom Center reinforces this emphasis on tolerance and mixture, such as a TV/film script titled "Milk in the Coffee" that concludes with a scene of the protagonists, a mixed-race couple, dancing together at a club. Selvon's treatment is emphatically egalitarian: "CUT TO DISCOTHEQUE WITH LOUD 'SOUL' MUSIC/SINGING . . . LOTS OF YOUNG PEOPLE, BOTH BLACK AND WHITE, DANCING, INCLUDING ANDREW AND BRENDA, BUT WITH *NO* SPECIAL FOCUS ON THEM . . . BRING UP CREDIT TITLES ON THIS SCENE—TO END" (manuscript notebook containing holograph drafts of radio and television plays, the opening lines of *Moses Ascending*, unfinished story, and various notes, dated 1973).

42. Ironically, the converse of this criticism could be leveled at *The Lonely Londoners,* as it does not present any real depictions of a white, English point of view. In a 1959 letter to Selvon held at the Harry Ransom Center, John Figueroa tactfully suggests, in response to the controversial scene in which Tiger essentially rapes the estate owner's wife, that the novel could have been improved by considering the woman's point of view.

43. In this context, it is useful to note that, as Selvon discussed with Dance ("Conversation with Samuel Selvon," 254), he was obliged by his publisher, Allen Wingate, to leave out an aggressive and sharply political interracial sex episode set in Britain in *An Island Is a World* (similar, it would seem, to the scene in *Turn Again, Tiger,* which Selvon brought out with a different publisher). A very stern 1954 letter from Charles Fry suggests that Selvon initially resisted the changes to his manuscript but, under threat of breach of contract, ultimately acquiesced. Although Paola Loreto's "The Male Mind and the Female Heart" attempts to redeem Selvon's sexual politics by arguing that his two "Tiger novels" evoke a gentle philosophy of gender complementariness, the consistent appearance of male sexual domination (especially across racial lines) suggests gender as a relative blind spot in Selvon's articulations of cosmopolitan equality. Critics who engage more skeptically with the gender dimensions of Selvon's work include Ashley Dawson, Curdella Forbes, and Lewis MacLeod.

44. Ernesto Laclau's "Universalism, Particularism, and the Question of Identity" provides a useful theoretical model for this way of thinking. In it, Laclau suggests the notion of the universal as consistently open and unstable, constructed only by being temporarily inhabited by various particularisms at any given time. Critics such as Bruce Robbins and Satya P. Mohanty have made similar arguments for the importance of universality in a more postcolonial vein.

45. Ronald Sutherland describes Selvon's vision of national identity in terms of an "umbrella consciousness of being Trinidadian" that transcends the islands' ethnic groupings ("Sam Selvon," 45). John Rothfork similarly argues for Selvon's fiction as an extended effort "to achieve a delicate balance to preserve ethnic traditions . . . while, on the other hand, not permitting ethnic and communal identity to annul commitment to the larger society" ("Race and Community," 10). These flexible models of belonging, however, both stop at the level of the national, rather than engaging with the international possibilities of this type of model that Selvon's novels also suggest.

5.   The Lyrical Enchantments of Roger Mais

1. Gladys Lindo's letters to Swanzy betray a consistent tone of unease regarding Mais, while Swanzy's letters (to Lindo, as well as to Calder Marshall and Collymore) reveal his pronounced dislike of Mais's first novel, as well as Mais's forward, aggressively confident personality. These letters can be found in the Henry Swanzy Papers, held in the University of Birmingham's library.

2. During his brief stint in Europe, Mais also exhibited paintings in both London and Paris, and the *Times* obituary refers to him as both novelist and painter.

3. For convenience, the page numbers for this collection of Mais's novels will be used in the following discussion. Manley's introduction comprises a separate entry in the bibliography.

4. "Jazz and the West Indian Novel" appears in the essay collection *Roots*. For a further example of Brathwaite's politicized treatment of Mais, see the overtly nativist take Brathwaite provides in his article "Roger Mais" in the *Dictionary of Literary Biography*.

5. Sylvia Wynter's two-part "We Must Learn to Sit Down Together and Talk about a Little Culture" takes explicit aim at what she sees as Carr's "acquiescent" aestheticizing take on Mais. Kwame Dawes, too, has taken issue with Carr's readings in "Disarming the Threat of Rasta Revolution in Mais's *Brother Man.*"

6. Hawthorne is surely correct in descrying Romantic and individualist strains within Mais's writing; however, the clear-cut dichotomy she sets up between these traits and a nationalist outlook seems to rely on a largely unexamined conception of nationalism as a static, monolithic political orientation.

7. This quotation is cited from a typescript of extracts from reviews of *The Hills Were Joyful Together* in the Roger Mais Collection, UWI, Mona (hereafter the Mais Collection). It is identified as a review appearing somewhere on the BBC under the title "Books to Read," on 8 June 1953.

8. This, too, comes from the Mais Collection.

9. This quotation may also be found in the Mais Collection. No author is identified.

10. The author is anonymous; the review appears as "Review of *The Hills Were Joyful Together*" in the bibliography.

11. The drawings referred to by the reviewer were Mais's own, which appeared in the original edition (and were also included in Sangster's three-volume reissue). Much of Mais's art, too, appears to be influenced by European modernist trends, perhaps especially Fauvism and Cubism.

12. Carr notes in 1967 that "apart from a sensitive reading of [*Black Lightning*] by Mr. Kenneth Ramchand (*Public Opinion* June 10, 1966) the novel has received virtually no attention" ("Roger Mais," 25). Jeannette B. Allis's normally exhaustive *West Indian Literature: An Index to the Criticism* provides only the Ramchand piece to which Carr refers under its listing of reviews of *Black Lightning*. Certainly none of the major London publications appears to have reviewed the novel, even if they had reviewed one or both of Mais's previous works.

13. D'Costa's introduction to the Heinemann edition of *Black Lightning* expresses her ambivalent attitude toward the novel, which she characterizes as a "flawed experiment" (7).

14. A number of critics have identified this Lawrentian element in Mais's work, including Carr ("Roger Mais"), Creary ("Prophet Armed"), and Gilkes (*West Indian Novel*), and even Brathwaite's reference to the "belly-centred" tradition within which he places Mais evokes Lawrence's investment in vital, instinctual language (*Roots*, 74).

15. In addition to Burack's work, see Michael Bell's *D. H. Lawrence: Language*

and Being and Robert E. Montgomery's *The Visionary D. H. Lawrence: Beyond Philosophy and Art* for assessments of Lawrence's pronounced interest in uniting mind and body, language and feeling.

16. Daphne Morris suggests that Mais served four months of his six-month sentence and was not badly treated in prison. In the words of one contemporary observer, Basil McFarlane, Mais's penning of the article was regarded "as the most critical of his entire career" and the act "by which his name became a household word throughout Jamaica" ("Roger Mais").

17. These sections can indeed be hard to decipher, and critics, though rarely actively interpreting the passages themselves, describe them with a variety of terms. Karina Williamson presents them as "a kind of prose-poetry charged with symbolism" ("Roger Mais," 145); Barrie Davies characterizes them as "broken poetry" with traces of surrealism ("Novels of Roger Mais," 141); and Ramchand refers to them as "authorial choruses" (*West Indian Novel,* 180). The notion of a chorus is now most prominent, though this seems to arise from the much more consistent (and actually choric) appearance of similar chapter beginnings in *Brother Man,* as well as Mais's use of the chorus device in the Jamaican production of his play, *Atalanta at Calydon,* in 1950.

18. Critics who single out the scene for such discussion include Carr, D'Costa, Hawthorne, Ramchand, and Williamson. In her monograph, D'Costa perceptively observes that the more troubling fissures within the group are also present underneath the social delight at the fish fry, asserting that "all later action, all later developments, derive from this scene" (20).

19. Naipaul (in a *Caribbean Voices* review of *The Hills Were Joyful Together*) and subsequently Brathwaite ("Unborn Body") have noted the often ungainly mixture of Jamaican and American vernacular language in Mais's novels. This song, while plainly meant to evoke Jamaican folk culture, seems, in orthographic terms, much closer to a southern US African American spiritual.

20. The chronology of events is not always clearly marked in the novel, but the succeeding two chapters portray many of the other characters in the yard going to bed after the fish fry, such that it is hard to make sense of the intervening chapter on Surjue as anything other than contemporaneous with those that follow it.

21. Singh suggests that a dominant theme of entrapment pervades *The Hills Were Joyful Together,* extending from the literal imprisonment of Surjue out to the less obvious but no less serious restraint imposed upon the rest of the yard by societal systems of oppression and control. This observation is a useful one, and it suggests in some ways that Surjue can be read as an archetype for the rest of the characters in the novel or, in terms of D'Costa's notion of "group-as-hero," as the most extreme (and visible) limit-case of the group's activity.

22. It emerges in the following sentences that Surjue actually, rather than metaphorically, sees something—the nearby church on fire—but the heavy symbolism of this sight, with its suggestion that Jamaica's inhumane penal policy destroys the charity and forgiveness embodied in the church and its teachings, only reinforces the sense that Surjue has now been enlightened about the world.

23. Others who emphasize the emotional aspect of Mais's aesthetic include D'Costa, Grandison, and Wynter.

24. Hawthorne notes something similar in another short story, "The Wine Is More Precious than the Skin," observing the protagonist's narratorially approved attempts to gain understanding beyond the mundane, everyday meanings of the material and social world.

25. The novel is rightly lauded by critics as the first Caribbean novel to represent a Rastafarian character in a sympathetic light. In "Disarming the Threat of Rasta Revolution in Mais's *Brother Man*," Dawes convincingly lays out the ideological significance of Mais's representation of Brother Man, arguing that many of the character's views (including on the use of marijuana, as well as sexual propriety) function as limitations on social critique, reflecting an interest in making the book's views more palatable to middle-class sensibilities. Brathwaite's "Brother Mais" (in *Roots*) also notes the extremes to which the novel goes to romanticize the moral purity of Rastafarianism.

26. Interestingly, a riddle (thought to be a product of Papacita's teaching) is also told in this chorus, and there is superstitious gossip about the ghost of Old Mag blessing Brother Man in the street. The less savory aspects of the chorus, however, appear to be eclipsed at the end of the chorus by the hymn singing.

27. It is rather remarkable that this jeering mob is explicitly made up of mostly women and children. For a comprehensive examination of the troubling gender implications in the novel, see Dawes's "Violence and Patriarchy: Male Domination in Roger Mais's *Brother Man*."

28. The contrast between mechanical and human often appears in Mais's work in the form of eating, whereby approved characters like Brother Man eat with evident natural enjoyment, whereas Girlie eats mechanically (20). Not surprisingly, Girlie's reading habits, too, are contrasted with Minette's epiphanic reading experience: when the novel introduces Girlie, she is "idly turning the pages of a magazine" (9).

29. Brathwaite's citations match the edition used here, and his orthographic choices have been preserved.

30. The prologue takes the form of a conversation between the narrator and God and, though complicated in its implications, ultimately asserts that God is comprised, most of all, of man (specifically the common, working man) and that the task of awakening humans to their own dignity is a holy task.

31. Another important scene of Amos playing alone occurs on p. 73, before Jake's accident and Amos's increasing importance to him; in this scene, too, the music inspires visions only in Amos.

32. This point of Mais's is also noted by Carr ("Roger Mais"), as part of the same passage cited in the discussion above.

33. Indeed, thought of in these terms, his novels get less "political" at the same time as they get less "experimental": that is, his most overtly political novel, *The Hills Were Joyful Together,* is also his most obviously experimental.

34. Before his death, Mais had been working on a novel, *In the Sight of This Sun,*

based on the biblical story of David and Bathsheba. The manuscript—fragmentary and unfinished—is preserved in the Mais Collection. The typescripts for two other earlier, unpublished novels—*Another Ghost in Arcady* and *Blood on the Moon*—are also held, along with much other material, in the same collection.

35. Mais's growing distrust of the political efficacy of aesthetic form might also be taken to reflect the inevitable contradictions of writing anticolonial literature in the seat of imperial power.

Coda

1. The legal categories of British citizenship became quite convoluted in the aftermath of this legislation, emerging into clarity only in 1981, when Margaret Thatcher's government passed the British Nationality Act. See Randall Hansen's *Citizenship and Immigration in Post-war Britain* for an exhaustive, technical, (and gruffly polemical) account of this history.

2. This award, it should be noted, was officially for *Miguel Street*. A look at the list of awardees from its inauguration in 1947 through the 1960s suggests the continuing struggle for institutional legitimation between the Amis-supported aesthetics of natural mimeticism and the more consciously experimental works of writers such as B. S. Johnson (winner in 1967) and Angela Carter (winner in 1969).

3. See Patrick French's richly detailed biography of Naipaul for a revealing account of this critical episode in Naipaul's life, in which he, interestingly, feels geographically disoriented in a provincial English railway station.

4. In an evocative echo of Amis's use of the Maugham prize money to write a novel satirizing the express purpose of the prize, Naipaul's own trip was financed by Eric Williams, then the chief minister of Trinidad and Tobago. French provides a good account of the ironies of the trip and its eventual published product (*World Is*, 201–3).

5. The interview was excerpted in "What Does Mr. Swanzy Want?," a program aired on BBC Radio Four, 27 Nov. 1998. Swanzy's rather tight-lipped and forcibly optimistic letters to Gladys Lindo and Frank Collymore, at the time he was certain of his new posting (in the Gold Coast) in late July and August, likewise suggest both his sadness and his relative unwillingness to give up editing the show.

6. Gail Low remarks a similar strain in the general publishing atmosphere of the time, in which the wishes of editors often concentrated on a folk or sociological aspect of the "traditional" Caribbean while artistic strivings toward modernism had less commercial appeal in Britain and were correspondingly played down in promoting the books ("Publishing Commonwealth," 86).

7. Naipaul's relationship with the show seems to have tapered off some time in the autumn of 1956, when he made his first trip back to the Caribbean after coming to Britain for university. At this time, Mittelholzer was the most regular editor on the show, along with various others. Characteristically, the aesthetic attitude of the shows on which Mittelholzer appears varies wildly, sometimes lauding experiments in dialect

or form, other times decrying the influence of Joyce and Dylan Thomas on Caribbean writers. French's biography suggests that Naipaul continued to have solid ties to the BBC at least until *Caribbean Voices* wound down in 1958.

8. As French's biography relates, the script was written by Naipaul but read by someone else, due to the fact that Naipaul arrived late to the recording session (*World Is,* 179–80).

9. This essay originally appeared in *BIM* in 1963. It is cited here in the collection of Brathwaite's critical writing *Roots,* published in 1993.

10. For accounts of Brathwaite's modernist-inflected experimentation, see esp. Hart, *Nations of Nothing But Poetry,* and Pollard, *New World Modernisms.*

11. If Brathwaite's attitude toward Naipaul changed, the reverse was also certainly the case. In an interview with French, Naipaul dismissively observed with regard to Brathwaite: "He's become very black; when I met him he wasn't so black" (French, *World Is,* 141). However crudely put, the trajectory Naipaul observes regarding his fellow Oxbridge author bears some truth. Brathwaite's initial poetry appearing in *Caribbean Voices* is all based on classical mythological sources ("Prometheus," "Persephone," and "Prometheus Unbound"), while his next set of poems to appear focuses on portraying European scenes, with an additional poem in memory of Dylan Thomas. Such topics are quite far removed from Brathwaite's later poetic output, influenced by his time in Ghana from 1955 to 1962.

12. This is not to say that the movements are entirely distinct or distinguishable: many authors plausibly falling into the category of the Windrush generation, notably Andrew Salkey, participated in CAM. However, both the political and the cultural contexts out of which these two important groupings emerged, as argued above, would seem to be appreciably different.

13. Anthony left England, spending two years in Brazil before returning to Trinidad in 1970. After publishing three novels—one each in 1963, 1965, and 1967—he did not produce another novel until 1973. Oddly, in that interval, his 1965 novel *The Year in San Fernando* was reissued in 1970 as the inaugural book of the Heinemann Caribbean Writers series, perhaps a testament to Naipaul's continuing prominence in British literary circles. Anthony's current critical reputation is not nearly as high as it was during the 1960s, and his work surely, if even only on the grounds of history, deserves more scrutiny.

14. Walmsley notes that Merle Hodge was credited as a copresenter with Salkey, but no record of her participation exists.

15. One of Harris's most comprehensive critics, for example, is Hena Maes-Jelinek, who was a central figure in the institutionalization of Commonwealth Literary Studies. Indeed, her edited collection of that group's 1974 conference, *Commonwealth Literature and the Modern World,* contains a lecture that Harris himself delivered there, as well as three other papers given on his work.

Bibliography

Allen, Walter. Review of *The Hills Were Joyful Together,* by Roger Mais. *New States-man,* 25 April 1953, 497.

Allis, Jeannette B. *West Indian Literature: An Index of Criticism, 1930–1975.* Boston: G. K. Hall and Company, 1981.

Amis, Kingsley. "Fresh Winds from the West." *Spectator,* 2 May 1958, 565–6.

———. *I Like It Here.* 1958. London: Penguin Books, 1968.

———. "The Legion of the Lost." *Spectator,* 15 June 1956, 830–31.

———. *Lucky Jim.* 1954. London: Penguin Books, 1961.

———. *Socialism and the Intellectuals.* Fabian Tract 304. London: Fabian Society, 1957.

Appiah, Kwame Anthony. "Is the Post- in Postmodernism the Post- in Postcolonial?" *Critical Inquiry* 17, no. 2 (1991): 336–57.

Ashcroft, Bill, Gareth Griffiths, and Helen Tiffin. *The Empire Writes Back.* London: Routledge, 1989.

———. *Post-Colonial Studies: The Key Concepts.* London: Routledge, 2001.

Attridge, Derek. "Innovation, Literature, Ethics: Relating to the Other." *PMLA* 114, no. 1 (1999): 20–31.

Bader, Rudolph. "George Lamming." In *International Literature in English: Essays on the Major Writers,* edited by Robert L. Ross, 143–52. New York: Garland Publishers, 1991.

Ball, John Clement. *Imagining London: Postcolonial Fiction and the Transnational Metropolis.* Toronto: University of Toronto Press, 2004.

Barratt, Harold. "Dialect, Maturity, and the Land in Sam Selvon's *A Brighter Sun:* A Reply." *English Studies in Canada* 8 (1981): 329–37. Reprinted in Nasta, *Critical Perspectives on Sam Selvon,* 187–95.

Baugh, Edward. *Frank Collymore: A Biography.* Kingston: Ian Randle Publishers, 2009.

Beebe, Maurice. "What Modernism Was." *Journal of Modern Literature* 3, no. 5 (1974): 1065–84.

Begam, Richard, and Michael Valdez Moses, editors. *Modernism and Colonialism: British and Irish Literature, 1899–1939.* Durham: Duke University Press, 2007.

Bell, Michael. *D. H. Lawrence: Language and Being.* Cambridge: Cambridge University Press, 1992.

Benítez-Rojo, Antonio. *The Repeating Island: The Caribbean and the Postmodern Perspective.* Translated by James E. Maraniss. Durham: Duke University Press, 1992.

Bentley, Nick. "Black London: The Politics of Representation in Sam Selvon's *The Lonely Londoners.*" *Wasafiri* 39 (Summer 2003): 41–45.

———. "Form and Language in Sam Selvon's *The Lonely Londoners.*" *ARIEL* 36, nos. 3–4 (2005): 67–84.

Bergonzi, Bernard. *The Situation of the Novel.* London: Macmillan, 1970.

Birbalsingh, F. M. "Edgar Mittelholzer: Moralist or Pornographer?" *Journal of Commonwealth Literature* 7 (1969): 88–103.

———. "Samuel Selvon and the West Indian Literary Renaissance." *ARIEL* 8, no. 3 (1977): 5–22.

Bloomfield, Paul. Review of *The Hills Were Joyful Together,* by Roger Mais. *Manchester Guardian,* 24 April 1953, 17.

Boehmer, Elleke. *Colonial and Postcolonial Literature: Migrant Metaphors.* Oxford: Oxford University Press, 2005.

Booth, Howard J., and Nigel Rigby, editors. *Modernism and Empire.* Manchester: Manchester University Press, 2000.

Bourdieu, Pierre. *Distinction: A Social Critique of the Judgement of Taste.* Translated by Richard Nice. Cambridge: Harvard University Press, 1984.

———. *The Field of Cultural Production: Essays on Art and Literature.* Edited and translated by Randal Johnson. New York: Columbia University Press, 1993.

———. *The Rules of Art: Genesis and Structure of the Literary Field.* Translated by Susan Emanuel. Stanford: Stanford University Press, 1996.

Bradbury, Malcom. *Eating People Is Wrong.* 1959. London: Arrow Books Limited, 1990.

———. *The Modern British Novel.* London: Penguin, 1995.

———. "'No, Not Bloomsbury': The Comic Fiction of Kingsley Amis." In *Critical Essays on Kingsley Amis,* edited by Robert H. Bell, 60–75. London: G. K. Hall & Co., 1998.

Brathwaite, L. E. (Kamau). "The New West Indian Novelists: Part One." *BIM* 8, no. 31 (1960): 199–210.

———. "Roger Mais." In *Dictionary of Literary Biography: Twentieth-Century Caribbean and Black African Writers,* edited by Bernth Lindfors and Reinhard Sander, 125: 78–81. Detroit: Gale Research, 1993.

———. *Roots.* Ann Arbor: University of Michigan Press, 1993.

———. "The Unborn Body of the Life of Fiction: Roger Mais's Aesthetics with Special Reference to *Black Lightning.*" *Journal of West Indian Literature* 2, no. 1 (1987): 11–36.

Breiner, Laurence A. "Caribbean Voices on the Air: Radio, Poetry, and Nationalism in the Anglophone Caribbean." In *Communities of the Air,* edited by Susan M. Squier, 93–108. Durham: Duke University Press, 2003

Brown, Nicholas. *Utopian Generations: The Political Horizon of Twentieth-Century Literature.* Princeton: Princeton University Press, 2005.

Burack, Charles Michael. *D. H. Lawrence's Language of Sacred Experience: The Transfiguration of the Reader.* New York: Palgrave Macmillan, 2005.

Butler, Janet. "The Existentialism of George Lamming: The Early Development of a Writer." *Caribbean Review* 11, no. 4 (1982): 15, 38–39.

Carr, Bill. "Roger Mais: Design from a Legend." *Caribbean Quarterly* 13, no. 1 (1967): 3–28.

Casanova, Pascale. *The World Republic of Letters.* Translated by M. B. DeBevoise. Cambridge: Harvard University Press, 2004.

Casillo, Robert. *The Genealogy of Demons: Anti-Semitism, Fascism, and the Myths of Ezra Pound.* Evanston: Northwestern University Press, 1988.

Chang, Victor. "Edgar Mittelholzer." In *Fifty Caribbean Writers,* edited by Daryl Cumber Dance, 325–40. Westport, CT: Greenwood Press, 1986.

Charques, R. D. Review of *The Hills Were Joyful Together,* by Roger Mais. *Spectator,* 17 April 1953. 494.

Cheng, Vincent J. *Joyce, Race, and Empire.* Cambridge: Cambridge University Press, 1995.

———. "Of Canons, Colonies, and Critics: The Ethics and Politics of Postcolonial Joyce Studies." In *Re: Joyce: Text, Culture, Politics,* edited by John Brannigan, Geoff Ward, and Julian Wolfreys, 224–45. Houndmills, Basingstoke: Macmillan Press, 1998.

Childs, David. *Britain since 1945: A Political History.* London: Routledge, 2001.

Clarke, Austin, Jan Carew, Ramabai Espinet, and Ismith Khan, with Frank Birbalsingh. "Sam Selvon: A Celebration." *ARIEL* 27, no. 2 (1996): 49–63.

Clarke, Richard. "Lamming, Marx and Hegel." *Journal of West Indian Literature* 17, no. 1 (2008): 42–53.

Cleary, Joe. "The World Literary System: Atlas and Epitaph." *Field Day Review* 2 (2006): 197–219.

Collier, Eugenia. "Dimensions of Alienation in Two Black American and Caribbean Novels." *Phylon* 43, no. 1 (1982): 46–56.

Conquest, Robert. "Commitment and the Writer." In *International Literary Annual, Volume 1,* edited by John Wain, 13–23. London: John Calder, 1958.

Creary, Jean. "A Prophet Armed: The Novels of Roger Mais." In *The Islands In Between,* edited by Louis James, 50–63. London: Oxford University Press, 1968.

Cullingford, Elizabeth. *Yeats, Ireland, and Fascism.* New York: New York University Press, 1980.

Dabydeen, David, and Nana Wilson-Tagoe. *A Reader's Guide to West Indian and Black British Literature.* Kingston-upon-Thames: Rutherford Press, 1987.

Dakers, Andrew. "Novelist from Jamaica." *John O'London's Weekly,* 1 May 1953, 387.

Dalleo, Raphael. "Authority and the Occasion for Speaking in the Caribbean Literary Field: Martin Carter and George Lamming." *Small Axe* 20 (June 2006): 19–39.

Damrosch, David. *What Is World Literature?* Princeton: Princeton University Press, 2003.

Darwin, John. *Britain and Decolonisation: The Retreat from Empire in the Post-War World.* New York: St. Martin's Press, 1988.

Dash, J. Michael. *The Other America: Caribbean Literature in a New World Context.* Charlottesville: University of Virginia Press, 1998.

da Silva, A. J. Simoes. *The Luxury of Nationalist Despair: George Lamming's Fiction as Decolonizing Project.* Amsterdam: Rodopi, 2000.

Davies, Barrie. "The Novels of Roger Mais." *International Fiction Review* 2 (1974): 140–43.

Dawes, Kwame S. N. "Disarming the Threat of Rasta Revolution in Mais's *Brother Man.*" *Commonwealth Novel in English* 7–8 (1997): 81–109.

———. "Violence and Patriarchy: Male Domination in Roger Mais's *Brother Man.*" *ARIEL* 25, no. 3 (1994): 29–49.

Dawson, Ashley. *Mongrel Nation: Diasporic Culture and the Making of Postcolonial Britain.* Ann Arbor: University of Michigan Press, 2007.

D'Costa, Jean. Introduction to *Black Lightning,* by Roger Mais, 7–22. London: Heinemann, 1983.

———. *Roger Mais: "The Hills Were Joyful Together" and "Brother Man."* Critical Studies of Caribbean Writers, edited by Mervyn Morris. London: Longman, 1978.

DeKoven, Marianne. *Rich and Strange: Gender, History, Modernism.* Princeton: Princeton University Press, 1991.

Dickinson, Swift. "Sam Selvon's 'Harlequin Costume': *Moses Ascending,* Masquerade, and the Bacchanal of Self-Creolization." *MELUS* 21, no. 3 (1996): 69–106.

Diepeveen, Leonard. *The Difficulties of Modernism.* New York: Routledge, 2003.

Donnell, Alison. "Heard but Not Seen: Women's Short Stories and the BBC's *Caribbean Voices* Programme." In *The Caribbean Short Story: Critical Perspectives,* edited by Lucy Evans, Mark McWatt, and Emma Smith, 29–43. Leeds: Peepal Tree Press, 2011.

———. *Twentieth-Century Caribbean Literature: Critical Moments in Anglophone Caribbean Literary History.* London: Routledge, 2005.

Doyle, Laura, and Laura Winkiel. *Geomodernisms: Race, Modernism, Modernity.* Bloomington: Indiana University Press, 2005.

Edmondson, Belinda. *Making Men: Gender, Literary Authority, and Women's Writing in Caribbean Narrative.* Durham: Duke University Press, 1999.

Edwards, Brent Hayes. *The Practice of Diaspora: Literature, Translation, and the Rise of Black Internationalism.* Cambridge: Harvard University Press, 2003.

Edwards, Nadi. "George Lamming's Literary Nationalism: Language between *The Tempest* and the Tonelle." *Small Axe* 11 (March 2002): 59–76.

Eliot, T. S. "Tradition and the Individual Talent." In *Selected Essays,* 3–11. New York: Harcourt, Brace and Company, 1950.

Elton, Geoffrey Rudolph. "Various Pursuits." Review of *An Island Is a World*, by Samuel Selvon. *Times Literary Supplement*, 27 May 1955, 281.

Emery, Mary Lou. *Jean Rhys at "World's End": Novels of Colonial and Sexual Exile*. Austin: University of Texas Press, 1990.

———. *Modernism, the Visual, and Caribbean Literature*. Cambridge: Cambridge University Press, 2007.

Esty, Jed. *A Shrinking Island: Modernism and National Culture in England*. Princeton: Princeton University Press, 2004.

Eysteinsson, Astradur. *The Concept of Modernism*. Ithaca: Cornell University Press, 1990.

Fabre, Michel. "From Trinidad to London: Tone and Language in Samuel Selvon's Novels." In Nasta, *Critical Perspectives on Sam Selvon*, 213–22.

———. "Samuel Selvon." In King, *West Indian Literature*, 152–62.

Fanon, Frantz. *The Wretched of the Earth*. Translated by Constance Farrington. New York: Grove Press, 1963.

Ferrall, Charles. *Modernist Writing and Reactionary Politics*. Cambridge: Cambridge University Press, 2001.

Forbes, Curdella. "' . . . And the Dumb Speak': George Lamming's Theory of Language and the Epistemology of the Body in *The Emigrants*." *Literature and Psychology* 48, no. 4 (2002): 6–32.

———. *From Nation to Diaspora: Samuel Selvon, George Lamming and the Cultural Performance of Gender*. Kingston: University of the West Indies Press, 2005.

Fraser, F. E. F. "Roger Mais: A New Judgement." *Public Opinion*, 15 June 1957, 7.

Freeman, Gwendolen. Review of *The Lonely Londoners*, by Samuel Selvon. *Times Literary Supplement*, 21 December 1956, 761.

French, Patrick. *The World Is What It Is: The Authorized Biography of V. S. Naipaul*. New York: Afred A. Knopf, 2008.

Friedman, Susan Stanford. "Planetarity: Musing Modernist Studies." *Modernism/modernity* 17, no. 3 (2010) 471–99.

Fryer, Peter. *Staying Power: The History of Black People in Britain*. London: Pluto Press, 1984.

Gasiorek, Andrzej. *Post-war British Fiction: Realism and After*. London: E. Arnold, 1995.

Gikandi, Simon. *Maps of Englishness: Writing Identity in Colonial Culture*. New York: Columbia University Press, 1996.

———. "Preface: Modernism in the World." *Modernism/modernity* 13, no. 3 (2006): 419–24.

———. *Writing in Limbo: Modernism and Caribbean Literature*. Ithaca: Cornell University Press, 1992.

Gilkes, Michael. "Edgar Mittelholzer." In King, *West Indian Literature*, 127–38.

———. "The Spirit in the Bottle—A Reading of Edgar Mittelholzer's *A Morning at the Office*." *World Literature Written in English* 14 (1975): 237–52.

———. *The West Indian Novel*. Boston: Twayne Publishers, 1981.

Gilroy, Paul. *The Black Atlantic: Modernity and Double Consciousness*. Cambridge: Harvard University Press, 1993.

———. *"There Ain't No Black in the Union Jack": The Cultural Politics of Race and Nation*. Chicago: University of Chicago Press, 1991.

Glass, Ruth. Assisted by Harold Pollins. *London's Newcomers: The West Indian Migrants*. Cambridge: Harvard University Press, 1961.

Grandison, Winnifred B. "The Prose Style of Roger Mais." *Jamaica Journal* 8, no. 1 (1974): 48–54.

Griffith, Glyne. "Deconstructing Nationalisms: Henry Swanzy, *Caribbean Voices* and the Development of West Indian Literature." *Small Axe* 10 (September 2001): 1–20.

———. *Deconstruction, Imperialism and the West Indian Novel*. Kingston: University of the West Indies Press, 1996.

Hale, Lionel. Review of *A Brighter Sun*, by Samuel Selvon. *London Sunday Observer*, 3 February 1952.

Hall, Stuart, Chas Critcher, Tony Jefferson, John N. Clarke, and Brian Roberts. *Policing the Crisis: Mugging, the State and Law and Order*. London: Palgrave Macmillan, 1978.

Hansen, Randall. *Citizenship and Immigration in Post-war Britain: The Institutional Origins of a Multicultural Nation*. Oxford: Oxford University Press, 2000.

Harris, Wilson. *Tradition, the Writer and Society: Critical Essays*. London: New Beacon Books, 1967.

Harrison, John R. *The Reactionaries*. London: Gollancz, 1966.

Hart, Matthew. *Nations of Nothing But Poetry: Modernism, Transnationalism, and Synthetic Vernacular Writing*. New York: Oxford University Press, 2010.

Harvey, W. J. "Have You Anything to Declare? or, Angry Young Men: Facts and Fictions." In *International Literary Annual, Volume 1*, edited by John Wain, 47–59. London: John Calder, 1958.

Hawthorne, Evelyn J. *The Writer in Transition: Roger Mais and the Decolonization of Caribbean Culture*. New York: Peter Lang, 1989.

Head, Dominic. *The Cambridge Introduction to Modern British Fiction, 1950–2000*. Cambridge: Cambridge University Press, 2002.

Hearne, John. "Roger Mais: A Personal Memoir." *BIM* 6, no. 23 (1955): 146–50.

Heppenstall, Rayner. "Divided We Stand: On 'the English Tradition.'" *Encounter* 15, no. 3 (1960): 42–45.

Heusel, Barbara Stevens. "Parallax as a Metaphor for the Structure of Ulysses." *Studies in the Novel* 15, no. 2 (1983): 135–46.

Hewison, Robert. *Culture and Consensus: England, Art, and Politics since 1940*. London: Methuen, 1995.

———. *In Anger: Culture in the Cold War, 1945–60*. London: Methuen, 1988.

Hilton, Frank. "Britain's New Class." *Encounter* 10, no. 2 (1958): 59–63.

Hinds, Donald. *Journey to an Illusion: The West Indian in Britain*. London: Heinemann, 1966.

Howard, G. Wren. Letter ("Mr. Roger Mais"). *London Times,* 24 June 1955, 13.

Howard, William J. "Edgar Mittelholzer's Tragic Vision." *Caribbean Quarterly* 16, no. 4 (1970): 19–28.

Hulme, Peter. "The Profit of Language: George Lamming and the Postcolonial Novel." In *Recasting the World: Writing after Colonialism,* edited by Jonathan White, 120–36. Baltimore: Johns Hopkins University Press, 1993.

Hutcheon, Linda. "'Circling the Downspout of Empire': Post-Colonialism and Post-modernism." *ARIEL* 20, no. 4 (1989): 149–75.

Ingrams, Elizabeth. "*The Lonely Londoners:* Sam Selvon and the Literary Heritage." *Wasafiri* 33 (Spring 2001): 33–41.

James, C. L. R. "Letter to the Editor." *Times Literary Supplement,* 28 September 1962, 766.

James, Louis. "Writing the Ballad: The Short Fiction of Samuel Selvon and Earl Lovelace." In *Telling Stories: Postcolonial Short Fiction in English,* edited by Jacqueline Bardolph, 103–8. Amsterdam: Rodopi, 2001.

Jameson, Fredric. *Fables of Aggression: Wyndham Lewis, the Modernist as Fascist.* Berkeley: University of California Press, 1979.

——. *Marxism and Form.* Princeton: Princeton University Press, 1974.

——. *The Political Unconscious: Narrative as a Socially Symbolic Act.* Ithaca: Cornell University Press, 1982.

Jenkins, Elizabeth. Review of *A Brighter Sun,* by Samuel Selvon. *Manchester Guardian,* 1 February 1952, 4.

Jennings, Elizabeth. "The Better Break." Review of *The Emigrants,* by George Lamming. *Spectator,* 1 October 1954, 411–12.

Johnson, Pamela Hansford. Review of *Kaywana Blood,* by Edgar Mittelholzer. *New Statesman and Nation,* 8 February 1958, 176.

Jonas, Joyce. *Anancy in the Great House: Ways of Reading West Indian Fiction.* New York: Greenwood Press, 1990.

Joseph, Margaret Paul. *Caliban in Exile: The Outsider in Caribbean Fiction.* Westport, CT: Greenwood Press, 1992.

Joyce, James. *A Portrait of the Artist as a Young Man.* Viking Critical Library edition, edited by Chester G. Anderson. New York: Penguin, 1977.

Kalliney, Peter. *Cities of Affluence and Anger: A Literary Geography of Modern English-ness.* Charlottesville: University of Virginia Press, 2007.

——. "Metropolitan Modernism and Its West Indian Interlocutors: 1950s London and the Emergence of Postcolonial Literature." *PMLA* 122, no. 1 (2007): 89–104.

King, Bruce, editor. *West Indian Literature.* 2nd edition. London: Macmillan, 1995.

Kortenaar, Neil ten. "George Lamming's *In the Castle of My Skin:* Finding Promise in the Land." *ARIEL* 22, no. 2 (1991): 43–53.

Laclau, Ernesto. "Universalism, Particularism, and the Question of Identity." In *The Identity in Question,* edited by John Rajchman, 93–108. New York: Routledge, 1995.

Lamming, George. "Caribbean Creative Expressions." Speech, 1995 Jamaican National

Literary Awards. Transcript copy in West Indies Collection, University of the West Indies, Mona, Jamaica.

——. "The Coldest Spring in Fifty Years: Thoughts on Sam Selvon and London." *Kunapipi* 20, no. 1 (1998): 4–10.

——. *Coming, Coming Home: Conversations II.* Philipsburg, St. Martin: House of Nehesi Publishers, 2000.

——. *Conversations: George Lamming: Essays, Addresses, and Interviews, 1953–1990.* Edited by Richard Drayton and Andaiye. London: Karia Press, 1992.

——. *The Emigrants.* 1954. London: Allison & Busby, 1980.

——. "George Lamming Talks to Caryl Phillips." *Wasafiri* 26 (Autumn 1997): 10–17.

——. Interview. With Ian Munro and Reinhard Sander. In *Kas-kas: Interviews with Three Caribbean Writers in Texas: George Lamming, C. L. R. James, Wilson Harris,* by Ian Munro and Reinhard Sander, 5–21. Austin: African and Afro-American Research Institute, University of Texas at Austin, 1972.

——. Interview. With Philip Nanton. Unpublished. Bathsheba, Barbados: 1998.

——. "An Interview with Mr. George Lamming." *Umma: A Literary Magazine from the University of Dar es Salaam* 5 (1975): 100–103.

——. *In the Castle of My Skin.* 1953. Ann Arbor: University of Michigan Press, 2001.

——. *Natives of My Person.* 1972. London: Picador, 1974.

——. *Of Age and Innocence.* 1958. London: Allison & Busby, 1981.

——. *The Pleasures of Exile.* 1960. Ann Arbor: University of Michigan Press, 1995.

——. *Season of Adventure.* 1960. London: Allison & Busby, 1979.

——. *Sovereignty of the Imagination: Conversations III.* Philipsburg, St. Martin: House of Nehesi Publishers, 2009.

——. "The Sovereignty of the Imagination: An Interview with George Lamming." Interview with David Scott. *Small Axe* 12 (September 2002): 72–200.

——. "This Time of Day." BBC Radio interview. 8 April 1965.

——. "Tribute to a Tragic Jamaican." *BIM* 6, no. 24 (1957): 242–44.

——. *Water with Berries.* 1971. New York: Longman, 1972.

——. "Writing and Publishing in the West Indies: An Interview with George Lamming." With Ian Munro. *World Literature Written in English* 19 (April 1971): 17–22.

Laski, Marghanita. Review of *Shadows Move Among Them,* by Edgar Mittelholzer. *Observer,* 25 March 1951, 7.

Lawrence, D. H. *Lady Chatterley's Lover.* 1928. New York: Grove Press, 1959.

——. "The Novel and the Feelings." In Lawrence, *Study of Thomas Hardy and Other Essays,* 201–5.

——. *Study of Thomas Hardy and Other Essays,* edited by Bruce Steele. Cambridge: Cambridge University Press, 1985.

——. "Why the Novel Matters." In Lawrence, *Study of Thomas Hardy and Other Essays,* 193–98.

Lazarus, Neil. "The Politics of Postcolonial Modernism." In *Postcolonial Studies and*

Beyond, edited by Ania Loomba, Suvir Kaul, Matti Bunzl, Antoinette Burton, and Jed Esty, 423–38. Durham: Duke University Press, 2005.

Lehmann, John, editor. *The Craft of Letters in England: A Symposium.* London: Cresset Press, 1956.

———. "Foreword." *London Magazine* 4, no. 2 (1957): 9–11.

———. "Foreword." *London Magazine* 5, no. 3 (1958): 7–9.

Lejeune, Anthony. "Without Benefit of Story." Review of *Thunder Returning,* by Edgar Mittelholzer. *Times Literary Supplement,* 10 March 1961, 149.

Lerner, L. D. "Literature as the Subject of Itself." *Twentieth Century* 16 (1957): 545–55.

Lessing, Doris. "The Small Personal Voice." In *Declaration,* edited by Tom Maschler, 187–201. London: MacGibbon & Kee, 1957.

Levin, Harry. "What Was Modernism?" *Massachusetts Review* 1 (1960): 609–30.

Lewis, Peter. *The Fifties.* New York: Lippincott, 1978

Lodge, David. "The Modern, the Contemporary, and the Importance of Being Amis." *Critical Quarterly* 5 (1963): 335–54.

Loreto, Paola. "The Male Mind and the Female Heart: Selvon's Ways to Knowledge in the 'Tiger Books.'" *Caribana* 5 (1996): 117–25.

Low, Gail. "Publishing Commonwealth: The Case of West Indian Writing, 1950–1965." *EnterText* 2, no. 1 (2001–2): 71–93.

———. *Publishing the Postcolonial: Anglophone West African and Caribbean Writing in the U.K. 1948–1968.* London: Routledge, 2011.

MacClancy, Jeremy. "The Latest Form of Evening Entertainment." In *A Concise Companion to Modernism,* edited by David Bradshaw, 75–94. Oxford: Blackwell Publishers, 2003.

MacKay, Marina, and Lyndsey Stonebridge, eds. *British Fiction after Modernism: The Novel at Mid-Century.* Basingstoke: Palgrave Macmillan, 2007.

Mackenzie, Norman, editor. *Conviction.* London: MacGibbon & Kee, 1959.

MacLeod, Lewis. "'You have to start thinking all over again': Masculinities, Narratology, and New Approaches to Sam Selvon." *ARIEL* 36, nos. 1–2 (2005): 157–81.

Malouf, Michael G. *Transatlantic Solidarities: Irish Nationalism and Caribbean Poetics.* Charlottesville: University of Virginia Press, 2009.

Maes-Jelinek, Hena, editor. *Commonwealth Literature and the Modern World.* Brussels: Didier, 1975.

Mais, Roger. "The Critics Criticised II." *Public Opinion,* 17 May 1952, 5.

———. *Face, and Other Stories.* Self-published. Roger Mais Collection, University of the West Indies, Mona, Jamaica.

———. "Form and Substance in Fiction." Unpublished manuscript. Roger Mais Collection, University of the West Indies, Mona, Jamaica.

———. *And Most of All Man.* Self-published. Roger Mais Collection, University of the West Indies, Mona, Jamaica.

———. "Now We Know." *Public Opinion,* 11 July 1944, 2.

———. *The Three Novels of Roger Mais.* Kingston: Sangster's Book Stores, 1966.

Manley, N. W. "Introduction: Roger Mais—The Writer." In *The Three Novels of Roger Mais*, by Roger Mais, v–viii. Kingston: Sangster's Book Stores, 1966.

Mao, Douglas, and Rebecca Walkowitz. "The New Modernist Studies." *PMLA* 123, no. 3 (2008): 737–48.

Marshall, Arthur Calder. "Caribbean Voices." *Times Literary Supplement*, 5 August 1955, xvi–xvii.

———. "In Search of a Future." Review of *The Emigrants*, by George Lamming. *Times Literary Supplement*, 8 October 1954, 637.

———. "Time and Change." Review of *Of Age and Innocence*, by George Lamming. *Times Literary Supplement*, 21 November 1958, 669.

———. "Uprooted Blooms." Review of *Turn Again, Tiger*, by Samuel Selvon. *Times Literary Supplement*, 19 December 1958, 733.

———. "Vagaries of the Soul." Review of *Latticed Echoes*, by Edgar Mittelholzer. *Times Literary Supplement*, 5 February 1960, 77.

———. "Youth in Barbados." Review of *In the Castle of My Skin*, by George Lamming. *Times Literary Supplement*, 27 March 1953, 203.

Marshall, Harold. Review of *Latticed Echoes*, by Edgar Mittelholzer. *BIM* 8, no. 31 (1960): 217–18.

Marwick, Arthur. *British Society since 1945*. Harmondsworth: Penguin, 1982.

Marx, John. *The Modernist Novel and the Decline of Empire*. Cambridge: Cambridge University Press, 2005.

McDonald, Avis G. "'Within the Orbit of Power': Reading Allegory in George Lamming's *Natives of My Person*." *Journal of Commonwealth Literature* 22, no. 1 (1987): 73–86.

McDougall, Russell. "Sound, Depth and Disembodiment in Mittelholzer's *My Bones and My Flute*." In *Re-siting Queen's English: Text and Tradition in Post-Colonial Literatures*, edited by Gillian Whitlock and Helen Tiffin, 79–89. Amsterdam: Rodopi, 1992.

McEwan, Neil. *The Survival of the Novel: British Fiction in the Later Twentieth Century*. Totowa, NJ: Barnes & Noble, 1981.

McFarlane, Basil. "Roger Mais, Novelist and Painter Poet and Patriot." *Public Opinion*, 2 July 1955, 4.

McGoogan, Ken. "Saying Goodbye to Sam Selvon." *ARIEL* 27, no. 2 (1996): 65–75.

McLeod, John. *Postcolonial London: Rewriting the Metropolis*. London: Routledge, 2004.

McWatt, Mark. "Critical Introduction." In *My Bones and My Flute*, by Edgar Mittelholzer, v–xx. Harlow: Longman, 1986.

Mead, Matthew. "Empire Windrush: The Cultural Memory of an Imaginary Arrival." *Journal of Postcolonial Writing* 45, no. 2 (2009): 137–49.

Melas, Natalie. *All the Difference in the World: Postcoloniality and the Ends of Comparison*. Stanford: Stanford University Press, 2007.

Menand, Louis. *Discovering Modernism: T. S. Eliot and His Context*. Oxford: Oxford University Press, 1987.

Metcalf, John. Review of *The Harrowing of Hubertus*, by Edgar Mittelholzer. *Spectator*, 19 February 1954, 216.

Middlemas, Keith. *Power, Competition, and the State*. Vol. 1, *Britain in Search of Balance, 1940–61*. Stanford: Hoover Institution Press, 1986.

Mignolo, Walter. "The Many Faces of Cosmo-polis: Border Thinking and Critical Cosmopolitanism." *Public Culture* 12, no. 3 (2000): 721–48.

Miller, Tyrus. *Late Modernism: Politics, Fiction, and the Arts Between the World Wars*. Berkeley: University of California Press, 1999.

Mittelholzer, Edgar. *The Adding Machine: A Fable for Capitalists and Commercialists*. Kingston: Pioneer Press, 1954.

——. *The Aloneness of Mrs. Chatham*. London: Library 33, 1965.

——. "Amiable Mr. Britten." *BIM* 3, no. 12 (1950): 288–91.

——. *Children of Kaywana*. London: Nevill, 1952.

——. "The Cure for Corruption." *Barbados Sunday Advocate*, 4 April 1954, 8.

——. "A Dying Integrity." *Barbados Sunday Advocate*, 4 July 1954, 8.

——. *The Harrowing of Hubertus*. London: Secker & Warburg, 1954.

——. "Heredity and Environment." *Barbados Sunday Advocate*, 2 February 1954, 8.

——. "Is There a West Indian Way of Life?" *Kyk-over-al* 6, no. 20 (1955): 200–201.

——. *The Jilkington Drama*. London: Abelard-Schuman, 1965.

——. *Kaywana Blood*. London: Secker & Warburg, 1958.

——. "Literary Criticism and the Creative Writer." 1952. Reprinted in *Kyk-over-al* 33–34 (1986): 116–19.

——. "Malicious Morality." *Barbados Sunday Advocate*, 17 October 1954, 8.

——. *A Morning at the Office*. 1950. Harmondsworth: Penguin Books, 1964.

——. *My Bones and My Flute*. London: Secker & Warburg, 1955.

——. *Of Trees and the Sea*. London: Secker & Warburg, 1956.

——. "The Piling of Clouds." Letter to the editor. *Times Literary Supplement*, 1 December 1961, 865.

——. *The Piling of Clouds*. London: Putnam & Company, 1961.

——. "Postscript (re: Roger Mais)." *Kyk-over-al* 6, no. 20 (1955): 164–65.

——. "Sexual Inverts." *Barbados Sunday Advocate*, 25 July 1954, 8.

——. *Shadows Move among Them*. London: Nevill, 1951.

——. "Something Fishy." *BIM* 2, no. 6 (1945): 36–38, 99–101.

——. "The Spiritual Beyond." *Barbados Sunday Advocate*, 14 March 1954, 8.

——. *A Swarthy Boy*. London: Putnam & Company: 1963.

——. *A Tale of Three Places*. London: Secker & Warburg, 1957.

——. *Thunder Returning*. London: Secker & Warburg, 1961.

——. *A Tinkling in the Twilight*. London: Secker & Warburg, 1959.

——. "Truth and Legend." *Barbados Sunday Advocate*, 28 March 1954, 8.

——. *Uncle Paul*. London: Macdonald, 1963.

——. *The Weather in Middenshot*. London: Secker & Warburg, 1952.

——. *With a Carib Eye*. London: Secker & Warburg: 1958.

Mittelholzer, Jacqueline. "'The Idyll and the Warrior': Recollections of Edgar Mittelholzer." *BIM* 17, nos. 66–67 (1983): 33–89.

———. "My Husband—Edgar Mittelholzer." *BIM* 15, no. 60 (1976): 303–9.

Mohanty, Satya P. *Literary Theory and the Claims of History: Postmodernism, Objectivity, Multicultural Politics.* Ithaca: Cornell University Press: 1997.

Montgomery, John. *The Fifties.* London: George Allen & Unwin, 1965.

Montgomery, Robert E. *The Visionary D. H. Lawrence: Beyond Philosophy and Art.* Cambridge: Cambridge University Press, 1994.

Morgan, Edwin. Review of *The Aloneness of Mrs. Chatham,* by Edgar Mittelholzer. *New Statesman and Nation,* 14 May 1965, 772.

Morris, Daphne. "Roger Mais." In *Fifty Caribbean Writers: A Bio—Bibliographical Sourcebook,* edited by Daryl Cumber Dance, 303–17. Westport, CT: Greenwood Press, 1986.

Morris, Mervyn. "The Poet as Novelist: The Novels of George Lamming." In *The Islands In Between,* edited by Louis James, 86–99. London: Oxford University Press, 1968.

Morrison, Blake. *The Movement: English Poetry and Fiction of the 1950s.* Oxford: Oxford University Press, 1980.

Muir, Edwin. "Indirections." Review of *The Emigrants,* by George Lamming. *Observer,* 19 September 1954, 13.

Mukherjee, Arun. "Interrogating Postcolonialism: Some Uneasy Conjunctures." In *Interrogating Post-Colonialism: Theory, Text and Contexts,* edited by Harish Trevedi and Meenakshi Mukherjee, 13–20. Shimla: Indian Institute of Advanced Study, 1996.

Munro, Ian. "The Early Work of George Lamming: Poetry and Short Prose, 1946–1951." In *Neo-African Literature and Culture: Essays in Memory of Janheinz Jahn,* edited by Bernth Lindfors and Ulla Schild, 327–45. Wiesbaden: B. Heymann, 1976.

———. "George Lamming." In King, *West Indian Literature,* 163–75.

———. "The Theme of Exile in George Lamming's *In the Castle of My Skin.*" *World Literature Written in English* 20 (November 1971): 51–60.

Naipaul, V. S. *Half a Life.* London: Picador, 2002.

———. *The Middle Passage: Impressions of Five Societies—British, French, and Dutch— in the West Indies and South America.* 1962. New York: Vintage Books, 2002.

———. *Mr. Stone and the Knights Companion.* London: A. Deutsch, 1963.

———. Review of *Of Age and Innocence,* by George Lamming. *New Statesman and Nation,* 6 December 1958, 826–27.

———. Review of *Turn Again, Tiger,* by Samuel Selvon. *New Statesman and Nation,* 6 December 1958, 826–27.

Nair, Supriya. *Caliban's Curse: George Lamming and the Revisioning of History.* Ann Arbor: University of Michigan Press, 1996.

———. "'Invented Histories': Cultural Production in George Lamming's *Season of Adventure.*" In *Reading the Shape of the World: Toward an International Cultural Studies,* edited by Henry Schwarz and Richard Dienst, 167–82. Boulder: Westview Press, 1996.

Nanton, Philip, editor. *Remembering the Sea: An Introduction to Frank A. Collymore.* Bridgetown: Central Bank of Barbados, 2004.

Nasta, Susheila, editor. *Critical Perspectives on Sam Selvon.* Introduction by Susheila Nasta. Washington, DC: Three Continents Press, 1988.

"New Fiction." Review of *Of Age and Innocence,* by George Lamming. *London Times,* 13 November 1958, 15.

Ngai, Mbatau Kaburu Wa. "The Relationship between Literature and Society and How It Emerges in the Works of G. Lamming, V. S. Naipaul, and W. Harris." *Busara* 8, no. 2 (1976): 53–67.

Nicholls, Peter. *Ezra Pound: Politics, Economics, and Writing.* Atlantic Highlands, NJ: Humanities Press, 1984.

———. *Modernisms: A Literary Guide.* Berkeley: University of California Press, 1995.

North, Michael. *The Dialect of Modernism: Race, Language, and Twentieth-Century Literature.* New York: Oxford University Press, 1994.

———. *The Political Aesthetic of Yeats, Eliot, and Pound.* Cambridge: Cambridge University Press, 1991.

O'Callaghan, Evelyn. *Woman Version: Theoretical Approaches to West Indian Fiction by Women.* Warwick University Caribbean Studies. London: Macmillan, 1993.

———. *Women Writing the West Indies, 1804–1939: "A hot place, belonging to us."* London: Routledge, 2004.

Osborne, John. *Look Back in Anger.* 1957. London: Faber and Faber, 1996.

Paquet, Sandra Pouchet. *The Novels of George Lamming.* London: Heinemann Educational Books, 1982.

Patterson, Anita. *Race, American Literature, and Transnational Modernisms.* Cambridge: Cambridge University Press, 2008.

Patterson, Sheila. *Dark Strangers: A Study of West Indians in London.* London: Tavistock, 1963.

Paul, Kathleen. *Whitewashing Britain: Race and Citizenship in the Postwar Era.* Ithaca: Cornell University Press, 1997.

Phillips, Caryl. *A New World Order: Essays.* New York: Vintage, 2002.

"A Place in the Sun." Review of *The Pleasures of Exile,* by George Lamming. *London Times,* 28 July 1960, 13.

Plotz, John. "One-Way Traffic: George Lamming and the Portable Empire." In *After the Imperial Turn: Thinking with and through the Nation,* edited by Antoinette Burton, 308–23. Durham: Duke University Press, 2003.

Pollard, Charles. *New World Modernisms: T. S. Eliot, Derek Walcott, and Kamau Brathwaite.* Charlottesville: University of Virginia Press, 2004.

Powell, Anthony Dymoke. "Caribbean Melting-Pot." Review of *A Morning at the Office,* by Edgar Mittelholzer. *Times Literary Supplement,* 28 April 1950, 257.

Prendergast, Christopher. "The World Republic of Letters." In *Debating World Literature,* edited by Christopher Prendergast, 1–25. London: Verso, 2004.

Pritchett, V. S. "A Barbados Village." Review of *In the Castle of My Skin,* by George Lamming. *New Statesman and Nation,* 18 April 1953, 460.

———. "These Writers Couldn't Care Less." *New York Times,* 28 April 1957, 1, 39.

Proctor, James. *Dwelling Places: Postwar Black British Writing.* Manchester: Manchester University Press, 2003.

Puri, Shalini. *The Caribbean Postcolonial: Social Equality, Post-Nationalism, and Cultural Hybridity.* New York: Palgrave Macmillan, 2004.

Quigly, Isabel. Review of *An Island Is a World,* by Samuel Selvon. *Spectator,* 15 April 1955, 480.

———. Review of *The Lonely Londoners,* by Samuel Selvon. *Spectator,* 14 December 1956, 882.

Quinton, Anthony, et al. "The New Novelists: An Inquiry." *Essays in Criticism* 5, no. 11 (1958): 13–31.

Rabinovitz, Rubin. *The Reaction against Experiment in the English Novel, 1950–1960.* New York: Columbia University Press, 1967.

Rahim, Jennifer. "(Not) Knowing the Difference: Calypso Overseas and the Sound of Belonging in Selected Narratives of Migration." *Anthurium* 3, no. 2 (2005).

Ramazani, Jahan. *A Transnational Poetics.* Chicago: University of Chicago Press, 2009.

Ramchand, Kenneth. "The Artist in the Balm-Yard: *Season of Adventure.*" *New World Quarterly* 5, nos. 1–2 (1969): 13–21.

———. "Black Lightning." *Public Opinion* ("Roger Mais Supplement"), 10 June 1966, 5.

———. "Celebrating Sam Selvon." *Journal of Modern Literature* 20, no. 1 (1996): 45–50.

———. "Introduction." In *An Island Is a World,* by Samuel Selvon, v–xxv. Toronto: TSAR Publications, 1993.

———. "An Introduction to This Novel." In *The Lonely Londoners,* by Samuel Selvon, 3–21. Harlow: Longman, 1985.

———. *The West Indian Novel and Its Background.* 1970. London: Heinemann, 1983.

Ramraj, Victor. "The Philosophy of Neutrality: The Treatment of Political Militancy in Samuel Selvon's *Moses Ascending* and *Moses Migrating.*" In Zehnder, *Something Rich and Strange,* 77–84.

———. "Samuel Dickson Selvon." *ARIEL* 27, no. 2 (1996): 7–10.

Raven, Simon. "The Kingsley Amis Story." Review of *I Like It Here,* by Kingsley Amis. *Spectator,* 17 January 1958, 79.

Raymond, John. Review of *Shadows Move Among Them,* by Edgar Mittelholzer. *New Statesman and Nation,* 19 May 1951, 573–74.

Review of *Brother Man,* by Roger Mais. *London Times,* 7 July 1954, 10.

Review of *Latticed Echoes,* by Edgar Mittelholzer. *London Times,* 28 January 1960, 15.

Richardson, Maurice. Review of *An Island Is a World,* by Samuel Selvon. *New Statesman and Nation,* 23 April 1955, 586.

———. Review of *The Lonely Londoners,* by Samuel Selvon. *New Statesman and Nation,* 29 December 1956, 846.

Rickards, Colin. "A Tribute to Edgar Mittelholzer." *BIM* 11, no. 42 (1966): 98–105.

Ritchie, Harry. *Success Stories: Literature and the Media in England, 1950–1959.* London: Faber and Faber, 1988.

Robbins, Bruce. "Race, Gender, Class, Postcolonialism: Toward a New Humanistic Paradigm?" In *A Companion to Postcolonial Studies,* edited by Henry Schwarz and Sangeeta Ray, 556–73. Malden, MA: Blackwell Publishing, 2000.

Roberts, W. Adolphe. Foreword to *The Adding Machine: A Fable for Capitalists and Commercialists,* by Edgar Mittelholzer. Kingston: Pioneer Press, 1954, vii–viii.

Rohlehr, Gordon. "Literature and the Folk." In *My Strangled City and Other Essays,* 52–85. Port-of-Spain: Longman Trinidad, 1992.

———. "The Problem of the Problem of Form." In *The Shape of That Hurt and Other Essays,* 1–65. Port-of-Spain: Longman Trinidad, 1992.

Rosenberg, Leah. *Nationalism and the Formation of Caribbean Literature.* New York: Palgrave Macmillan, 2007.

Ross, Alan. "Struggle for Existence." Review of *A Brighter Sun,* by Samuel Selvon. *Times Literary Supplement,* 15 February 1952, 121.

———. "Troubled Waters." Review of *My Bones and My Flute,* by Edgar Mittelholzer. *Times Literary Supplement,* 11 November 1955, 669.

Rosselli, John. "Mood of the Month—V." *London Magazine* 5, no.9 (1958): 39–43.

Rothfork, John. "Race and Community in Sam Selvon's Fiction." *Caribbean Quarterly* 37, no. 4 (1991): 9–22.

Ruck, S. K., editor. *The West Indian Comes to England: A Report by the Family Welfare Association.* London: Routledge & Kegan Paul, 1960.

Rushdie, Salman. "Outside the Whale." In *Imaginary Homelands: Essays and Criticism 1981–1991,* 87–101. London: Granta Books, 1991.

Said, Edward. *Culture and Imperialism.* New York: Vintage Books, 1993.

———. *Orientalism.* New York: Pantheon Books, 1978.

Salick, Roydon. *The Novels of Samuel Selvon: A Critical Study.* Westport, CT: Greenwood Press, 2001.

———. "Sam Selvon's *I Hear Thunder:* An Assessment." *ARIEL* 27, no. 2 (1996): 117–29.

Sandhu, Sukhdev. *London Calling: How Black and Asian Writers Imagined a City.* London: Harper Perennial, 2004.

Sangari, Kumkum. "The Politics of the Possible." *Cultural Critique* 7 (Autumn 1987): 157–86.

Schwarz, Bill, editor. *The Locations of George Lamming.* Warwick University Caribbean Studies. Oxford: Macmillan, 2007.

Scott, David. *Conscripts of Modernity: The Tragedy of Colonial Enlightenment.* Durham: Duke University Press, 2004.

Scott, J. D. "In the Movement." *Spectator,* 1 October 1954, 399–400.

Selvon, Samuel. *A Brighter Sun.* 1952. London: Longman, 1976.

———. "Conversation with Samuel Selvon." In *New World Adams: Conversations with West Indian Writers,* by Daryl Cumber Dance, 247–59. Leeds: Peepal Tree Press, 2008.

———. *Foreday Morning: Selected Prose, 1946–1986.* Edited by Kenneth Ramchand and Susheila Nasta. Harlow: Longman, 1989.

———. *The Housing Lark.* 1965. Boulder: Lynne Rienner Publishers, 1990.

———. "Interview with Sam Selvon." With Reed Dasenbrock and Feroza Jussawalla. In *Tiger's Triumph: Celebrating Sam Selvon,* edited by Susheila Nasta and Anna Rutherford, 114–25. London: Dangaroo Press, 1995.

———. "Interview with Sam Selvon." With Peter Nazareth. In Nasta, *Critical Perspectives on Sam Selvon,* 77–94.

———. *An Island Is a World.* 1955. Toronto: TSAR Publications, 1993.

———. *The Lonely Londoners.* 1956. Harlow: Longman, 1985.

———. *Moses Ascending.* 1975. London: Heinemann, 1984.

———. *Moses Migrating.* Harlow: Longman, 1983.

———. "'Oldtalk': Two Interviews with Sam Selvon." With John Thieme and Alessandra Dotti. In Zehnder, *Something Rich and Strange,* 117–34.

———. "Place Out of the Sun." Review of *They Seek a Living,* by Joyce Eggington. *Evening Standard,* 26 March 1957, 12.

———. "Sam Selvon Talking: A Conversation with Kenneth Ramchand." In Nasta, *Critical Perspectives on Sam Selvon,* 96–104.

———. "Sam Selvon: The Open Society or Its Enemies?" Interview with Frank Birbalsingh. In *Frontiers of Caribbean Literature in English,* edited by Frank Birbalsingh, 54–67. London: Macmillan, 1996.

———. "Samuel Selvon: Interviews and Conversations." With Michel Fabre. In Nasta, *Critical Perspectives on Sam Selvon,* 64–76.

———. "The Spade Who Looked for Justice." Review of *City of Spades,* by Colin MacInnes. *Evening Standard,* 3 September 1957, 12.

———. *Turn Again, Tiger.* New York: St. Martin's Press, 1959.

Seymour, A. J. "An Introduction to the Novels of Edgar Mittelholzer." *Kyk-over-al* 8 (December 1958): 60–74.

———. Review of *Latticed Echoes,* by Edgar Mittelholzer. *Kyk-over-al* 9, no. 27 (1960): 134–37.

Sheller, Mimi. *Consuming the Caribbean: From Arawaks to Zombies.* London: Routledge, 2003.

Sherry, Vincent. *Ezra Pound, Wyndham Lewis, and Radical Modernism.* New York: Oxford University Press, 1993.

———. *The Great War and the Language of Modernism.* Oxford: Oxford University Press, 2003.

Shrapnel, Norman. Review of *The Lonely Londoners,* by Samuel Selvon. *Manchester Guardian,* 4 December 1956, 4.

Sinfield, Alan. *Literature, Politics, and Culture in Postwar Britain.* Berkeley: University of California Press, 1989.

Singer, James Burns. "The Caribbean Mixture: Variations and Fusions in Race and Style." *Times Literary Supplement,* 10 August 1962, 578.

Singh, Sydney. "*The Hills Were Joyful Together:* Art and Society." *World Literature Written in English* 29, no. 1 (1989): 110–20.

Slemon, Stephen. "Modernism's Last Post." *ARIEL* 20, no. 4 (1989): 3–17.

Smith, Faith. *Creole Recitations: John Jacob Thomas and Colonial Formation in the Late Nineteenth-Century Caribbean.* Charlottesville: University of Virginia Press, 2002.

Smith, Stevie. Review of *The Harrowing of Hubertus,* by Edgar Mittelholzer. *Observer,* 23 October 1955, 12.

Spender, Stephen. *The Struggle of the Modern.* Berkeley: University of California Press, 1963.

Steiner, George. "On Difficulty." In *On Difficulty and Other Essays,* 18–47. Oxford: Oxford University Press, 1978.

Stephens, Michelle Ann. *Black Empire: the Masculine Global Imaginary of Caribbean Intellectuals in the United States, 1914–1962.* Durham: Duke University Press, 2005.

Stern, James. Review of *The Emigrants,* by George Lamming. *London Magazine* 2, no. 5 (1955): 109–10.

Stevenson, Randall. *The British Novel since the Thirties: An Introduction.* Athens: University of Georgia Press, 1986.

"Storm-Tossed." Review of *A Brighter Sun,* by Samuel Selvon. *Times Literary Supplement,* 11 February 1972, 145.

Sutherland, Ronald. "Sam Selvon—The Caribbean Connection." *Toronto South Asian Review* 2, no. 1 (Spring 1983): 44–46.

Swartz, David. *Culture and Power: The Sociology of Pierre Bourdieu.* Chicago: University of Chicago Press, 1997.

Symons, Julian Gustave. "Caught in the Trap." Review of *A Tale of Three Places,* by Edgar Mittelholzer. *Times Literary Supplement,* 29 March 1957, 189.

———. "Uncommitted Talents." *Times Literary Supplement,* 29 August 1952, iii.

Szeman, Imre. *Zones of Instability: Literature, Postcolonialism, and the Nation.* Baltimore: Johns Hopkins University Press, 2003.

Taylor, D. J. *After the War: The Novel and English Society since 1945.* London: Chatto & Windus, 1993.

Taylor, Patrick. *The Narrative of Liberation: Perspectives on Afro-Caribbean Literature, Popular Culture, and Politics.* Ithaca: Cornell University Press, 1989.

Thieme, John. Review of *The Novels of George Lamming,* by Sandra Pouchet Paquet. *Wasafiri* 1, no. 1 (1984): 21–22.

———. "The World Turn Upside Down: Carnival Patterns in *The Lonely Londoners.*" *Toronto South Asian Review* 5 (1986): 191–204.

Thiong'o, Ngugi wa. "Freeing the Imagination: George Lamming's Aesthetics of Decolonization." *Transition: An International Review* 100 (2009): 164–69.

Thorpe, Michael. "Sam Selvon (1923–1994)." *World Literature Today* 69, no. 1 (1995): 86–88.

Toynbee, Philip. "Experiment and the Future of the Novel." In *The Craft of Letters in England: A Symposium,* edited by John Lehmann, 60–73. London: Cresset Press, 1956.

Tylden-Wright, David. "Irreconcilable Worlds." Review of *Brother Man,* by Roger Mais. *Times Literary Supplement,* 9 July 1954, 437.

Van O'Connor, William. *The New University Wits and the End of Modernism.* Carbondale: Southern Illinois University Press, 1963.

Viswanathan, Guari. *Masks of Conquest: Literary Study and British Rule in India.* New York: Columbia University Press, 1989.

Wagner, Geoffrey. "Edgar Mittelholzer: Symptoms and Shadows." *BIM* 9, no. 33 (1961): 29–34.

Wain, John. "Along the Tightrope." In *Declaration,* edited by Tom Maschler, 69–90. London: MacGibbon & Kee, 1957.

———. "Correspondence." *London Magazine* 4, no. 3 (1957): 55–57.

———. "How It Strikes a Contemporary." *Twentieth Century* 16 (1957): 226–36.

———. *Hurry on Down.* 1953. London: Penguin Books, 1979.

———. Review of *Of Trees and the Sea,* by Edgar Mittelholzer. *Observer,* 29 July 1956, 9.

———. "A Writer's Prospect—IV." *London Magazine* 3 (November 1956): 59–64.

Walcott, Derek. "Selvon Has Returned to the Old Form." Review of *The Housing Lark,* by Samuel Selvon. *Trinidad Sunday Guardian,* 27 June 1965, 7.

Walkowitz, Rebecca L. *Cosmopolitan Style: Modernism beyond the Nation.* New York: Columbia University Press, 2006.

Walmsley, Anne. *The Caribbean Artists Movement 1966–1972: A Literary and Cultural History.* London: New Beacon Books, 1992.

Walvin, James. *Passage to Britain: Immigration in British History and Politics.* Harmondsworth: Penguin, 1984.

"What Does Mr. Swanzy Want?" BBC Radio Four, 27 November 1998.

White, Antonia. Review of *A Morning at the Office,* by Edgar Mittelholzer. *New Statesman and Nation,* 13 May 1950, 552.

Williams, Patrick. "'Simultaneous uncontemporaneities': Theorising Modernism and Empire." In *Modernism and Empire,* edited by Howard J. Booth and Nigel Rigby, 13–38. Manchester: Manchester University Press, 2000.

Williams, Raymond. *The Politics of Modernism: Against the New Conformists.* Edited by Tony Pinkney. London: Verso, 1999.

Williamson, Karina. "Roger Mais: West Indian Novelist." *Journal of Commonwealth Literature* 2 (December 1966): 138–47.

Wilson, Angus. "Arnold Bennett's Novels." *London Magazine* 1, no. 9 (1954): 59–67.

———. "Mood of the Month—III." *London Magazine* 5, no. 4 (1958): 40–4.

Woolf, Virginia. *Collected Essays.* 2 volumes. New York: Harcourt, Brace & World, 1967.

———. "How Should One Read a Book?" In Woolf, *Collected Essays,* 2: 1–11.

———. "Modern Fiction." In *Collected Essays,* 2: 103–10.

———. "Reading." In *Collected Essays,* 2: 12–33.

Wyndham, Francis. "The New West Indian Writers." *BIM* 7 (January–June 1959): 188–90.

———. Review of *A Morning at the Office,* by Edgar Mittelholzer. *Observer,* 7 May 1950, 7.

Wynter, Sylvia. "We Must Learn to Sit Down Together and Talk about a Little Culture: Reflections on West Indian Writing and Criticism." *Jamaica Journal* 2, no. 4 (1968): 24–32, and *Jamaica Journal* 3, no. 1 (1969): 27–42.

Zehnder, Martin, editor. *Something Rich and Strange: Selected Essays on Sam Selvon.* Leeds: Peepal Tree Press, 2003.

Index